BOSTON
GUIDE

BE A TRAVELER - NOT A TOURIST!

CRITICAL ACCLAIM FOR
OPEN ROAD TRAVEL GUIDES!

*Whether you're going abroad or planning a trip in the United States, take Open Road along on your journey. Our books have been praised by **Travel & Leisure, The Los Angeles Times, Newsday, Booklist, US News & World Report, Endless Vacation, American Bookseller, Coast to Coast**, and many other magazines and newspapers!*

Don't just see the world – experience it with Open Road!

ABOUT THE AUTHOR

Julie M. Fenster is a freelance writer who makes her home in DeWitt, New York. Ms. Fenster is the author of three books about classic cars, and numerous magazine articles on history, cars, and travel, which have appeared in American Heritage magazine, The New York Times, The Los Angeles Times, USAir magazine, and many others.

Ms. Fenster is also a consultant to the popular series, *The American Experience*, produced by Boston's public television station WGBH. In addition to *Boston Guide*, her next travel guide for Open Road Publishing will be *America's Grand Hotels* (Fall 1997), a unique combination of travel planner and historical guide to the opulent 19th and early 20th century hotels that still define elegance and style for experienced travelers.

HIT THE OPEN ROAD -
WITH OPEN ROAD PUBLISHING!

Open Road Publishing now has guide books to exciting, fun destinations on four continents. As veteran travelers, our goal is to bring you the best travel guides available anywhere!

No small task, but here's what we offer:

• All Open Road travel guides are written by authors with a distinct, opinionated point of view – not some sterile committee or team of writers. Our authors are experts in the areas covered and are polished writers.

• Our guides are geared to people who want great vacations, great value, and great tips for both standard tourist sights and fun, unique alternatives.

• We're strong on the basics, but we also provide terrific choices for those looking to get off the beaten path and experience the country or city – not just see it or pass through it.

• We give you the best, but we also tell you about the worst and what to avoid. Nobody should waste their time and money on their hard-earned vacation because of bad or inadequate travel advice.

• Our guides assume nothing. We tell you everything you need to know to have the trip of a lifetime – presented in a fun, literate, no-nonsense style.

• And, above all, we welcome your input, ideas, and suggestions to help us put out the best travel guides possible.

BOSTON GUIDE

BE A TRAVELER - NOT A TOURIST!

Julie M. Fenster

OPEN ROAD PUBLISHING

2nd Edition

To my mother and father who helped me to find Boston. And to the memory of Mary Ellen Reinman, who loved Boston: a wit was she.

Text Copyright ©1999 by Julie M. Fenster
Maps Copyright ©1999 by Open Road Publishing
- All Rights Reserved -

Library of Congress Catalog Card No. 99-74389
ISBN 1-892975-14-9

Front and top back cover photo by Kimberly Grant, Boston; bottom back cover photo courtesy of Greater Boston Convention & Visitors Bureau. Maps by Rob Perry; hotel, restaurant and sights maps updated by James Ramage.

TABLE OF CONTENTS

1. INTRODUCTION   13

2. OVERVIEW   14

3. A SHORT HISTORY   22

4. PLANNING YOUR TRIP   38
Boston in White or Green   38
Weather & What to Wear   40
Information in Advance   41
Annual Events   42
24-Hour Town   43
Currency Exchange   40
Medical & Dental Care   44
Good Numbers to Know   44
Boston Publications   44

5. ARRIVALS & DEPARTURES   45
By Air   45
By Land   46

6. GETTING AROUND TOWN   48
Parking   50
Walking   50
Tours   51

7. BEST PLACES TO STAY   52
A Good Bargain   52
Close to Everything, Downtown   53
Close to Everything, The Back Bay   54

Button-Down Business Address   54
Squeaky, Shiny Clean   55
With Family   56
If It Were Romance   56

8. CHILD'S PLAY   58
Children's Boston   58
Parent's Boston   61

9. WHERE TO STAY   65
Waterfront   68
The Charles River   70
Downtown   71
Financial District   73
Beacon Hill   74
The Theater District   75
Around The Public Garden   77
The Back Bay   79
Kenmore Square   85
Airport   87
Cambridge   87
Bed & Breakfasts in Town   88
Hostel   90

10. WHERE TO EAT   92
Open Anytime   93
Local Chains   97
Barbecue   99
Big Business   102
Children, Too   104
Italian   105
Lots of Food   107
Neighborhood Places   109
Off-Beat, Near The Hynes Convention Center   110
Pizza   112
Real Boston   114
Romantic   117
Sandwiches   118
Seafood   120
Serious About Food   122
The Theater District   123
2 Cool 4 U   125

Tourist Places   126
World Cuisines   128
Bakeries   130

11. SEEING THE SIGHTS   134

The Must-Sees   134
   The Public Garden   135
   Faneuil Hall   139
   John F. Kennedy Library   141
   Museum of Fine Arts   142
   New England Aquarium   143
   USS Constitution   145
   Isabella Stewart Gardner Museum   148
   Harvard Museum of Cultural & Natural History   149
The Freedom Trail   151
   The Freedom Trail: Boston Proper   151
   The Freedom Trail: The North End   155
   The Freedom Trail: Charlestown   157
Other Sights   159
   The Black Heritage Trail   159
   Boston Architectural Center   160
   The Children's Museum   160
   The Computer Museum   161
   The First Church of Christ, Scientist   163
   Hart Nautical Collections   163
   MIT Museum   164
   Museum of Science, Mugar Omni Theater,
     & Charles Hayden Planetarium   166
   The New England Holocaust Memorial   168
   Sports Museum of New England   168
Running In   169
   Harrison Gray Otis House   169
   The Gibson House   170
   Frederick Law Olmsted National Historical Site   170
   Longfellow National Historical Site   171
   Other Historic Homes   171

12. WALKING TOURS   173

Three Walking Tours   173
   Harvard University   173
   The Back Bay   179
   A Half-Hour on Beacon Hill, & A Couple Hundred Years   183

Views   187
Walks to Nowhere   188
   The Boston Common   188
   The Esplanade   189

13. NIGHTLIFE   192

After Work   192
Before Dinner   193
The Heart of the Evening   194
Music & People   194
Jazz   195
Irish Pubs   195
Comedy   196
Brewhouses   197
Late Night Dance Clubs   198
At Night Without All That Jazz   199

14. CULTURE   201

Music   202
Theater   205
Goings On, On Campus   206
Film   207
Author Signings, Lectures, & Readings   209
Art Galleries   210
Libraries   211

15. SPORTS & RECREATION   214

Spectator Sports   214
The Bigs   215
   Baseball   215
   Basketball & Hockey   216
   Football & Soccer   216
   Horse Racing   217
   Other Spectator Sports   217
   The Boston Marathon   218
Participant Sports   218

16. SHOPPING   221

Antiques   223
Books   224
Choclate & Candy   226
Clothes   226

Food   227
Galleries   229
Gifts   229
For the House   230
Jewelry   230
Magazines   230
Models   231
Music   231
Nostalgia   231
Souvenirs   232
Stationery   232
Toys   234

17. EXCURSIONS & DAY TRIPS   236

Day Trips   236
　Lexington & Concord   236
　Nahant   239
　Salem   239
　Plymouth   240
　Whale Watching   240
Overnight   242
　Nantucket   242
　Rhode Island & Connecticut   243
　Vermont   244
Cape Cod   248

INDEX   259

MAPS

Boston Area   *17*
The "T"   *49*
Boston Hotels   *66-67*
Boston Restaurants   *94-95*
Boston Sights   *136-137*
Excursions   *237*

SIDEBARS

Digging the Big Dig   19
The Boston Juggernaut   32
Growth Through Annexation   36
Boston's Firsts   37
Fun Alternatives   39
Boston's Area Code   41
Pronunciation Guide   43
Who Are Those Guys, Anyway?   51
The Zoo   59
What's Going On For Kids   62
B&B Services   86
Besting The Best   100
Restaurant Rows   131
Hotel Sweets & Specials   133
Going Halfies   135
Boston's Mr. Bulfinch   140
Boston By Boat   151
Freedom Trail Tours & Events   156
The Freedom Trail: Information For Major Stops   159
Free For All   163
Only in Boston   173
Guided Tours   178
Pictures For Your Mind   186
The River Came First   191
The Littlest History Of The Littlest Bar   193
Irish Music Updates   196
Beer On The Hoof Or Beer On The Trolley   198
Hot Spots   200
Boston Symphony Insider Tips   203
Ticket Tricks   205
We Had Theaters, Then   208
What's On At The Galleries?   210
A Boston Christmas In The Year 3000   213
Dot-Com: Sports Information   215
Where It's Always Spring ...   218
Indulgences   219
Edible Wild Plant Classes   220
Boston Sales Tax   223
Book Worlds   226
How To Eat In Quincy Market – A Battle Plan   228
How Quincy Market Came To Life   233
The Filene's Basement Game   235
New England Inns – Worth a Trip All By Themselves   246-247
At Home on Cape Cod   257

BOSTON GUIDE

1. INTRODUCTION

If I just could, I would spend every day the same way. It would be in Boston, and would start with a walk up one of the long streets in the Back Bay. Perhaps Boylston or Newbury: vital things happen to them every day. Another restaurant, yet another store, today's special, a different window at a gallery, a sale, a sign, an opening. Every few days, however, I'd walk on Commonwealth Avenue instead, that cathedral of a street. Beacon Street and Marlborough are incognito by comparison, and they would have their time, too, if I could spend every day the same way.

Meandering is the only way to cross the Public Garden, although I would pick up the pace a bit in the Common, because it is bigger, arriving at the old Athenaeum Library just in time to slump into a small sofa, the one near the window overlooking the Granary Burial Ground. I say, "just in time" because the sun only wends its way past the office buildings and onto that small sofa for a short span of time each morning. As long as it did, I would be there, reading all the magazines that neither I nor anyone else has ever heard of – those are the kind of magazines that the Athenaeum receives, in addition to all the rest.

I would then cross the upper part of the Common to Winter Street, and have lunch at Locke-Ober: old wood and red leather, hectic in the anteroom, straightened out to the last mint in the dining rooms. Before long, the whole team of tuxedoed waiters would know without a word what I wanted: apple pie, followed by apple pie, followed by apple pie. Three courses. A quick swoop through Filene's Basement, just down Winter Street, to see what's hit rock-bottom in their sale-system, and then to Suffolk Downs, which is a few stops away on the T, with a short ride on the bus they call a jitney. If there were a day game at Fenway Park, I'd go there instead. If Suffolk were dark and the Red Sox were away, however, I could always do what Franklin Roosevelt would do when he was a student at Harvard, playing hooky from his classes to go down to the harbor all afternoon to look at the ships.

If I just could, that is how I would spend every day, a *boulevardier* in the city of Boston, with never a dull moment. The hope is that you can use this book to spend days that are even better, and that your being a visitor, there will be no "if" about it. You just can. The city is easy to love and uncommonly welcoming. Except – don't block my sun at the Athenaeum.

2. OVERVIEW

The tale of Boston is often told in terms of revolution: religious, political, or literary. Don't be deluded. The story of Boston is the story of dirt. Real dirt, the stuff that holds up the ground, has made Boston what it is today, and there is hardly a shovelful in the whole city that has stayed put since the beginning. Whole hills disappeared. So did bodies of water. Few places, outside of Holland, have had so much work to do.

The fault lies with the **Puritans**. They landed at Charlestown in 1630, didn't like it particularly and immediately looked across the **Charles River** to the **Shawmut Peninsula**, a rocky, marshy, nearly treeless point – all but an island, really, with one uncertain tail of land connecting it to a bulkier piece of the mainland. Fresh water abounded and access to the ocean was convenient. But anyone could see that it was no place to put a teeming city of hundreds of thousands of people. For some reason, a few dozen Puritans moved there anyway, and called it Boston.

Whenever land became tight – that is to say, whenever you could smell the dump in a good neighborhood – Bostonians would come out of their houses and eye one of the peninsula's hills, the most conspicuous of which were the inspiration for the nickname, **Tremont** (for "Trimountain"). One by one, hills were chopped up and pushed into the drink to make more land. When all the others were completely gone, **Beacon Hill** was shaved by about 60 feet, and after that, Boston had to look elsewhere for its dirt. Samuel Adams, Henry Thoreau, transcendentalists, and rebels: much has been written on the subject of how Bostonians perceive the world around them. And the answer turns out to be: in wheelbarrows.

Having been created by the barrow, Boston has never stretched into a gaping city. The very longest walk you could take from one end to another would be eight miles. (London is fifty miles across.) Even so, most of the places of interest to visitors are not even that farflung. Boston fashions itself a "walker's city," and it is true. Nearly flat, except for that famous plateau (Beacon Hill), most neighborhoods are pocked with squares, grassy malls, or parks, ready with places to sit. Let one neighborhood lead to another. Or take to the parks.

Frederick Law Olmsted's well-planned system, called the **Emerald Necklace**, spans greater Boston in a five-mile course, practically unbroken by streets or pavement.

AROUND THE TOWN

The Puritans never established much of a reputation for kidding, and when they called their city the "Hub of the Universe," they did so with a steady eye. The very hub of the Hub is the same now as it was then: the **Common**, that un-municipal park, which has belonged to the people, not the city, of Boston since 1634.

Boston has arrayed itself around the Common in a pattern that has changed remarkably little through the years. Perhaps the fact that Boston never had any land to waste accounts for the way that many of its neighborhoods have been well-maintained for generations.

BEACON HILL

Using the Common's Frog Pond (no one ever once recorded seeing a frog in it) as the hub of the hub of the Hub, **Beacon Hill** is just to the north, a veritable crowd of red-brick townhouses craning for a view, either of the Common, or of the Charles River, on the other side of the hill. Most of the quiet streets there are strictly residential.

Louisburg Square is considered the city's best address, while **Charles Street** is probably its most pleasant shopping stretch, especially if you like antiques. Moving to the east of Beacon Hill (or clockwise around the Common), the **State House** is a point of division between Beacon Hill and downtown. The State House is a state house, despite the fact that Massachusetts is a commonwealth.

ABOUT DOWNTOWN

Near the top of Beacon Hill, downtown Boston is rather long-faced and serious with business blocks, though it does make room for **King's Chapel** and the **Athenaeum Library**. Just beyond downtown to the northeast, **Faneuil Hall** and the **Quincy Market** rest on what was once waterfront. Beyond them is the **North End**: the tip of the Shawmut Peninsula where the Puritans first settled their new town. For the past hundred years, though, the North End has had a distinctly Italian personality.

The part of downtown east of the Common is **Downtown Crossing**, the hotbed of shopping that is fanned by the likes of **Filene's Basement**. Even further east of the stores and the pedestrian malls, Boston's financial district rises bullishly around **Post Office Square**.

To the east of all, the **Harbor** is still lively, with day-cruiseboats leaving from **Long Wharf** jutting out next to the **New England Aquarium**. Nearby, **Rowes Wharf** is much more than its 18th-century namesake: a new but not modern complex including residences, a hotel, offices, and perches indoors and out from which to look at the harbor.

CHINATOWN & THE THEATER DISTRICT

To the southeast of the Common, **Chinatown** is so distinct that crossing Kneeland St. at Washington St. is equivalent to stepping off into another country. Tyler St., near Kneeland, is lined with restaurants, though the small vegetable markets, noodle factories, and bakeries on nearby streets are an even more intriguing way to gather a feast. Next to Chinatown, exactly south of the Common, the Theater District has been in the same place for hundreds of years and so, over a shorter span, have a few of Boston's beautiful theaters, including the **Colonial** and the enormous **Wang Center**.

The **South End** is south of the Common, on the other side of that vehicular river called the Massachusetts Turnpike. Reclaimed townhouses

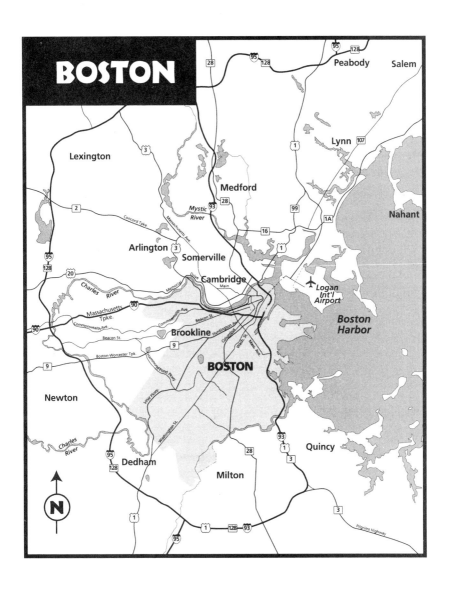

and tiptop restaurants are making it a better address than it has ever been before.

THE BACK BAY

Completing the sweep around the Common, the **Back Bay** lies on its neat grid to the west, built on landfill starting 140 years ago. Few cities have a second chance at creating themselves: Boston had that chance with its 450-acre Back Bay, and instituted building codes to ensure that it would be ordered and yet varied in appearance. **Commonwealth Avenue**, surely the most beautiful residential street in the country, seems to emerge naturally from the Public Garden at its western end. The **Prudential Center** and **Copley Place** are the neighborhood's slick shopping areas (and each is much more besides), while **Newbury Street** is filled with small shops bursting with imagination.

Through the Back Bay, Commonwealth Avenue leads to **Kenmore Square**, which is just a long pop fly from **Fenway Park**, the home of the Red Sox. Another pop fly away (maybe off Babe Ruth's bat), is the actual Fenway, a managed wetland. The **Museum of Fine Arts** borders it, as does the **Isabella Stewart Gardner Museum**. In the same general vicinity, many excellent hospitals, including the **Harvard Medical School**, cluster in the Longwood Medical area.

OVER THERE

Charlestown is part of Boston now, retaining the **USS Constitution**, **Bunker Hill**, and the village atmosphere of a place apart. Another section, flowering with more and more places of interest to visitors, is the developing waterfront of **South Boston**.

Separate from Boston as a city, and across the Charles River geographically, **Cambridge** has a very different look, marked by light-industrial districts, clapboard houses, and two very famous campuses. **Harvard** is there, and so is the **Massachusetts Institute of Technology**. The comfortable suburb of **Brookline**, adjoining Boston to the southwest, is another separate town without which Boston would not be Boston.

DIGGING THE BIG DIG

The **Central Artery/Tunnel Project** is no mere road construction: it is major surgery for the city of Boston. Whole highways are being tucked underground, so that the traffic that now crawls over them will zoom through tunnels, leaving only greenspace above. The project has been the talk of the town since construction started in 1989, under a nickname that sums it up: the **"Big Dig."** By the time it is finished in 2004, the Big Dig will have sent 541,000 truckloads of pure Boston – 13 million cubic yards of it – out to landfills. By then, the Central Artery elevated highway will have been largely replaced by one tunnel, while the Massachusetts Turnpike will extend under the city to take travelers all the way out to Logan Airport.

In the meantime, local residents are persevering through long delays and gnarled traffic patterns – grumbling heartily all the while, as though either one of those were new for Boston. Tourists have made an attraction of the main construction sites, where gaping holes give a dizzying, prehistoric look to the city. The Big Dig has its own visitor's center, suited to children or adults, at Milk Street on the Central Wharf, right next door to the New England Aquarium. Admission is free. For more information on the Big Dig, call 951-6362; website, www.bigdig.com.

The Central Artery may be ugly, but as a wall of cars, it has protected the North End since 1959 from infiltration by modern development. After the highway is dismantled in 2003, the North End will be, as it were, reconnected to the rest of Boston. That sounds at first like cause for rejoicing, except that the North End has long been disconnected from time itself, being a true old-fashioned Italian-American neighborhood, oblivious to change. Now that neighborhood is bracing itself for new winds from the city, but then, air will blow a bit differently all over Boston, once the Big Dig is done.

IN THE HARBOR

Boston Harbor is part of the city too: 50 square miles sprinkled with islands. Many of the islands, even some of the 31 included in a state-park system, are a travesty of garbage, abandonment, or cruel excavation.

However, others are beautiful and often historic places. **Little Brewster Island**, for example, is home to the oldest continuously manned light-house in the country. Ferries leaving from Long Wharf offer scheduled service in the summer to Little Brewster and four other harbor islands.

EXCURSIONS & DAY TRIPS

To the north is the **North Shore**. To the south is the **South Shore**. For many people, especially in the summertime, that is all that there is to know about the region outside of the city. A debate ensues about their relative merits, but to flip a coin over it and start with the North Shore, towns like **Marblehead**, **Manchester**, **Gloucester**, and **Rockport** speak of seafaring days. **Salem** is more famous now for its darkest hour, when witch-burning was considered justice, as is recounted by a museum there. One of the finest small museums anywhere is also in Salem – the **Peabody Essex Museum** is devoted to the region's trading days, especially with the Far East.

The South Shore is generally more relaxed, with longstanding resort towns such as **Cohasset, Scituate**, and **Duxbury**. There are more and better beaches to the south than north. **Plymouth** is about 35 miles south of Boston, and just a few years older. Not much in the way of English settlement is older than Plymouth, of course, and the **Plimouth Plantation** is an extensive outdoor museum that tries to recreate the original settlement.

Cape Cod is no mere excursion. It is a way of life, and it starts about an hour by car from Boston, or about three hours by ferry, straight across the bay to **Provincetown**. Cape Cod is also the main route to the islands, **Martha's Vineyard** and **Nantucket**. Both are worth the trip, if you like the ocean looking to be comfortable with the shore, and the well-kept places on it.

Newport, Rhode Island does not have good beaches, but then, nobody who lived in the elephantine mansions lining the ocean there ever minded about that. It is not, after all, a good idea to go swimming when you're weighted down with rocks, even sparkling ones. Many greathouses are now open to the public.

Closer to Boston, the towns of **Lexington** and **Concord** are quintessential New England towns, in addition to their historical importance. Concord has a museum concerned with the events of the Revolution, as well as the work of literary figures such as Henry Thoreau, who spent an important sojourn at nearby **Walden Pond. Louisa May Alcott's** family home is also in town, and open to the public. Keep in mind that in the spring, each town stages re-enactments of the British attacks that started the Revolutionary War.

And the British, you may recall, came to regret ever leaving the cozy confines of Boston.

3. A SHORT HISTORY

FROM COMPANY TO COLONY

John Winthrop had never even been outside of England before he set sail for the New World on March 22, 1630. Yet he was brimming with confidence. He must have been. He started writing a history of New England, while he was still on the boat on the way over.

One would think that the history of New England, as New England, could have been written on the back of a postcard in 1630: the region had only been settled by the first Europeans in 1621 in Plymouth. Admittedly, a lot had happened there, and in subsequent settlements at Salem and Charlestown, but as Winthrop knew very well, in his sheer confidence, even more was going to happen in Boston. That is why he spent the rest of his time on the boat, the *Arabella,* writing rules and laws, a new philosophy for his new city. Only good things were to happen in Boston, that was the basis of the Covenant that Winthrop wrote. According to the Covenant, it was up to the colonists to "do justly, to love mercy and to walk humbly with our God." It was up to God to "dwell among us as his own people, and command a blessing on us in all our ways."

Winthrop stipulated that God would be presumed to have entered into the Covenant when the *Arabella* arrived safely in New England. It did, and Winthrop began looking for a location for his special colony. "We must consider that we shall be as a City upon a hill," he wrote, "The eyes of all people are upon us. Soe that we shall deal falsely with our God in this work we have undertaken, and so cause him to withdraw his present help from us, we shall be made a storey and a by-word throughout the world." Winthrop had no intention of letting that happen.

The **Massachusetts Bay Colony** was founded by "Puritans," who considered themselves victims of religious persecution. For that reason, they were seeking a better life in the New World; but in organization, it was a company first, and government sprang from the company. The members of the company elected a governor – John Winthrop, of course – and a cabinet. First, there were laws, and then there was Boston.

The first 150 settlers may have brought the company charter with them, but they didn't bring water, and that was the issue they fretted about for several weeks after landing at **Charlestown**, where the only spring was covered at high tide by sea water.

One of the standing snobberies of New England is that someone has always been there longer than you have. The Rev. William Blackstone had roots in New England going back years – at least a few of them – when the Puritans arrived, and he moseyed over from his house on the Shawmut Peninsula to greet the newcomers. The Shawmut Peninsula was only across the Charles River from Charlestown. Blackstone had emigrated with a previous group of pioneers, all the rest of whom had packed up and gone home to England. Moving to the peninsula to live all alone, he had tucked himself into a house on the site of the present Louisburg Square. Apparently, it has always been the best address. Blackstone told Winthrop that there was plenty of fresh water on the Shawmut Peninsula and invited the new colony to locate there.

Pausing only long enough to name the new place, "Boston," after a city in England – a country the Puritans otherwise professed to disdain – about one thousand colonists eventually moved to an area located where downtown is today, near the present Washington St. between Milk and State streets. The typical house was a rectangular wooden hut with a thatched roof and a fireplace at one end. The bottom floor was a kitchen/living room/master bedroom, and the children or servants slept in the loft.

As Thomas O'Connnor noted in *Bibles, Brahmins and Bosses, A Short History of Boston*, the New England coast was practically devoid of native Americans when the Puritans arrived to found Boston. A plague in about 1617 decimated the population, and wars between tribes further reduced the numbers, such that only about 500 Indians populated the coast of what is now Massachusetts. Relations with the Indians were amicable enough, though one English woman who had a romance with an Indian was punished for it: as John Dunton wrote in a letter of 1686, she "had an Indian cut out exactly in red cloth, and sewed upon her right Arm, and enjoyned to wear it Twelve Months."

That may have been peculiar, but it was certainly not harsh for the day. For kissing a woman in the street, a man was whipped or fined; for cursing, a hot iron was applied to the tongue; for stealing, a thief had to pay back four times what he took, and stealing was the least known of the major offenses. Women who were "scolds" were tied to their front doors for a few hours. Cheating, according to John Dunton, was, however, looked upon as "a commendable Piece of Ingenuity" (John Dunton had just been cheated out of £400).

The capital crimes were murder, adultery, and witchcraft. In *The History of New England,* John Winthrop later recounted one murder trial that took place almost as soon as Boston was founded in the autumn of 1630: a disturbed woman killed her own three year-old daughter, on a revelation from Satan that by doing so "she might free it from future misery." The woman, named Dorothy Talbye, was hung.

The merest revelation was the most serious danger known to the Puritans. They founded their "city on a Hill" very firmly on the teachings of the Bible. There was to be no sudden wisdom, either from Satan or from God. There were to be no surprises.

When Anne Hutchinson arrived in Boston with her husband and family in 1634, she seemed a winning candidate for happiness in Boston. The Hutchinsons were pious and prosperous. Mrs. Hutchinson, however began to feel a certain religious fervor from the inside out, without need of the words of the Bible or of a church. Goodness came from within, she maintained, not merely from going through the motions of obeying laws, rules, and commandments. Mrs. Hutchinson spoke to others about her revelations in weekly meetings at her house. In 1637, she was called up on charges before the General Court. Interrogated directly by John Winthrop, she proved herself resourceful, wily, and articulate. Winthrop, a Cambridge graduate, was continually frustrated in his probing to find a legal cause on which to punish her. In addition, he looked clumsy and ill-informed in their parries.

About to be cleared, Mrs. Hutchinson used her public forum to expound on her exalted revelation ... and that gave Winthrop his chance. He pounced on the fact that revelations were flagrantly contrary to the Massachusetts Bay Colony. Unlike those eccentrics and innocents convicted as witches, Mrs. Hutchinson was truly a danger to the Colony, if the colony was determined to remain a strictly controlled religious community. What was wrong was not that she had had an original idea, but that her idea would render the Puritan hierarchy of churches and rules practically useless. Mrs. Hutchinson was banished to Rhode Island. She was later scalped by Indians near the Hudson River. There is a statue in her honor in front of the State House.

The early history of Boston was neither accidental nor casual. Winthrop and his followers were thinking hard every step of the way. Not many people in England went to college in the early 1600s. It took either a great deal of money or a fine early education, and probably both. Yet Boston counted over one hundred Cambridge and Oxford graduates in its founding population of about 5,000. The emphasis on education was put into law, and Boston had a system of elementary schools; a public "prep" school (**Boston Latin**) and a college (**Harvard**), in place only a dozen years after the founding of the city.

Good livings were made in Boston supplying oncoming waves of immigrants – every religious clamp-down in England meant another windfall for Boston. But the truly great fortunes were made when the city organized New World trade around itself. Boston merchants and shippers had built 78 wharves by 1708 to tie their city literally to the sea, but they couldn't keep up, and in one 18th-century complaint, pedestrians said they had to climb over the bowsprits of ships tied up right at the street. In 1710, the original **Long Wharf** was America's first engineering marvel – people came from all around to see it take 800 feet back from the sea.

Trade was heaviest between America and England, of course, with manufactured goods and raw materials going in both directions. The route to the Caribbean became important, with Boston merchants as the invisible partners in slave trade with Africa. Boston merchants would trade anything; later in the century, a man made a fortune shipping ice to countries as far away as India – which is as far away as can be from Boston. Under British rule, American merchants were forbidden to trade with China, and so that important route would develop – very quickly – only after 1783.

The old Company gave way to Massachusetts' status as a regular Royal Colony at the end of the 1600s. The crown sent a Royal Governor, whose main function was to absorb the constant tensions between London and its unruly subjects in Boston. The colony had started out as a private entity, and its residents chafed ever afterward at outside rule. Nonetheless, the Royal Governor and his entourage had one welcome function in the first half of the 18th century. They were emissaries of style, keeping rich Bostonians up-to-date on how things were being done, in those far-off places where they were done right. The Puritan work ethic may have remained, with a certain degree of its self-restraint, but Puritan fashions gave way in a blast to powdered wigs, gold jewelry, and bright satin clothing. The same was happening all over America.

THE REVOLUTIONARY WAR

By comparison to other corners of the British Empire, the American colonies were an expensive proposition. In the first place, the Americans had developed into tough traders, not acquiescent suppliers, and they cut most of the fat from British profit margins. In addition, the thirteen colonies occupied an expansive territory, much of which required military protection from the Indians and the French, as in the war that ended in 1763.

To subsidize the army that was stationed in America, Great Britain imposed a **Stamp Tax** (on most paper goods and documents) in 1765. It wasn't entirely unfair, under the circumstances – but it was the first time that Americans had been directly taxed. And there was no pretense of self-government about it: it was "taxation without representation."

During the subsequent year, colonists in places up and down the seaboard spoke out, riling themselves into activity. Among other things, angry Bostonians stoned the house occupied by the lieutenant-governor, one Thomas Hutchinson, grandson of Anne Hutchinson. The Hutchinsons ... ever ill-treated by Boston. Across America, boycotts and protests carried the point and the Stamp Act was repealed in 1766. However, a revolutionary machine had been created by it, and put into motion.

Samuel Adams was foremost in that machine, which took shape as the **"Sons of Liberty,"** in Boston. Having inherited and disposed of a small fortune, Adams became, to all appearances, a wastrel as a young man, spending his days chatting wherever and with whomever he could, while his wife, Elizabeth, found ways to make ends meet for their family. Unlike most true wastrels, however, Samuel Adams emerged with great knowledge of human nature, which he put to use in the revolutionary movement. He spoke out frequently at **Faneuil Hall**, and displayed a great skill for organization, as well.

Soon enough, other means of taxation brought forth other protests: more boycotts. Even Thomas Hutchinson, who proclaimed his basic faith in Boston even as his house was being pelted, began to despair in 1770, after attending a Town Meeting: "We are sinking into perfect barbarism ... The spirit of anarchy which prevails in Boston is more than I am able to cope with." Later that same year, the anarchy took hold of a spring night, as a contingent of British soldiers, answering a fire-call, was met by a small mob of Americans. The Americans were disposed only to resent the soldiers, and show it at every opportunity; there was no specific protest about the mob. In the melee and confusion, the soldiers thought they heard the order to fire their guns – it must have been the voice of one of the Americans, taunting them – but five in the crowd were killed. "**The Boston Massacre**" inflamed the anarchy, as Hutchinson had called it, that was already loose in the city and if it were not for the leadership that followed, the mob may well have ruled with nothing but base resentment.

Instead, Boston produced the leaders who turned the angry mobs into a force of inevitable reason, and who helped shape the Revolution for the entire nation. At the head of the movement was a physician of high social standing, **Dr. Joseph Warren**. Two years after the Boston Massacre, March 5, 1772, he delivered a rousing speech at Faneuil Hall. The speech, even in excerpts, tells as much about the people in the audience, as it does about the man who delivered it:

"In vain, we crossed the boisterous ocean, found a new world, and prepared it for the happy residence of LIBERTY – In vain we toiled – In vain, we fought – We bled in vain, if you, or our offspring, want valour to repel the assaults of her invaders! – Stain not your birthright; be wise in your deliberations, and determined in your exertions for the preservation of your liberties. Follow not the dictates of passion, but enlist yourself under the sacred banner of reason."

And then Dr. Warren recalled the Covenant that launched Boston: the first time, as a colony; in his own time, as part of a republic: "If you perform your part, you may have the strongest confidence, that THE SAME ALMIGHTY BEING who protected your pious and venerable forefathers – who enabled them to turn a barren wilderness into a fruitful field, who so often made bare his arm for their salvation, will still be mindful of you, their offspring."

The following year, the British tried yet again to exert new rule over their American colonies. Legally, they had every right to do so, but in practical terms, the situation was long past legalities. Through the waiver of the import duty on the product of the ailing British East India Company, the **Tea Act of 1773** would have affected most colonists only by lowering the price they paid for tea ... Pay less for tea! Pay less for tea! The colonists were outraged.

It took Samuel Adams to tell them why. It was a case of manipulation, from his point of view. The standing tax on other teas remained: a tax that colonists had learned to avoid through smuggling. Waiving government charges on British East India Tea, in effect, subsidized it and made it even cheaper than the smuggled kinds – and that represented a flagrant attempt by the British to dictate what kind of tea the colonists would drink. Adams could not abide any hint of manipulation from London, and insisted that the first load of British East India tea should never even land on American soil. On December 16, 1773, he and several dozen other men left the **Old South Church**, going home only long enough to disguise themselves as Mohawk Indians, before meeting each other again at the Harbor, into which they dumped £13,000 worth of tea from newly arrived ships.

It was not merely a symbolic act, it was a costly one, equivalent to destroying millions of dollars in property today. The following June, the British slapped back hard, and right at Boston, closing its port and pouring soldiers into the town. The colonial government was replaced by a military one, headed by **General Thomas Gage**. The population of Boston dropped from 16,000 to 5,000 in a matter of months. There wasn't much livelihood left, except for one: preparing secretly for war. The plight of Boston became the rallying point of revolutionary sentiments throughout the colonies.

On April 19, 1775, a contingent of Gage's troops left Boston on a mission that had become a regular chore for them in the vicinity of Boston: looking for stores of ammunition. They were headed for **Concord**, but paused for several hours in Cambridge. Meanwhile, the Americans put a communication plan into motion, by which they flashed a warning from the steeple of the **Old North Church**, regarding the movement of troops: one lantern if the British moved by land, two if they moved by sea.

Paul Revere was one of the two riders who saw the message and took it on horseback to the town of **Lexington**, where "Minute Men" could ready themselves for a fight. On the way, Revere was caught by British troops – his stirrups and the girth of his saddle were cut – but he kept riding. When the British arrived at Lexington, the first skirmish of the Revolutionary War ensued. The Americans had a knack for slogans, and they called what happened "the shot heard round the world." Samuel Adams wrote in his diary, "What a glorious morning is this!"

The fight was for real. In mid-June, **George Washington** of Virginia, was appointed Commander-in-Chief of the entire Continental Army: it was **John Adams** of Boston (the future president) who proposed him, on the basis that a Southern general in command of a war starting in Boston would knit all of the thirteen colonies together. It would take until July

4th, however, for Washington to make his preparations and reach the Boston area.

In the meantime, Dr. Warren was the colonel in charge of the Massachusetts militia, and he rather aggressively stationed his troops close by Boston, on **Breed's Hill** across the Charles River in Charlestown. The British attacked on June 17th, but the hastily constructed fortifications of the Americans held back the first wave, aided by reinforcements from New Hampshire. Accounts vary as to whether the Americans were fighting so very valiantly, or the British, especially the junior officers, were performing so very badly. But the entire war could easily have ended that day on Breed's Hill, at the battle known ever since (in a consensus error) as **Bunker Hill**. Once more the British tried to advance and once more they retreated in disarray. On the third try, they captured the hill, but again lost the opportunity for a true victory by failing to follow the Americans. It was a case in military history of one side – the Americans – losing the battle and winning the war, because the British were off-balance in their perception of American strength and strategy throughout the rest of the war.

One of the many heroes of the day was Dr. Joseph Warren, who stood in the field of battle and exhorted the men not to give up at any cost. But the cost, as it turned out, was Dr. Warren's life, as Abigail Adams wrote in a letter to her husband, "... Our dear friend, Dr. Warren, is no more, but fell gloriously fighting for his country; saying, better to die honourably in the field, than ingloriously hang on the gallows. Great is our loss."

By July, George Washington arrived in Cambridge and accepted command of the Army. Awaiting the arrival of artillery through most of the rest of the year, he devised a good plan for retaking Boston, but that is not what made him such a natural leader from the start. The fact is that he ended up implementing an even better plan devised by his subordinates. That, and the fact that it was executed successfully in March 1776, made it apparent that the army was in the right hands. Boston was liberated, but the year of siege had been harsh; disease, hunger, and downright cold had punished the city, which saw almost no further action through the rest of the Revolutionary War.

Boston emerged unhappy from the Revolution. It was a tired, old-fashioned town, still ravaged by the siege. Money was scarce, and there was very little construction in Boston through the end of the century, other than the monumental new State House of 1798. Prosperity returned only slowly, even as commerce in New York whizzed ahead in the aftermath of the war. The British were gone, but so was their sense of style, and as late as 1800, a young man returning from his education in Europe was shocked to notice that upper-class Bostonians were still wearing the brightly colored clothes, the wigs, and short breeches they'd worn since long before the war.

BOSTON WANTS TO SECEDE FROM THE UNION

The end of British rule meant one thing to Boston sea captains: the route to China was finally open. In 1784, a Boston ship named, with high expectations, the *Empress of China*, was the first to arrive in Canton, the only trade port open to foreigners at the time. At first, Americans took tea in trade for ginseng, an herb rare in China that grew plentifully in New England. Soon Americans sent fur-pelts to China in exchange for Chinese porcelain, known as export-porcelain, because it was specially commissioned by the traders. Boston dominated the lucrative China trade through the 19th century, and many Chinese people emigrated to the town starting around 1800. In many ways, Boston was regaining its old confidence.

Then Thomas Jefferson defeated Boston's own John Adams to become the president of the United States. Jefferson's perspective on the country was slightly different than that of the average Bostonian. They believed in a strong national government; he did not. They believed that trade and manufacturing were to be protected at all costs; he believed that farming was the basis of the national structure. Most important, probably, they believed that Boston was essential to the new Republic; he seemed to think it of it as a little city, up north.

The leading Bostonians were conservative Federalists, who had replaced a monarchy with a central government, but who were otherwise comfortable with a rather British sense of order and even hierarchy. They

THE BOSTON JUGGERNAUT

Samuel Adams (1722-1803) - *A penniless but well-educated man, Adams rose to the occasion of the revolution, making speeches over the years that kept the effort on a single track: independence. Showing a talent for organization, he helped convene the First Continental Congress, and later served as Massachusetts' second governor.*

John Hancock (1737-1793) - *Inherited a fortune and a thriving business from his uncle, Thomas Hancock. John Hancock was a poor businessman himself, but, as a member of Boston's upper class, made an important early contribution to the revolutionary effort simply by attaching his family's name to it. After the war was over, he became Massachusetts' first governor under the republic.*

John Adams (1735-1826) - *Samuel Adams' second cousin. John Adams also served in the Continental Congress, helped frame the Declaration of Independence, and made his mark in national politics after the war. Adams ran against Washington for president, served as his vice president under the system then in effect. In 1796, John Adams was elected the second president.*

Abigail Adams (1744-1818) - *one of the most astute and engaging of colonial commenters, through her letters and diaries. She was the wife of one president, John Adams, and the mother of another, John Quincy Adams.*

Dr. Joseph Warren (1741-1775) - *physician, who participated in the Boston Tea Party and led the troops at the Battle of Bunker Hill, where he was killed.*

Paul Revere (1734-1818) silversmith and businessman, who made himself useful to the Sons of Liberty, notably when he rode to Lexington to warn of the approach of the British. His later service as an officer in the Continental Army ended in scandal, though he was ultimately given an honorable discharge.

liked the British very much, in fact, now that the family fight was in the past. What they didn't like was the **War of 1812**, which shut the Boston harbor down and pitted America against the British. The talk around town throughout the war was of peace, even a separate New England peace with Britain. Finally, there was also serious talk of secession: of organizing the New England states into a separate country. A proposal reached the desk of the president, **James Madison**, for Massachusetts to secede. He just put it aside and ignored it, which is what the nation in general did for awhile to Boston, a city living in the past politically.

INTELLECTUAL BOSTON & THE ABOLITIONIST MOVEMENT

"I don't go to hear Mr. Emerson; I don't understand him. But my daughters do ..." That was the general sentiment around Boston in the 1840s and 1850s, according to an observer of the day. **Ralph Waldo Emerson** was an eminent writer, but he galvanized a generation in and around Boston through his lectures, asserting by his statements and example that the United States had something vital to contribute to the world of letters.

Emerson was a Harvard graduate, but he considered that the greatest influence on his thinking was his Aunt Mary, a woman with the soul of a Puritan and the intellectual curiosity of a university full of professors. They talked at the end of each day, and wrote each other lively letters: hers was the quintessential Bostonian mind that shaped Emerson's as the model American one. The Boston writers who followed Emerson, either personally or in his wake, proved his point that America was ready to come forth with good writing: Herman Melville; Henry David Thoreau; Louisa May Alcott; Nathaniel Hawthorne; Henry Wadsworth Longfellow; Margaret Fuller; Oliver Wendell Holmes, and John Greenleaf Whittier, among them.

Another voice on the lecture circuit was that of **William Lloyd Garrison**, who published the newspaper *The Liberator*. Southern politicians wrote to their counterparts in Boston, asking them to quash *The Liberator*, because it was vehemently anti-Slavery. They weren't alone in fearing its influence, either: in 1834, a mob of pro-Slavery Bostonians dragged Garrison from his office, with a rope around his neck. A friend of Garrison's later described the riot: *"To the Common!" shouted the mob.*

'To the Common!' The first thought of the whole vast crowd – all maddened as one man is mad – was to drag the poor man to Boston Common – a beautiful park in front of the State House – there to hang him upon the great elm, the `Tree of Liberty,' on which Quakers had been hanged in the early Puritan days." The mayor himself led a force of strongmen to retrieve Garrison from the midst of the mob, long before they reached the tree.

Boston's in-fighting over the Slavery issue only amplified the anti-Slavery, or abolitionist, voices that riled crowds at meetings; the smallest of them in front parlors, the largest at Faneuil Hall. Blacks as well as whites held leadership positions in most of Boston's abolitionist groups. However, the focus for many of the African-Americans living on the north slope of Beacon Hill was personal: assisting runaway slaves.

The vehemence of the argument in Boston propelled the national debate, yet the city was not of a single mind on the issue of Slavery; in fact, once the war broke out in April 1861, recruiting speeches on the Common never once mentioned Slavery or the abolition of it. The only appeal that united Boston was that the Civil War was a battle to save the Union (the same one that some Bostonians had tried to break up in 1814).

BOSTON'S IMMIGRANT EXPERIENCE

Boston expanded in two lasting ways at the middle of the 19th-century. The Back Bay was filled in with train-loads of dirt from a nearby town, adding 450 acres and a new face to the look of the city. And immigration turned the Anglophilic old place into a city of many, many new faces. Up to one thousand immigrants arrived each day by the 1890s, from every nation, but notably from Italy, China, Ireland, and from the Jewish ghettos of Poland or Russia. The same was happening all over America, of course, but Boston, for all its liberal leanings, was built on a hard core of conservatism.

A **Restriction League of Boston** formed to try and stop immigration; that was one reaction. Other groups formed to try and assimilate the newcomers, embracing and educating them. Some historians maintain that the city's cultural institutions – the Symphony, the Museum of Fine Arts, the Museum of Natural History, and so on – formed with hidden urgency at the end of the 19th century, so that the Old Guard could establish a standard American culture, in the most public way possible.

Politically, the most influential of the immigrant groups were the Irish. Starting in mid-century, when there was not so much as a single policeman of Irish descent, they worked the election process to advantage, with the result that an Irish-American mayor in the 20th century was the norm, to which there have been only a few exceptions. Among the Irish-American mayors was **John Fitzgerald**, called by the memorable nickname, "Honey Fitz," who took office in 1907; his grandson and namesake, **John Fitzgerald Kennedy**, went from local congressman to senator to the presidency. His election in 1960 ended Boston's 136 year dry spell; JFK was the first president from Boston since John Quincy Adams (John Adams' son) won the 1824 election.

THE CITY GROWS

In the midst of change and influx, there was one thing that Bostonians did not do: they did not move away. Remarkably, the **North End**, the **Back Bay**, and **Beacon Hill** have remained stable residential neighborhoods for at least the past hundred years. In the 20th century, the city has not so much evolved in that way as it has changed through dramatic steps, for better or for worse, and major construction projects. The **Esplanade**, the park along the Charles River, was developed in 1910 and finished in the 1930s.

The **Fitzgerald Expressway**, a product of the 1950s, is almost never known as that: "Central Artery," is its mundane name. It is an elevated highway that sweeps past downtown and hacks the North End off of the rest of the city, as no water or chasm could.

The **Back Bay** was anchored in 1965 by the **Prudential Center**, an ambitious complex for its time, encompassing high-rise apartments and office buildings, with shopping on the ground floor. It was everything that the low-rise, architecturally mellow, Back Bay was not, yet it merged into the neighborhood nonetheless. **Scollay Square** was Boston's *demi-monde* through most of the century, but in the 1960s, it was cleaned out, as if with steel wool, to be replaced and renamed: **Government Center**. The new buildings are much less colorful – determinedly so – even if more productive than their predecessors.

The **West Side**, just beyond Government Center, was an old neighborhood that underwent urban renewal at about the same time, with the result that there isn't much there anymore. The West Side has almost always been something of a backwater neighborhood, but nowadays, it is showing some signs of life.

GROWTH THROUGH ANNEXATION

Boston was founded in 1630 as a town of 793 acres. Through annexation of whole towns, such as Charlestown and Dorchester, and extensive landfill, the city covers 24,000 acres today.

Mayor Josiah Quincy, elected in the 1820s, was one of Boston's most effective officials ever, and was the force behind construction of an elegant new marketplace in front of Faneuil Hall. By the 1960s, however, the four buildings there were practically abandoned – except by Durgin-Park, the restaurant that is permanent, if anything is permanent. At the end of the decade, a local architect named Ben Thompson submitted a plan to renovate Quincy Market into small shops. The newly realized **Faneuil Hall Marketplace** opened in 1976, a gift to the city: one that it already had. Today, much of Boston's energy is directed toward the harborfront area of **South Boston**, choice real estate that is in transition from outdoor work as a port, to button-down work as a business area.

Ben Thompson once said that, "The fact that Boston's past touches us daily is the most modern thing about the city." That past is not concentrated in one district, or even along the **Freedom Trail**. Walk around anywhere, and you will notice that all of Boston's years are out in the open, still. They were all of them years of arrival, in a sense.

Boston's history is closely associated with colonial days, and the fight for independence. There might not have been a Revolutionary War without Boston; there might not have been a Civil War, either. Boston pushed hard in both. Yet, the history that is all around in Boston is earlier than that. And later, too. It goes back to Winthrop's Covenant, not in its pious aspect, but in its sense of arrival, at a place where you must make good things happen – not just that you "can" make them happen, but that you *must*. That's the Covenant that lasted, and in the eyes of those who felt it, or still feel it, Boston *is* a city on a Hill.

BOSTON'S FIRSTS

Some of these were not originally a part of Boston proper, denoted by an asterisk, but they are all today part of the greater Boston experience:

America's first ...	date ...
St. Patrick's Day Celebration	March 17, 1737
Thanksgiving (a fasting day) *Massachusetts Bay Colony	February 22, 1631
college (Harvard) *Cambridge	October 28, 1634
post office	1639
public school supported by taxes *Dorchester	May 20, 1639
book published: The Whole Book of Psalmes Faithfully Translated Into English Metre *Cambridge	1640
coffee house (operated by a woman)	1670
underground sewer	1704
street lighting	1719
small-pox vaccinations	1800

4. PLANNING YOUR TRIP

BOSTON IN WHITE OR GREEN

Snow becomes Boston, and Childe Hassam painted the Back Bay in white as an urban idyll. Even so, the temperature can also rise from within – Boston warms up whenever its Celtics or Bruins get hot. And though its Christmas traditions are locked in time, Boston completely reinvented New Year's Eve, renaming it "First Night."

Summer, alas, will never see some of Boston's best moods. Neither will the crowds who flock to town in that season. The only predictable drawback to visiting in winter is that certain museums and tours close up shop for the winter, about Dec. 1 through April 1 (check individual schedules).

Obviously, seasonal attractions like golf courses close for the season, but here are some of the other specific sites that hibernate, as well:
• Longfellow National Historic Site
• Nichols House Museum
• Harvard University tours (closed for winter-break)
• Swan Boats, Public Garden
• Boston Tea Party Ship & Museum
• Whale watch cruises
• Most walking tours
• Bunker Pavilion (Monument stays open)

FUN ALTERNATIVES

Here are examples of a few of the ways to salvage the day, and your dignity.

IF YOU ARE SHUT OUT OF ...	GO STRAIGHT TO ...
All the whale watching cruises	**Long Wharf** for a Boston Harbor Cruise, Tel. 227-4321, to George's Island, about 1 1/2 hours roundtrip, and reservations are not necessary
Durgin-Park	**Jacob Wirth's**, 31 Stuart St., Tel. 338-8586. About as old as Durgin-Park, not quite the stupendous food, but at least as much old-fashioned atmosphere
Hayden Planetarium at the Science Museum	**J.B. Coit Observatory** at Boston University, 725 Commonwealth Ave., Tel. 353-2630. Visitors are welcomed on clear Wednesday nights, to look at the real thing: the universe

In summertime, Boston breaks out with things to do: and with the color of balloons at Quincy Market and of roses at the Public Garden; of red stockings at Fenway Park, of blue water embracing the old peninsula from the harbor and the river, and of green hugging it even closer in the parks known as the **Emerald Necklace**. It is also bursting with other people – which is not so bad: they're just trying to have fun, too. However, it is bad when they, those other people, arrive somewhere before you do.

If you are even a little flexible, there are always other options, even at the last minute, and this book will list many of them. It is a good idea, though, to make reservations for restaurants and for tours, especially cruises and whale-watches, as early as possible – as soon as you have your hotel booking in hand.

If the world happens to revolve around you, though – as it does me – then booking in advance will seem totally unnecessary until the moment somebody is closing a door on your nose. See the sidebar on the previous page for some ideas if you get shut out of your first choice.

WEATHER & WHAT TO WEAR

The two most common phenomena are fog and wind, neither of which is likely to be ruinous to the average day. Fog can cause delays in departures of tour boats, though, and it can certainly take the view out of the view at the John Hancock building. As to the wind: give some thought about which hat to wear and how to tie back your hair, especially if you are going anywhere near the harbor. Even Quincy Market can be gusty.

The average temperature for summer ranges between 60-85°F; for Fall and Spring, 37-68°F, and in Winter, 23-40°F. *For an updated message regarding the weather, call 936-1234.* To learn what the next three hours are expected to bring, take a look at the top of the old Hancock Building, at the corner of Clarendon and Berkeley streets in the Back Bay. The light on top is coded by color: blue (clear); flashing blue (cloudy); red (rain); flashing red (snow); flashing red in summertime (Red Sox game rained out).

In the wintertime, a snowstorm can make the streets slushy, with deep puddles at the corners. Only about two such snowfalls occur per month, but just in case, bring waterproof shoes or boots. For fair weather, the note to make on shoes is that many sidewalks in Beacon Hill, Charlestown, and at Quincy Market/Faneuil Hall are paved in cobble or brick, so wear something fairly sturdy to go walking.

In matters of dress, Boston is more careful than most other cities. Jackets and ties, and equivalent dress for women, are expected in most of the nicer restaurants and required by some, such as Anthony's Pier Four.

Obviously, in our day and age, you can generally wear anything you like, but Bostonians usually go a notch above the norm; around town, you'll see sweaters rather than sweatshirts, walking shorts, rather than jogging togs, and polo shirts rather than T-shirts.

BOSTON'S AREA CODE

*The area code for Boston is **617**. Unless otherwise noted, that is the code for all of the telephone numbers listed in this book. The region has two other area codes: **781** and **978**. There may be some pattern to the service of those two, inasmuch as 781 forms (more or less) the closer of two concentric rings around Boston. It would have baffled Paul Revere, though: Lexington doesn't even have the same area code as Concord.*

INFORMATION IN ADVANCE

Contact the Greater Boston Convention & Visitor's Bureau for a copy of the publication, *Boston Travel Planner* – it has what this book cannot give, the schedules for specific events in each new season. It is free of charge. For $5.25, you can order a complete *Visitor Information Kit*, including a guidebook (now, what do you need that for?), a good map, a coupon-booklet, and other brochures.

The Bureau can be reached through any of the following means:

• **Greater Boston Convention and Visitors Bureau**, *Two Copley Place, Suite 105, Boston, MA 02116-6501. Tel. 617/536-4100, Fax 617/424-7664; Toll free: 888/733-2678 (U.S. and Canada only); Website: www.bostonusa.com*

Other numbers for events and schedules:

• **Cambridge Office for Tourism**, *Tel. 800/862-5678 or 617/441-2884*
• **Massachusetts Office of Travel & Tourism**, *Tel. 617/727-3201; Website: www.mass-vacation.com*

ANNUAL EVENTS

Boston has its own calendar: the same exact things as last year. And sometimes, the century before that. These are a few of the highlights, which can be exhilarating, but can also make for tight times in hotel bookings:

January	**First Night** - *December 31-January 1; Tel. 536-4100 or 542-1399.* Invented in Boston in 1975, First Night is a non-alcoholic smorgasbord of music and entertainment, at dozens of sites around the city. One ticket, at $10, is good for admission to any and all of them, though reservations are necessary for some
February	**Food, Wine & Arts Celebration** - *all month (and beyond)*
March	**The New England Spring Flower Show** - *second week*; since 1871
April	**Boston Marathon** - *3rd Monday,* which is a state holiday called Patriots Day; since 1897. The race ends in the Back Bay at Copley Place.
May	**Graduation** at 53 colleges in the vicinity; Harvard and MIT are in June
June	**Summer Music Festival** - popular music, all summer long
July	**Harborfest**; *first week.* Boston Pops, fireworks, reading of the Declaration of Independence from the Old State House, and Chowderfest
October	**Head-of-the-Charles Regatta**, Charles River
December	**Holiday** performances of *Nutcracker, Child's Christmas in Wales, Black Nativity,* Handel's *Messiah,* and other long-standing traditions

24-HOUR TOWN

Most of Boston falls quiet at some point in the day - but not these stores and services:

- **Copy Cop**: *815 Boylston St. Tel. 267-9267.* Also 13 other locations: business services
- **CVS/pharmacy**: *Porter Square, Cambridge. Tel. 876-4037*
- **Dependable Cleaners**: *110 Newbury St. Tel. 267-1235.* Dry cleaning.
- **Bakery**: *Bova Bakery, 76 Prince St., North End. Tel. 523-5601.* Breads, cakes and pastries.
- **Post Office**: *South Station, Tel. 654-5326; Logan Airport, Tel. 567-1296*
- **Supermarket**: *Star Market, Prudential Center, except Saturday night, midnight to 6am.*

PRONUNCIATION GUIDE

You can clown around with Boston's accent, saying, "Pok the cah in Hah-vad Yod," but you can't mess with the town's passwords:

The Back Bay - not Back Bay

Bowdoin - Boe-din

Common - not Commons

Copley - Kop-lee (not Kope-lee)

Faneuil - Fannul

Peabody - Peabiddy

Public Garden - not Gardens

Quincy - Quinzey

Rowes - Rose

Tremont - Traymont

Worcester - Woohstur

CURRENCY EXCHANGE

- **BayBank**, *Tel. 788-5000*
- **Thomas Cook**, *Tel. 426-0016*

MEDICAL & DENTAL CARE

- **In-House Doctor**, *Tel. 859-1776*. 24-hour medical or dental housecalls.
- **Massachusetts Dental Society**, *Tel. 508/651-7511*. Referrals.
- **Beth Israel Hospital**, *330 Brookline Ave.*, *Tel. 667-8000*; 24-hour Emergency Room, *Tel. 667-3337 (TTY/TDD, Tel. 667-4195)*
- **Massachusetts General Hospital Physician Referral Service**, *Tel. 800/711-4644*; Monday-Friday, 8:30 am- 5:30 pm; main hospital number, *Tel. 726-2000*

GOOD NUMBERS TO KNOW

- **Emergencies** only, *Tel. 911*
- **Non-emergencies**, *Tel. 343-4200*
- **Travelers Aid Society**, *Tel. 542-7286*
- **Weather Recording**, *Tel. 936-1234 or 976-6200*

PUBLICATIONS

The *Boston Globe* publishes a complete events calendar in its Thursday editions. The *Boston Herald* is the city's other daily, with good sports and entertainment coverage. Weekly and bi-weekly papers focus on nightlife and the arts: *The Phoenix*, *TAB*, and *Improper Boston*.

In addition, each Boston neighborhood has a paper that covers the home turf in the same way as a small-town weekly. Among them are the *South End News* and the *Beacon Hill Times*. The *Cambridge Current* is a visitor's guide to timely happenings across the Charles River.

5. ARRIVALS & DEPARTURES

BY AIR

Logan Airport is the 11th busiest in the world. During the peak traffic times of 7-10 am, and 4:30-7:30 pm, one flight lands or takes off every 90 seconds. There are five terminals named by letter, with "E," for example, used for international flights. Over three dozen airlines operate flights through Logan; USAir and Delta offer the most complete domestic service.

The **main airport phone number** is *Tel. 567-5400*. For complete airport transportation information, including shuttles to the regions around Boston, call the **24 hour toll-free number**, *Tel. 800/23-LOGAN (235-6426)*.

Logan is located within the city limits in the section known as East Boston, across the harbor from downtown (and the Shawmut Peninsula). It is well-connected to downtown by water, rail, and road:

· **Massport Water Shuttle** – a seven-minute boat ride across the harbor, between Rowes Wharf (Atlantic Ave.) and a dock on the grounds of the airport. The cost for the ride is: adults, $8; senior citizens, $4; under 12, free. A water-shuttle leaves either side every 15 minutes, Monday-Friday, 6 am-8 pm. The service runs every half-hour on weekends: Friday, 8-11 pm; Saturday, 10 am-11 pm; Sunday, 10 am-8 pm. The view is spectacular and it's great to be on the water – especially during a traffic jam on land. *For information, call 330-8680 or 439-3131.* A free shuttle-bus takes passengers between the airport dock and the terminals (see the next paragraph for more information on the shuttle-bus).

- **The T** – Boston's subway system, called the T, has a stop at Logan, called "Airport" on the Blue Line. The cost to any stop in or near Boston is 85 cents (outlying towns will cost more), and the trip to a downtown stop, such as Park St., takes about 12 minutes. Free shuttle-buses, marked "**MASSPORT**," operate between all five terminals and both the T-stop and the water-shuttle dock. The buses are well-marked, but if you want to remember it, bus number 22 serves Terminals A and B, while bus number 33 serves Terminals C, D, and E. *For questions about the Airport-T, call the airport at Tel. 800/23-LOGAN (235-6426) or call the M.B.T.A., Tel. 722-3200.*

- **Taxis & Limousines** – a cab-ride will cost about $12-16 to a downtown or Back Bay address. However, traffic can sometimes slow the typical ride-time from about 20 minutes to ... well, much longer than 20 minutes. If you are squeezed for time during the rush hour, and the thought of a long wait in traffic makes you nervous, take either the T or the water shuttle (depending on the location in Boston). Two good taxicab companies are **Checker Cab Co.**, *Tel. 497-9000* and **Red Cab**, *Tel. 734-5000*. A bus/limousine will take somewhat longer in either direction than a cab, with stops for other passengers; the cost is about $8. Bus or limo companies that offer scheduled service are **Back Bay Coach**, *Tel. 698-6188*, and **City Transportation**, *Tel. 567-1888*.

- **Bus** – The MBTA runs a bus (route CT3) from all Logan terminals to such stops as the World Trade Center/Seaport District and the Longwood Medical Area. The fare is 60¢.

BY LAND
By Bus

Two companies serve Boston with scheduled routes. **Greyhound**, *Tel. 800/231-2222*, has connections to the rest of the country. **Peter Pan**, *Tel. 800/343-9999*, is focused on the northeast, including New York City and the gambling casinos on Native American lands in Connecticut. Both companies operate out of South Station.

By Car

If you're driving from points south, you'll most likely take I-95 straight into Boston. If you're coming from Cape Cod, you'll take Route 3 to Route 93 into town. And if you're approaching from the west, the main highway into town is Route 90, also known as the Mass Pike. For state **highway conditions**, call *800/828-9104.*

By Train

Amtrak connects Boston to many other cities all around the country; New York is a little more than four hours on an express train. The trip to New York takes only two hours and forty-five minutes on the new High Speed Train, which runs all the way to Washington from Boston. Amtrak trains also go due west to Albany and on to Chicago. All Amtrak trains make two stops in Boston: the Back Bay station (near Copley Square), and South Station (near downtown). Both connect with the T; South Station is also the bus terminal. *In Boston, Amtrak's telephone number is Tel. 482-3660; nationwide, call 800/USA-RAIL (872-7245).*

The **MBTA**, *Tel. 722-3200*, which operates the T, has extended commuter-train service to nearby towns well worth visiting, including historic Lowell and seaside Rockport.

6. GETTING AROUND TOWN

All public transportation – including buses, subway, commuter trains, and water shuttles – is operated by the **Massachusetts Bay Transportation Authority** (**MBTA**). The **buses** generally provide service to outlying areas of the city and suburbs.

The **subway** – which comes up for air outside of the central city – is called the "**T**," and it will take visitors within walking distance of most of the places they want to go. The T encompasses four lines, listed with some of their noteworthy stops:

- **Blue Line** – Suffolk Downs, Airport, Aquarium
- **Green Line** – Copley Square (Back Bay), Science Park (Museum of Science), Museum (Museum of Fine Arts)
- **Orange Line** – Community College (Charlestown), Back Bay/South End
- **Red Line** – Harvard, Charles/MGH (Beacon Hill), JFK/U.Mass (Kennedy Library)

Hours of operation for the T are as follows: service starts at 5 am weekdays, 6 am weekends; service ends each day with the last trains leaving Park St. (downtown) at 12:45 am. The cost of taking the T to any of the stops listed above, or to any other stops in the immediate vicinity of Boston, is 85 cents.

Boston city buses are also 85 cents. Passes for unlimited travel, called **Passports**, are sold as follows, one day, $5; three days, $9; seven days, $18.

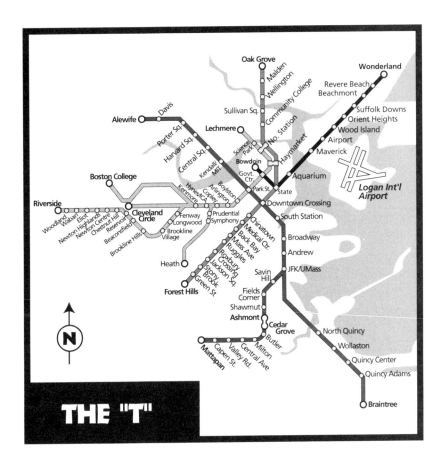

THE "T"

T-passports include discount coupons for attractions around town. Even so, you would have to travel quite a bit (six trips) to make the one–day pass worthwhile, but the others may make sense. The passports are sold at convenient locations, such as the **Visitor Information Center** *on the Boston Common (Tremont St. near Winter St.), or call 222–3200 for other locations.*

The MBTA also operates a commuter train service that goes to outlying towns as far away as Providence, with higher cost. *The MBTA can be reached at 222-3200; its website is www.mbta.com.*

You shouldn't forget that boats are practical forms of transportation in Boston. The MBTA oversees a **shuttle boat** between the Charlestown Navy Yard and Long Wharf ($1), *Tel. 227-4321.* Two other commuter routes, which may be fun just for the ride, go between Rowes Wharf and Hingham on the South Shore ($4), and between Long Wharf and Hull, also to the south ($3). The MBTA also operates the Airport water-shuttle, *Tel. 330-8680 or 439-3131* (see Chapter 5, *Arrivals & Departures*). **Boston Harbor Cruises**, *Tel.* 227-4321, runs a water-shuttle to the Kennedy Library from Long Wharf.

PARKING

The best thing to do with your car, once you're in Boston, is sell it. Get rid of it somehow for the duration of your trip, because some of the most inviting parts of the city have the tightest parking, including on that list Beacon Hill, Charlestown, and the North End. A couple of hotels in Boston proper that provide parking with the cost of a room are the **MidTown**, *220 Huntington Av., Tel. 262-1000 or 800/343-1177,* and the **Howard Johnson** location at *575 Commonwealth Av., Tel. 267-3100.*

Having said that you shouldn't take your car into certain popular neighborhoods expecting to find on-street parking, here is a list of parking garages in each:

- **Back Bay**: *Danker & Donohue, 341 Newbury St. Tel. 536-3380*
- **Beacon Hill**: *Charles St. Parking – 144 Charles St. Tel. 523-8432*
- **Financial District**: *Garage at Post Office Square, Tel. 423-1430*
- **Fenway Park**: *Pilgrim Parking – Yawkey Way; Tel. 859-0441*
- **North End**: *Kinney, 600 Commercial St.; Tel. 742-6759*
- **Midtown**: *Boston Common Underground Garage – under the Common, enter from Charles St., Tel. 523-7395*
- **Prudential Center**: *Back Bay, Tel. 267-2965*
- **Theater District**: *Kinney, 400 Stuart St., Tel. 572-7275*

WALKING

The only group that seems to have a lower regard for pedestrians than Boston drivers are the people who program Boston's crossing signals. I have shaken many a fist at both. A white "walk" sign means that it is the walker's turn to use the street. A flashing red "Don't Walk" sign means that the light will change at any second; proceed with caution – and alacrity. The white signs don't normally last long enough for Secretariat to get across. Under either the white or flashing red, though, step lively and watch the traffic.

Keep in mind that right-on-red turns are legal at most intersections and that the cars sometimes have the right-of-way. I could walk in my sleep in New York City or London, places where order prevails by comparison. I keep my eyes wide open in Boston.

TOURS

At least a half-dozen companies operate bus tours of the city. Here is a selection, with a prime attribute of each:

- **Boston Duck Tours**: *101 Huntington Ave, next to Prudential Center. Tel. 723-DUCK/723-3825.* Amphibious vehicles tour the city and then go right across the Charles River. An 80-minute tour costs $21.
- **Boston Trolley/Blue Trolley**: *Tel. 269-3626*; getting on and off allowed; call for pick-up locations.
- **Brush Hill Tours/Beantown Trolley/Gray Line**: *Tel. 236-2148*; complimentary pick-up from Boston hotels.
- **Old Town Trolley Tours**: *Tel. 269-7010*; getting on and off allowed; call for pick-up locations.

WHO ARE THOSE GUYS, ANYWAY?

You will note in Boston that everything from an alley to a park bench is named after someone. As in most cities, you can hear a name ten times a day, without ever having heard of the person who first made it famous:

Boylston - *Dr. Zabdiel, physician*
Copley - *John Singleton, 1738-1815, painter and large landowner*
Faneuil - *Peter, 1700-1742, merchant*
Harvard - *John, 1607-1638, clergyman*
Hatch (*Hatch Memorial Shell, on the Esplanade*) - *Edward*
Hynes - *Mayor John B.*
Logan - *Lt. Gen. Edward L., lawyer, judge, soldier (WWI)*
Quincy - *Mayor Josiah, 1772-1864*

7. BOSTON'S BEST PLACES TO STAY

About thirty years ago, standardization swept into the hotel industry, and it seemed for awhile that industrial designers were well on the way to determining the one medium hotel acceptable for all travelers. They never quite succeeded, though mass-produced hotel rooms are all around – and sometimes, let's face it, they are just right, in their medium way. However, sometimes, they are not. When I think of a half-dozen of my best friends, and try, as a mental exercise, to pick out one Boston hotel just right for all of them at once, the quiet complaints grow into squabbles, even in my imagination.

There are more than forty hotels listed in Chapter 9, *Where To Stay,* and they are all respectable and well-kept; they are all convenient to something, it is safe to say, and the listings specify the attractions in the immediate vicinity of each. But these are the stand-outs in different categories that may be important to completely different types of people.

A GOOD BARGAIN

MIDTOWN HOTEL, *220 Huntington Ave., Boston 02115. Tel. 262-1000, Fax, 262-8739; Reservations, Tel. 800/343-1177. Rates: $79-159. 159 rooms. Built circa 1968. Main amenities: free indoor parking; outdoor swimming pool.*

With rooms under or around $100 per night, the MidTown is a rarity in town. It also offers free indoor parking, another rarity, and a pretty swimming pool in the central court. If I were with a group, the MidTown would be a relaxed place to use as a base. It is a low, white building, more like a motel you'd find in a prosperous suburb, perhaps in California, than the high-rises and brownstones across the Back Bay.

The rooms are clean and comfortable, renovated in 1996, though I venture to doubt that you would borrow any of their decorating ideas for your own house. They are cheerfully ... basic. The hotel's public rooms, including the lobby, are more sleek, with an antique piece here and there. Located almost next door to the Colonnade Hotel, the MidTown is across the street from the Christian Science church campus, and within a block or two of Symphony Hall, the Hynes Convention Center, the Pru, and the thick of the Back Bay.

The MidTown's restaurant is called Tables of Content, serving all day.

CLOSE TO EVERYTHING, DOWNTOWN

OMNI PARKER HOUSE, *Tremont and School Sts., Boston 02108. Tel. 227-8600, Fax, 742-5729; Reservations, Tel. 800-843-6664. Rates: $119-249. 535 rooms. Built in 1927. Valet parking; room service; business services.*

The original Parker House Hotel was built in 1855, when Boston was only old, and not yet ancient. Because of that, it nabbed a pinpoint location in the midst of Boston's business, the state's government, and some of the nation's most important tourist attractions. The new Parker House, built in 1927 to replace the original one, is on the same spot, one of the city's most venerable hotels in its own right. In fact, it is the oldest major hotel in the country, in terms of continuous operation. There are older minor hotels, and there are older hotel buildings, ones built for some other business, but the Parker House has the distinction that in 1856 and on this very day, today, people came to Boston from all over the country with the entity called the Parker House on their minds.

The richly paneled lobby has that air of importance, bolstered by the continuing tradition that every U.S. President since Coolidge has been a guest. The Parker House presides in Tremont Street downtown, two blocks away from the Common or the State House.

CLOSE TO EVERYTHING, THE BACK BAY

THE LENOX HOTEL, *710 Boylston St., Boston 02116-2699. Tel. 536-5300, Fax 267-1237; Reservations, Tel. 800/996-3160; website: www.Lenoxhotel.com. Rates: $180-250; suite, $450. 214 rooms. Built in 1898. Main amenities: valet parking; small gym; room-service.*

The Lenox is a small but formal hotel, built in the last century, and renovated in 1996. It is in the midst of the Back Bay: across the street from the modern addition to the Public Library, two blocks from Copley Place, three to the Public Garden, and about four to the Pru and the Hynes centers. It is a half-block from the Copley T-stop.

A couple of world travelers that I know commented that for all of its convenience, the Lenox still has a quality of detachment. That is probably because it works hard to retain its own personality. With a combination of antiques and good reproductions; high, plaster-worked ceilings, and rich wallpapers, the Lenox is a well-defined hotel.

BUTTON-DOWN BUSINESS ADDRESS

FOUR SEASONS HOTEL, *200 Boylston St., Boston 02116. Tel. 338-4400, Fax 423-0154; Reservations, Tel. 800/332-3442. Rates: (single) $295-505; (double) $335-545; (suite) $850-2,950. 288 rooms. Opened 1985. Main amenities: valet parking; extensive gym and spa, with indoor pool; 24-hour room service.*

According to my own assiduous eavesdropping, the well-dressed people hovering around the concierge desk at the Four Seasons never tend to business errands with clients or colleagues closer than Madagascar. Flinging packages to Japan, placing calls to Chile, speaking three languages in the course of one sentence: it is not that other hotels can't handle the same high-powered executives. It is that it seems a waste of the Four Seasons' muscle to stay there without being on intra-planetary business. But perhaps it is not enough just to do business efficiently, one must be seen to be doing business efficiently, and the Four Seasons is an unassailable address. (Unless your stockholders check over your expense account ...)

The hotel's flagship restaurant is Aujourd'hui, considered one of the top restaurants in Boston. With a dining room on the second floor overlooking the Public Garden, it gets its name and much of its reputation from the effort that the chefs make in gathering local ingredients, fresh today (*aujourd'hui*). On the ground level, a more casual restaurant also faces the Garden.

SQUEAKY, SHINY CLEAN

BOSTON HARBOR HOTEL AT ROWES WHARF, *70 Rowes Wharf, Boston 02110. Tel. 439-7000, Fax, 330-9450; Reservations, Tel. 800/752-7077; website: www.bhh.com. Rates: $260-430. 230 rooms. Built: 1987. Main Amenities: valet parking, gym and spa, indoor pool, extensive business center, 24-hour room service.*

The Boston Harbor Hotel takes up most of one central building at Rowes Wharf, the complex of 18th century style buildings overlooking Boston Harbor. In the top echelon of Boston hotels, it has a settled grace that ought to take a lot longer than ten years to establish, yet that is its age. The hotel is immaculate, perhaps because it is relatively new, or because the construction values look to be old (that is, of a quality not often seen these days) – or perhaps because the housekeeping staff works hard at what they do.

One of my friends considers cleanliness to be the only criterion for a hotel, "clean" meaning, mind you, that it is neither dirty nor noxious from the smell of cleansers. And the Boston Harbor passes inspection. Having made a grand hotel seem like an operating theater, it might also be a good idea to describe its other charms. The Boston Harbor Hotel is elegant in a masculine way, with a collection of fine antique pieces, and endless lounges unraveling around views of the water on each of the two public floors. The harborside location is more than just picturesque, though. Guests arriving at the hotel by private boat have use of a 30-slip marina. Guests arriving in Boston by airplane can use the seven-minute Airport Water Shuttle, a motorboat service that goes directly to Rowes Wharf.

The Rowes Wharf Restaurant serves New England cooking as haute cuisine – and overlooks a good chunk of New England, too, in the form of Boston Harbor. From May to September, the hotel's cafe serves lunch and dinner outdoors at harborside.

WITH FAMILY

BOSTON MARRIOTT LONG WHARF, *296 State St., Boston 02109. Tel. 227-0800, Fax, 227-2867; Reservations, Tel. 800/228-9290. Rates: $265-295. 400 rooms. Built 1982. Main amenities: valet parking; gym with indoor pool; business center.*

Most guestrooms at the Marriott have private balconies overlooking the city and the harbor, from the second and third stories. For children (those old enough to know not to climb over the brick wall and fall), it would be a boon to have a room with a constant show of boats and birds. For all of the time that children wait in hotel rooms for their parents to get ready – a process that seems to take up most of the vacation – the spacious balconies would make it impossible to feel cooped up.

Shaped like a brick barn, the Marriott Long Wharf is indeed aligned at the base of the specified wharf, just across Atlantic Avenue from Faneuil Hall. Light and airy throughout the inside, it is especially fitting for families, with Christopher Columbus Park on one side of it, harbor-tour boats departing from their docks on the other, and the New England Aquarium nearby. The Aquarium subway stop is connected to the hotel, giving guests convenient access to other parts of the city via the Blue Line; the airport is just two stops away.

Seafood comes to mind on Long Wharf, and that is the basis of the hotel's primary restaurant, the Oceana. There is also a California-style grill for casual meals.

IF IT WERE ROMANCE

THE ELIOT, *370 Commonwealth Ave., Boston 02215. Tel. 267-1607, Fax, 536-9114; Reservations, Tel. 800/443-5468. Rates: (all rooms are suites) single, $205-225; double, $245-265. two bedroom suites, $375-450. 91 rooms. Built in 1925. Amenities: Valet parking; all rooms have kitchenettes.*

The Eliot has the sort of qualities that inculcate the best possible mood in the least possible crowd (two people): privacy, quiet, class, and a pleasant location, among them. All of its guestrooms are suites, with kitchenettes, for a homelike sense of coziness. In fact, for a long time, the Eliot was a residential hotel, where Harvard old boys and Radcliffe old girls could live out their years comfortably, next door to their school club on Commonwealth Avenue.

In 1990, the family that owned the hotel decided to turn it into a luxury "little hotel," a European-flavored category of which Boston then had none. The whole place was renovated, inside and out. I thought the Eliot looked great to begin with; I thought it looked even better after the renovation, but the improvements keep coming: a new ironwork portico, worthy of Brussels; new uniforms for the doormen; better planters, new fur hats for the doormen in the winter. Some people look to the top of the old John Hancock building to see what the weather is going to be; some of us look to the headgear of the Eliot doormen.

The Eliot is located at the western end of the Back Bay, one block from the Hynes T-stop; three blocks from the Hynes Convention Center, and about four, in the other direction, from Fenway Park. Breakfast is served in a small dining area. Clio's is the Eliot's high-visibility bistro, serving an overly ambitious menu of nouvelle cuisine.

8. CHILD'S PLAY

The first part of this chapter is organized the way that children visit a city – not the way that I do, and perhaps not as you do. The second part of the chapter is organized the way that parents see a city.

CHILDREN'S BOSTON

The following sections are arranged in order of importance from a kid's vantage.

Dinosaurs

The best exhibit is at the **Harvard University Museum of Cultural and Natural History**, *26 Oxford Street, Tel. 495-3045; Hours: Monday-Saturday, 9 am-5 pm; Sunday, 1-5 pm; Cost: Adults, $5; senior citizens and students, $4; ages 3-12, $3; Free every Saturday 9 am-Noon*. There are real skeletons, including a big sea-dino called a kronosaurus and the head of a triceratops. Also, other kinds of skeletons: mammoths, bears, big cats. Also a six-foot ant farm and a long room filled with birds – stuffed ones. Lots else. After school and on weekends, there are special programs for children, *Tel. 495-2341*.

The **Museum of Science**, *Science Park, Tel. 723-2500*, has some dinosaur bones – most of a stegosaurus – and a big, fake Tyrannosaurus. With something to do everywhere you look, the place is a funhouse of science, even besides the dinosaurs. Take the T to the Science park stop. Hours are Saturday-Thursday, 9 am-5 pm (to 7 pm in summer); Friday, 9 am-9 pm. Cost: adults, $8, senior citizens and children, $6.

Playgrounds
- **Back Bay**: corner of Commonwealth and Clarendon
- **The Common**: just about in the middle
- **North End**: Prince St. near Snowhill

Animals
The **Franklin Park Zoo**, *Columbia Rd., and Blue Hill Rd., South Boston, Tel. 442-2002, website: www.newenglandzoo.com,* has a Children's Area with farm animals to pet. The rest of the zoo was recently renovated and makes the world of the different animals come alive. If you're taking the T: orange-line to Forest Hills, or Red Line to Andrew Station; take the No. 16 bus from either one. Hours of operation: April-October, Monday-Friday, 10 am-5 pm., Saturday-Sunday, 10 am-6 pm.; November-April, daily, 9 am-4 pm. Cost: ages 12 and up, $6; seniors, students, $5; ages 4-11, $3; under 3 free.

The Sea Lion Show at the **New England Aquarium**, *Central Wharf off Atlantic Ave., Tel. 973-5200,* should delight the kids. Outside in the harbor, the sea lions don't do an act ... they actually participate in a program all about the Boston Harbor. If you're taking the T, your stop is Aquarium.

> ### THE ZOO
> *Recently renovated, the **Franklin Park Zoo** is a swell place for a short walk to learn something from the animals. It is divided into four main sections: African Tropical Forest; Bird's World; Children's Zoo, and Hooves and Horns. For a longer walk or jog, you can go on through the rolling lawns of Franklin Park, or play a round of golf.*

People Dressed-up
Usually, there's an actor who looks like **Benjamin Franklin** talking to children and other people in front of the Quincy Market.

The people onboard the *U.S.S. Constitution* at the Charlestown Navy Yard are real, for-real U.S. Navy sailors, though for their duty onboard the 18th-century warship, they revert to the official uniforms of about 1810.

Cool

The **MIT Museum**, *Tel. 253-4422*, has an exhibit of holograms, which are 3-D photographs made by a specialized scientific process that makes everyone who looks at one say, "My sainted aunt!" or something else indicating amazement.

Jillian's, *145 Ipswich St. at Landsdowne, next to Fenway Park, Tel. 437-0300; T-stop: Kenmore Square; Hours: Monday-Saturday, 11 am-2 am; Sunday, Noon-2 am,* is a restaurant with nine-zillion games – if you happen to like billiards, video games, arcade and pinball games, and virtual reality games.

The **Mapparium**, *250 Mass. Ave., Tel. 450-3790,* is a glass globe of the world that you walk right into, it being about 40 feet in diameter. But because it's glass, your voice carries in the weirdest ways; a whisper sounds like a shout. The T-stop is Symphony; hours are Monday-Saturday, 10 am-4 pm; no admission.

Starved for a Story

The **Somerville Public Library**, *Tel. 776-6531,* operates Dial-a-Story. Even over the phone, a good tale can be mesmerizing; the library records a new one every week.

Toys

F.A.O. Schwartz, *440 Boylston Street, Tel. 262-5000,* is a wonderland of a store, in which you can play with most of the toys to your heart's content. The clerks are ultra-nice about it, too.

Ice Cream

Some people know Newbury Street by the cross streets. More important geographically, however, are the ice cream places: between Mass. Ave. and Hereford, **J.P. Licks** (painted to look cow-like); between Gloucester and Fairfield, **Emack and Bolio's**, and so on. Unless I am mistaken, you'll never be caught in that terrible position of not being on the same block as an ice cream parlor.

Boats

The coolest thing is when the **Boston Duck Tour**, *Tel. 723-3825,* which uses amphibious vehicles, actually takes the plunge right into the Charles River, after a tour on wheels of the rest of the city.

But the best thing is a ride on a **Swan Boat**, no matter if you do have to wait in line to get on. They operate on the pond at the Public Garden, and there is a big swan at the back.

Tours

"Make Way for Ducklings" tour follows the route taken by the mother duck and her family in Robert McCloskey's book of the same title. For ages 5 and up, it takes an hour-and-a-half ($5), and is offered by the **Historic Neighborhoods Foundation**, *Tel. 426-1885.*

Beaches

The best thing about a beach is if you don't have to drive in the car for a year to get there.

Revere Beach is great. It is a mere 20 minutes from Government Center on the T, which is just like a train and not a subway after it crosses the harbor to East Boston. The beach is wide – the sand is kind of dark, but it packs well for castles – and the water stays relatively calm because the beach is part of the nook of a bay. The pavilions were recently renovated to their turn-of-the-century appearance, but who cares about that when Kelly's is right across the street, selling hot dogs, fish 'n chips, and really good roast beef sandwiches. Revere is not the most charming part of New England, but it's a good beach.

PARENTS' BOSTON

We didn't come all the way to Boston to eat ice cream all day.

Museum Programs

The following have special programs for children. They vary in content and frequency throughout the year, but are usually held on Saturday mornings. Some exhibits are free, others charge admission.

• **John F. Kennedy Library**, *Columbia Point, Dorchester, Tel. 929-4523*
• **Harvard University Museum**, *Tel. 495-2341*
• **Museum of Science**, *Tel. 589-0300*
• **USS Constitution Museum**, *Tel. 426-1812*

Convenient

A warehouse (literally) of activities for children aged about three to six, the **Children's Museum**, *300 Congress Street, Tel. 426-8855*, is located downtown, not far from shopping and other attractions. Other museums listed in this chapter may prove to be more memorable, – and less expensive – but the Children's Museum is a kid's world unto itself, a cross between an indoor playground and a school fair. Darting around with parents in tow, children can try weaving, see themselves on TV, learn about Native American life, or crawl through a tunnel, among other things.

For more information, see Chapter 11, *Seeing the Sights*.

Theater

The **Boston Children's Theater**, *647 Boylston Street. Tel. 424-6634*, features children in the audience, children up onstage. Tickets range $10-12.

WHAT'S GOING ON FOR KIDS

The Boston Parents' Paper, P.O. Box 1777, Boston 02130; Tel. 522-1515, is a newspaper with listings and advertisements pertaining to children's theater, special events, and story-telling at bookstores around town. Available at Bread & Circus; call for other locations.

Music

The **Boston Symphony Orchestra Youth Concerts**, *Symphony Hall, Massachusetts Ave, Tel. 266-1492; T: Symphony*, usually present three programs for children each season.

Toys

No Kidding! A Toy Store, *19 Harvard St., Brookline, Tel. 739-2477*, is a different kind of toy store: not a Barbie or a Ninja in sight. Better than all that: for example, card games for ages 5 and up, made locally, Slamwich, $9.95; Rat-a-tat Cat, $9.95. Also: Dog Dice, for ages 6 and up, $15.99. Toys you've never heard of. What a relief.

Animals

The **City of Boston Park Rangers**, *Tel. 635-7383*, offer free tours, including wilderness waks within the city limits at Franklin Park, and seasonal programs such as "Signs of Spring." They also offer a "Make Way for Ducklings Walk," specially designed for ages 2-6.

Tours

Boston By Foot, *Tel. 367-2345*, a non-profit tour organization, offers **Boston By Little Feet**, a tour of the downtown portion of the Freedom Trail for children aged 6 to 12 and their parents. Each child navigates with his or her own map. The Old South Meeting House sponsors a tour called **Ben and Kids**, *Tel. 482-6439*, a two-hour walk for children 8 and older, accompanied by parents.

Storytelling

The New England Aquarium offers frequent storytimes and children's special events, for free, at the World of Water Gift and Bookshop, *Tel. 973-0204*, next to the Aquarium on Central Wharf. Not all of the stories are tales of the sea, but most are.

Treat

The **Bova Bakery**, *76 Prince Street, Tel. 523-5601*, in the North End decorates cupcakes into works of happy art, plump clown faces and elf heads ($2.50 each). The North End has many bakeries, but none with such a sense of fun.

Something Different

The **Ritz-Carlton**, *15 Arlington Street, Tel 536-5700,* has a series of programs designed, according to a hotel brochure, "to introduce young ladies and gentlemen to The Ritz-Carlton traditions." There is a Teddy Bear Tea; a Day of Social Savvy (etiquette) and special holiday programs, in addition to the Junior Chef Debut at which children "explore the Pastry Shop and Garde Manger (food pantry)," among other things.

Beaches

The best thing about a beach is if you don't have to look for a parking place. **Manchester** is a seaside town of white clapboard houses and tiny downtown stores. The sea nips almost into town at a grassy town park, and Singing Beach is up a sloping road called Beach Street just north of that.

The best way to get there is by taking the MBTA commuter train from North Station, a ride of just under an hour that takes in the ocean views along the way. Children will likely enjoy the train ride, and besides, there are two good reasons not to drive to Manchester: the traffic can easily clog on the way out of Boston, and there is very little convenient parking within one mile of the beach. The sand leads down another slope to the water.

9. WHERE TO STAY

A good night's sleep in Boston will cost you somewhere in the range of, say, $15 to $3,000. Therein lies the decision, ranging through everything from a clean bed at the hostel to a suite at the Four Seasons.

Three new hotels are scheduled to open in downtown Boston in the year 2000, with more to follow, and so the supply of hotel rooms is still growing. But not fast enough: when a big convention or a festival hits town, veritably the whole city can be sold out, and so reservations in Boston are always recommended.

The prices listed below are standard room rates, for use only as a guide, because they may well be subject to haggling, prodding, and poking for special packages, in addition to market fluctuation. All over America, booking travel is becoming about as fun and nearly as fair across the board as buying a new car, so have all of your affiliations handy, from the Flipper Fan Club on up, because being a member of a club, almost any club, may land you a discount. Even if you have never worked a day in your life, you might as well make it a habit to ask for the corporate hotel room rate. It seems un-American to make people pay different prices for the same exact thing, but that's part of the hotel business now, at many places.

Weekend rates vary in both directions from the weekday rates in Boston. At downtown hotels, they are usually less, while on the water, in the summer, they are quite a bit more. All hotel rooms in Massachusetts carry a tax at least 9.7 percent; the tax is 12.45 percent in Boston. Parking will cost $10-25 per day, where there is a charge.

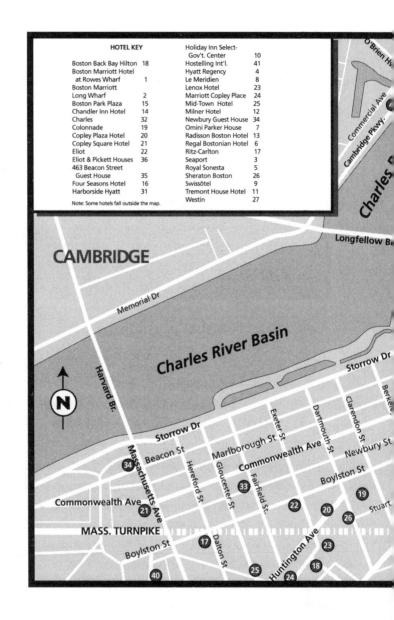

HOTEL KEY

Boston Back Bay Hilton	18
Boston Marriott Hotel at Rowes Wharf	1
Boston Marriott Long Wharf	2
Boston Park Plaza	15
Chandler Inn Hotel	14
Charles	32
Colonnade	19
Copley Plaza Hotel	20
Copley Square Hotel	21
Eliot	22
Eliot & Pickett Houses	36
463 Beacon Street Guest House	35
Four Seasons Hotel	16
Harborside Hyatt	31
Holiday Inn Select- Gov't. Center	10
Hostelling Int'l.	41
Hyatt Regency	4
Le Meridien	8
Lenox Hotel	23
Marriott Copley Place	24
Mid-Town Hotel	25
Milner Hotel	12
Newbury Guest House	34
Omini Parker House	7
Radisson Boston Hotel	13
Regal Bostonian Hotel	6
Ritz-Carlton	17
Seaport	3
Royal Sonesta	5
Sheraton Boston	26
Swissôtel	9
Tremont House Hotel	11
Westin	27

Note: Some hotels fall outside the map.

CAMBRIDGE

O'Brien Hwy

Commercial Ave

Cambridge Pkwy.

Charles

Longfellow Br.

Memorial Dr

Charles River Basin

Storrow Dr

Harvard Br.

N

Storrow Dr

Berke

Clarendon St.

Dartmouth St.

Exeter St.

Newbury St

Marlborough St.

Beacon St

Hereford St.

Gloucester St.

Fairfield St.

Commonwealth Ave

Boylston St.

Commonwealth Ave

Massachusetts Ave

Stuart

MASS. TURNPIKE

Boylston St.

Dalton St.

Huntington Ave

CHARLESTOWN

Inner Harbor

93

Charlestown Br.

Commercial St
Charter St

Prince St

Lowell St.
Causeway St
Canal St
Portland St.
Merrimac St.
New Chardon St.
Congress St
Salem St
Hanover St
Blackstone St
North St

Blossom St

9
Cambridge St

5

30

2

93

Commercial St

Atlantic Ave.

Hancock St
Bowdoin St
Somerset St
Myrtle St
Joy St
Court St
State St

35

Vernon St

School St
6
Bromfield St
Milk St
Broad St

Beacon St

7

Park St
Tremont St
Washington St
Franklin St
Devonshire St
High St
1

Boston
Common

Summer St
8
J. F. K. EXPWY.

Charles St

Essex St

Fort Point Channel

3

Garden

Charles St
Kneeland St
Beach St
Atlantic Ave.
Congress St
Summer St

12
11
10

Washington St
Tremont St
South St
J. F. K. EXPWY.

PIKE (Underground)

**BOSTON
HOTELS**

Having stayed at hotels from which it was a long walk just to get to the bus that went to the subway, I count location as a matter of importance on a short trip, and so the hotels below have been grouped by neighborhood. Each listing also includes nearby points of interest and T-stops.

WATERFRONT
The Harbor

1. BOSTON HARBOR HOTEL AT ROWES WHARF, *70 Rowes Wharf, Boston 02110. Tel. 439-7000, Fax 330-9450; Reservations, Tel. 800/752-7077; website, www.bhh.com. Rates: $260-430. 230 rooms. Built: 1987. Main Amenities: valet parking, gym and spa, indoor pool, extensive business center, 24-hour room service.*

Rowes Wharf was not much more than a long wooden dock when it belonged to Mr. John Rowe in the 18th century. More than 200 hundred years later, a quite different incarnation of Rowes Wharf opened in 1987: no mere dock, but a cathedral-sized complex that blends harborlife with citylife, encompassing residences, offices, boat slips, and the Boston Harbor Hotel at the heart of it. For all of its modern luxury, though, Rowes Wharf is still grandly 18th century at heart, with its soft red-brick hues, its rotunda and arches – and its observatory.

The Boston Harbor Hotel takes up most of one central building at Rowes Wharf. In the top echelon of Boston hotels, it has a settled grace that ought to take a lot longer than ten years to establish. Its collection of fine antique pieces certainly helps, as do endless lounges unraveling around views of the water on each of the two public floors. The harborside location is more than just picturesque, though. Guests arriving at the hotel by private boat have use of a 30-slip marina. Guests arriving in Boston by airplane can use the seven-minute Airport Water Shuttle, a motorboat service that goes directly to Rowes Wharf and avoids Boston's other, notoriously wretched, type of traffic on the way from Logan. To the cityside of the hotel, the financial district and Faneuil Hall are each about three blocks away; the only drawback, for pedestrians, is that a busy and rather dank thoroughfare, Atlantic Avenue, separates the Boston Harbor Hotel from the rest of Boston.

The Rowes Wharf Restaurant serves New England cooking as haute cuisine – and overlooks a good chunk of New England, too, in the form of Boston Harbor. From May to September, the hotel's cafe serves lunch and dinner outdoors at harborside.

2. BOSTON MARRIOTT LONG WHARF, *296 State Street, Boston 02109. Tel. 227-0800, Fax 227-2867; Reservations, Tel. 800/228-9290. Rates: $265-295. 400 rooms. Built 1982. Main amenities: valet parking; gym with indoor pool; business center.*

Shaped like a brick barn, the Marriott Long Wharf is indeed aligned at the base of the specified wharf, just across Atlantic Avenue from Faneuil Hall. Light and airy throughout the inside, the Marriott Long Wharf is especially fitting for families, with Christopher Columbus Park on one side of it, harbor-tour boats departing from their docks on the other, and the New England Aquarium nearby. The Aquarium subway stop is connected to the hotel, giving guests convenient access to other parts of the city via the Blue Line; the airport is just two stops away. Guestrooms have private balconies overlooking the city and the harbor, from an enviable vantage.

Seafood comes to mind on Long Wharf, and that is the basis of the hotel's primary restaurant, the Oceana. There is also a California-style grill for casual meals.

3. THE SEAPORT HOTEL, *One Seaport Lane, Boston 02210; Tel. 385-400; Reservations, 877/SEAPORT; website, www.seaporthotel.com. Built in 1997. 437 rooms. Rates: $240-335. Main amenities: indoor swimming pool and spa; indoor parking available; 24-hour room service; cats and dogs welcomed; internet-accessible computers in rooms; on-site auto mechanic. All rooms are non-smoking.*

The Seaport Hotel was completed in 1997 and was built with the future in mind. As that stretch of the old, ignored South End now known as the Seaport District develops, the Seaport Hotel will be at the heart. It is across the street from the World Trade Center, which has a quarter of a million square feet of convention space. It is also something like midway between Logan Airport, by way of the Ted Williams Tunnel, and the downtown Financial District.

And so, on paper, the Seaport Hotel was a good investment. It is also a pleasing hotel: a handsome brick tower, brisk and certainly well-groomed. The look throughout is contemporary, but softened in the rooms with wood furniture and seafaring artwork.

The Aura restaurant is an haute cuisine restaurant, serving seafood.

THE CHARLES RIVER

4. HYATT REGENCY, *575 Memorial Drive, Cambridge 02139. Tel. 492-1234, Fax 491-6906; 800-233-1234. Rates: $129-249. 469 rooms. Built 1976. Main amenities: adjacent indoor parking; gym and indoor pool; 24 hour room service.*

Someone that I know observed that you can't mention the Hyatt Regency without talking with your hands. It sits along the Charles River in Cambridge: quite a swank hotel. But the main thing about it is that is shaped as though the sides were big steps, used by a giant to walk up to the highest plateau of the roof, in the center. When you first say, "the Hyatt Regency," in any conversation, you wait through a rather blank moment and then, without even thinking, make steps in the air with your hands, connecting in the middle. Then the other person says, "Oh *that* hotel," and you can continue (this point should actually be added to the Pronunciation Guide to Boston in Chapter 4, *Planning Your Trip*)!

The Hyatt Regency has the atrium lobby by which the chain is known, though my favorite part of the whole indoor vista is the extensive train-set installed at ground level. The hotel's perch on the Charles lets many of the rooms have a sweeping view of Boston, this way or that; the best rooms face east, if you can arrange it. The Hyatt Regency is not walking distance to very much, other than the M.I.T. campus, and the core of that is about a quarter-mile away. However, free shuttles take guests to popular points in Cambridge and Boston.

The Hyatt has two restaurants, both of which are supposed to take advantage of the view. The one on the top floor, which serves seafood, is a revolving restaurant and it certainly succeeds in giving everyone a good look. The American restaurant on the second floor, however, is a frustration: it only has one really good table where the view is concerned. I would personally cut down the trees and rip out the curtains, if I were the Hyatt Regency, which I am not.

5. THE ROYAL SONESTA, *5 Cambridge Pkwy., Cambridge 02142. Tel. 491-3600, Fax 661-5956; Reservations, Tel. 800/766-3782. Rates: single, $170-220; double, $190-235; suites, $315-725. 400 rooms. Built in 1963; new wing, 1984. Main amenities: adjacent indoor-parking; gym with indoor/outdoor swimming pool; courtesy van to points in Boston and Cambridge.*

The Royal Sonesta anchors the Cambridge side of the Charles River Dam Bridge. In addition to its being convenient to Boston, even with its Cambridge address, the hotel takes in spectacular views of the city skyline, as well as life on the Charles River. It is half-a-bridge away from the Museum of Science, a whole bridge away from the Museum Park T-stop, and in the other direction it is across the street from one of the area's largest shopping malls, the Cambridgeside Galleria. Other than the mall, the neighborhood does not have many shops or restaurants within walking distance, and the Kendall Square and Harvard Square areas of Cambridge are a half-mile and a mile away, respectively.

The Royal Sonesta itself is contemporary, removing itself from the ranks of the standardization through the use of original artwork, none of which competes with the view, south or east, through the windows. Davio's (see Chapter 10, *Where to Eat*) is one of the Royal Sonesta's two restaurants. It serves Northern Italian cuisine. The other dining room is more American, and more casual..

DOWNTOWN
Government Area
6. REGAL BOSTONIAN HOTEL, *Faneuil Hall Marketplace, Boston 02109. Tel. 523-3600, Fax 523-2454; Reservations, Tel. 800/222-8888; website, www.regal-hotels.com/boston. Rates: $245-335, rooms; $450-725, suites.*

152 rooms. Built 1982. Main amenities: valet-parking; complimentary gym privileges nearby; 24-hour room-service.

Just across the street from the bright life of the Faneuil Hall Marketplace, and through a buffering courtyard, the Bostonian is a modern hotel with the impeccable manners of a townhouse. Guests are greeted as – as guests, rather than customers, and register sitting comfortably at a desk. Just a block or two from Government Center and about five from the financial or shopping districts, the Regal Bostonian is a suave hotel. Most of it is modern from the ground up, but unobtrusive even in the historic surroundings in which it sits. One whole section, the Harkness Wing, is a restoration of a 19th-century building. While no one is going to think they have stepped back in time, in the renovated wing many of the rooms retain older architectural details, such as exposed beams and working fireplaces.

Whether you stay at the Regal Bostonian or not, you might like to stop into the lobby to see several magnificent models of sailing ships, along with two other historical exhibits: one on Boston underground and the other on historic firefighting. Both exhibits would do any museum curator proud.

One of the city's most respected restaurants is the Seasons at the Regal Bostonian, a sophisticated room serving new American cuisine.

7. OMNI PARKER HOUSE, *Tremont and School Sts., Boston 02108. Tel. 227-8600, Fax 742-5729; Reservations, Tel. 800/843-6664. Rates: $119-249. 535 rooms. Built in 1927. Valet parking; room service; business services.*

The original Parker House Hotel was built in 1855, and it is only a slight exaggeration to state that everybody in the world stayed there. It was central to Boston's social, political, and literary worlds, at a time when all were formidable. One man who stopped at the old Parker House was John Wilkes Booth, who was recalled looking handsome and relaxed at a sunstreaked breakfast table, April 8, 1865, just before leaving for Washington to shoot Abraham Lincoln. But much better people than that loved the old Parker House through the years, and loved its restaurant – and loved its rolls, too, enough to make them famous throughout the country.

The new Parker House, built in 1927 to replace the first one, is now one of the city's most venerable hotels in its own right. In fact, it is the oldest major hotel in the country, in terms of continuous operation. There are older minor hotels, and there are older hotel *buildings,* ones without such an ancient antecedent, but the Parker House has the distinction that in 1856 and on this very day, today, people came to Boston from all over the country with the entity called the Parker House on their minds. The richly paneled lobby has that air of importance, bolstered by the continuing tradition that every U.S. President since Coolidge has been a guest. The Parker House presides in Tremont Street downtown, two blocks away from the Common and the State House.

FINANCIAL DISTRICT

8. LE MERIDIEN, *250 Franklin Street, Boston 02110. Tel. 451-1900, Fax 423-2844; Reservations, Tel. 800/300-9955. Rates: $265-335, single; $295-365, double; $475-1,300, suites. Weekend rates, $155-550. 326 rooms. Opened in 1981, in 1922 landmark building. Main amenities: valet parking; very good gym with indoor swimming pool; 24-hour room service; complimentary limousine shuttles (weekdays); extensive business center.*

A couple of Boston's hotels are more than just places to stay, they are European outposts: Swissôtel (see below) is one, Le Meridien, operated by Air France, is the other. The Meridien even managed to find a property in downtown Boston that could be just as much at home in Paris, and that is no common standard. In 1981, the hotel opened in the former home of the Boston Reserve Bank: a granite building, great with dignity, set on a corner at Post Office Square. Reserve Banks, no less than French hotels, go to lengths to impart an air of well-being, and so the Meridien inherited beautifully detailed interiors, including the two N.C. Wyeth murals (1923) that grace the Julien Bar. Their themes pertain to the history of finance, which is fitting, for the place sees at least as many bankers nowadays as it did back when it was the reception room for the Reserve.

Post Office Square is a natty park, neatly trimmed with grass, and vivid with the colors of flowers through much of the year. Located at the heart of the financial district, and surrounded by the skyscrapers to prove it, the Meridien is popular with business travelers during the week, but it gets romantic on weekends. Its all-chocolate buffet, for example, is fiscally clueless, but that's what Saturday afternoons are for.

9. SWISSÔTEL, *One Avenue de Lafayette, Boston 02111. Tel. 451-2600, Fax 451-0054; Reservations, Tel. 800/621-9200. 500 rooms. Built circa 1975. Main amenities: adjacent indoor parking; gym with indoor pool; 24-hour room service; business-equipped rooms available.*

Not much to look at on the outside – a tall blockhouse of black bricks – the Swissôtel does indeed operate on the inside with the precision and even the beauty of a ... Swiss watch. It is a good hotel for people in a hurry, and is used by the flight crews of several international airlines, including Swissôtel's parent, Swissair. All of the rooms feature multiple phone lines and voice mail, while Business Advantage rooms also include a fax machine and free credit card calls.

Some of the streets in the immediate vicinity of the hotel are scruffy, though it is only a matter of about three blocks to the Common or the Financial District. For quick errands – or a crisp shortcut to the Financial District, the Swissôtel is connected to the Lafayette Place office- and shopping-mall.

BEACON HILL

10. THE HOLIDAY INN SELECT-GOVERNMENT CENTER, *5 Blossom Street, Boston 02114. Tel. 742-7630, Fax 742-4192; Reservations, Tel. 800/465-4329. Rates: $179-219. 303 rooms. Built c. 1975. Main amenities: adjacent parking; gym and outdoor pool.*

A modern, white blank like the Holiday Inn building would never be allowed in the exquisite Beacon Hill section – and so it is across the street. The fact is that, while the architecture could be more charming (it couldn't be too much plainer), it doesn't interfere with the historic cityscape, from across Cambridge Street, and it is the closest of the bigger hotels to Beacon Hill. It is also a walk of only about four blocks to

Government Center, three to the Fleet Center, and one block to the Massachusetts General Hospital.

Even without much in the way of style, the Holiday Inn is perfectly competent, and made pleasant by the friendly air of the staff. Foster's is the hotel's bistro, specializing in seafood.

THE THEATER DISTRICT

11. TREMONT BOSTON – A WYNDHAM GRAND HERITAGE HOTEL, *275 Tremont Street, Boston 02116-5694. Tel. 426-1400, Fax 482-6730; Reservations, Tel. 800/996-3426. Rates: $119-249. 316 rooms. Built in 1926. Main amenities: valet parking; room service.*

Boston opened the nation's – and the world's – first grand hotel in 1827, the Tremont House. It was built on new innovations, including privacy in the guestrooms and formal sociability in the public spaces. There were also little inventions about the place, such as gaslight throughout; locks on the doors; indoor plumbing, and the electro-magnetic annunciator, by which guests could summon a bellboy without saying a word. Hence the word, "bellboy." And hence the bellboy, too: another Tremont invention. The original Tremont House is my favorite hotel of all time, even though it was torn down in 1895. The name still evokes the grandeur of an idea perfectly realized.

In the 1920s, another luxury hotel took the name "Tremont House" to a different location about a mile down the street. The hotel was recently renovated: the theatrical elegance of the original 1920's design being erased in favor of a streamlined and essentially plainer art deco look. In the fashion of a post office or train station of the WPA era, the lobby is now dominated by a big, bold mural. It doesn't quite manage to replace the banks of sparkling chandeliers that used to decorate the Tremont lobby – and everyone who walked through it. With its facelift, the Tremont no longer seems a handsome old dowager of a hotel, but a service-minded youngster. It is about three blocks from the Boston Common, about four blocks from Chinatown, and two blocks from the Essex T-stop.

The popular Roxy nightclub is in the Tremont House, along with a smaller, adjunct nightclub, and two standard restaurants.

12. THE MILNER HOTEL, *78 Charles Street South, Boston 02116. Tel. 426-6220, Fax 350-0360; Reservations: Tel. 800/453-1731, website, www.milner-hotels.com. Rates, $65-105. 64 rooms. Built in 1895. Main amenities: Laundromat; free breakfast (in fetching breakfast nook).*

The Milner is priced as a budget hotel, but you should go look at it, even if you don't stay there. It was built as a little charmer, with its dainty lobby so fully detailed in plasterwork, and so content with good proportion. I don't know that the current owners appreciate the lobby, though. They keep it in very good repair, but they seemed to go to great lengths to pick out a front desk made of some brown laminate invented but to depress dainty plasterwork. However, the breakfast nook off the lobby at the Milner is set up with cast-iron furniture on the original mosaic floor and it does suggest the old dignity of the place.

The Milner is located on Charles Street a half-block south of Stuart Street, in the Theater District. It is about two blocks from the Boston Common and the Public Garden, and about three blocks to the Boylston T-stop. As refurbished in 1995, the rooms would be very nice at a ski-lodge; they are quite plain for the city of Boston, but the hotel is respectable throughout. It could be the jewel of the city.

13. RADISSON BOSTON HOTEL, *200 Stuart Street, Boston 02116. Tel. 482-1800, Fax 457-2610; Reservations, Tel. 800/333-3333 (general Radisson number). 350 rooms. Built circa 1970. Main amenities: adjacent parking; indoor swimming pool; rooftop sundeck.*

With big rooms and big views from 24 floors, the old 57 Park Plaza recently came under the Radisson badge, with a new emphasis on accommodating business travelers. The Radisson is at a mid-point in the city, about five or six blocks from either downtown to the northeast or the Back Bay to the west. Most of Boston's commercial theaters are located in the adjoining streets. What makes the Radisson unique in Boston, though, is that it has its own theater: the 57, fully equipped for stage productions. At the time of writing, though, only one play has been "up," and it wasn't exactly a hit. So apparently being in the Theater District is easier than being in the Theater business.

The "57" is a local tradition (see Chapter 10, *Where to Eat*).

14. THE CHANDLER INN HOTEL, *26 Chandler Street, Boston 02116. Tel. 482-3450, Fax 542-3428; Reservations, Tel. 800/842-3450. Rates: $89-109. 56 rooms. Built circa 1920. Main amenities: breakfast included with room rate.*

As plain as an office building on the outside, the Chandler Inn, at nine stories, towers over its residential neighborhood in the South End, about five blocks from either the Back Bay or the Theater District. The lobby is workmanlike, and the rooms are spare though clean (each with private bath and telephone). The Chandler Inn is not for people looking for a home away from home, but rather for an honest and affordable place from which to tour the city. Parking is available three blocks away.

AROUND THE PUBLIC GARDEN

15. BOSTON PARK PLAZA, *64 Arlington Street, Boston 02116-3912. Tel. 426-2000, Fax 617-423-1708; Reservations, Tel. 800/225-2008, website, www.bostonparkplaza.com. Rates: $135-245. 960 rooms. Built in 1927. Main amenities: valet parking; standard gym, guest passes for local spa; 24-hour room service; business center.*

Staying at the Park Plaza is like traveling with an elegant great-aunt who happens to be prepared for any eventuality. And, while other hotels may well be willing to send out for anything that a guest might need, the Park Plaza may not have to do more than send downstairs, because so many of the major airlines, travel companies, and other services have storefronts in the same building. It is located about three blocks from the Theater District, and across the street from the Public Garden and the start of the Back Bay. The Park Plaza is a big, bustling hotel, seemingly seen every night on the local news as the backdrop for some political or social event. It is the first of the three hotels that would be hard to imagine

Boston being without. The others would be the Ritz-Carlton and the Parker House.

The Park Plaza Hotel has a large, casual restaurant of its own, the Cafe Rouge, in addition to one of the original Legal Seafoods locations in the city. The Swans Court overlooking the lobby serves Afternoon Tea and has many special, seasonal programs.

16. FOUR SEASONS HOTEL, *200 Boylston Street, Boston 02116. Tel. 338-4400, Fax 423-0154; Reservations, Tel. 800/332-3442. Rates: (single) $295-505; (double) $335-545; (suite) $850-2,950. 288 rooms. Opened 1985. Main amenities: valet parking; extensive gym and spa, with indoor pool; 24-hour room service.*

Across the country and around the world, Four Seasons and Ritz-Carlton hotels duke it out (sometimes over real Dukes, no doubt) for the best customers and the highest superlatives. In Boston, they have taken up their sides along the pristine Public Garden, eyeing each other at an angle. Neither can be faulted for trying, and succeeding, to make people comfortable. But there is a great difference in style. The Four Seasons is not a warm or cozy place, though the rooms are richly decorated (unlike the New York Four Seasons, in which the rooms are sleek to the point of looking unfinished). It is the lobby areas, glossy with marble, accentuated sparsely by antiques, that puts me in mind of a phrase I once read in an ad: "we operate at peak performance so that our guests may do the same." There is a hint of that challenge about the Four Seasons, distinctly a pit stop on the last lane, and if you're just a lazy sod who wants to be coddled, then a lot of the bracing attitude about the place will be wasted on you.

The hotel's flagship restaurant is Aujourd'hui, considered one of the top restaurants in Boston. With a dining room on the second floor overlooking the Public Garden, it gets its name and much of its reputation from the effort that the chefs make in gathering local ingredients, fresh today (*aujourd'hui*). On the ground level, a more casual restaurant also faces the Garden.

17. THE RITZ-CARLTON, *15 Arlington Street, Boston 02117. Tel 536-5700, Fax 536-1335; 800 241-3333. Rates: $245-385. 278 rooms. Built in 1927. Main amenities: valet parking; gym and passes to spa; 24-hour room-service; complimentary morning shuttle to financial district.*

Some automobiles are impressive because the engine makes a great big sound every time it does something. Others are impressive because they operate with practically no sound at all, and in hotel terms, the Ritz-Carlton is in the latter category. Though it is one of the most prestigious hotels in Boston, I would rank it much further down the list in pretension. The Ritz-Carlton greets those who enter with the intimate proportions of its lobby, and its softness: soft colors, soft carpets, the soft hum of people going about. The guestrooms are likewise designed without any sharp edges in style.

The Ritz-Carlton, built in 1927, has no pronounced sense of that era: most of an original set of art-deco murals were removed a dozen or so years ago, while the dining areas seem, if anything, turn-of-the-century in their high-ceilinged grace. The overall scheme is that pastel known as French Provincial. The official list of services is long enough, from same-day dry cleaning to babysitting to limousine shuttles around town (on weekdays). Unofficially, it includes practically anything that a guest needs.

THE BACK BAY

18. BOSTON BACK BAY HILTON, *40 Dalton Street, Boston 02115. Tel. 236-1100, Fax 867-6139; Reservations, Tel. 800/874-0663 (touch-tone phone only). Rates: $150-230, single; $170-250, double; $350-600, suites. 330 rooms. Built in 1982. Main amenities: adjacent indoor parking; gym with indoor swimming pool; room service; business services.*

The Hilton is the last in the line of high-rise hotels poised in a line over the Hynes Convention Center. On average, it is a third the size of the others, the Westin and Marriott at Copley Place and the Sheraton across the street. For better or for worse, the Hilton is not part of a complex, like the others. It's a free-standing hotel and its atmosphere is more reserved in the public rooms, including the lobby.

Boodles is the Hilton's English-style chophouse.

19. THE COLANNADE, *120 Huntington Ave, Boston 02116. Tel. 424-7000, Fax 424-1717; Reservations, Tel. 800/962-3030, website, www.colonnadehotel.com. Rates: $195-325. 285 rooms. Built 1971. Main amenities: adjacent parking; gym and rooftop swimming pool; 24-hour room service; all rooms have PC hookup.*

The Back Bay is about evenly divided between modern high-rise hotels with characteristics, and vintage hotels with character. The Colonnade is the best combination of the two, a privately owned, modern hotel that slows down just a bit, over the details. I may not always agree with the decorating schemes in the rooms, but at least they are not the nothingness of many modern hotel rooms. (Actually, they seem vaguely East European in the emphasis on comfy furniture and vivid hues.) The hotel is located across the street from the Christian Science church campus, and about one block each from the Hynes Convention Center, Symphony Hall, and Copley Center.

The Cafe Colonnade is a continental restaurant with the imagination of an impresario, staging special events that are seasonal, musical, or international.

20. FAIRMONT COPLEY PLAZA HOTEL, *138 Street James Avenue, Boston 02116. Tel. 267-5300, Fax 267-7668. Reservations: Tel. 800/527-4727, website, www.copleysquarehotel.com. Rates: $149-379. 373 rooms. Built in 1912. Main amenities: valet parking; small gym on site, privileges at local health club; 24-hour room-service; business center.*

The Copley Plaza is the backdrop of the Back Bay: its broad grey facade is literally the backdrop for all of Copley Square, and the interiors are the fantastical backdrop for a slice of the whole city's social life. The lobby and several of the other public halls sparkle with mirrors, gilt and cut-glass in the style of France before the Revolution. Whether you stay there, or just make it your business to walk through – bring sunglasses. The dining rooms and the Oak Bar settle into more subdued, Edwardian surroundings, while the guestrooms are traditional in an up-to-date way. John Singer Sargent lived in a corner suite for the last eight years of his life; the Copley Plaza has never slipped much from its position as Boston's grand hotel. Recent renovations gave it an even firmer grasp of that title.

In 1996, the Copley Plaza was purchased by the Fairmount Hotel group, which owns San Francisco's landmark hotel of the same name.

21. COPLEY SQUARE HOTEL, *47 Huntington Avenue, Boston 02116. Tel. 536-9000, Fax 236-0351; Reservations, Tel. 800/225-7062. Rates: (single) $135-165; (double) $155-185; (suite) $299. 143 rooms. Built in 1891. Main amenities: adjacent indoor parking; complimentary use of nearby gym; in-room safes.*

It's quite easy to confuse the Copley Square Hotel with the Copley Plaza Hotel by their names, but they are, of course, very different. That is to say, every hotel is quite different from the grandiose Copley *Plaza* Hotel, and in the case of the Copley *Square* Hotel, the result is a place more genteel than grand. The hotel is located one block from each of the following: Copley Square itself, Copley Place shopping/office/hotel complex, and the Prudential Center. It is a 19th century hotel, with rooms that benefit from vintage architectural details. The guest rooms are well-appointed, though they tend to be snug in size. The lobby is old-fashioned, in that the central part is a small front hall for transacting business, such as registering, while a spacious room with a corner view is the lounge, with some peace and quiet.

The Copley Square Hotel has a Hungarian restaurant called Cafe Budapest, a place that has taken its good reputation for granted, as far as I am concerned. The Original Sports Saloon doesn't look venerable, but it is as old as the hotel, now serving tasty ribs and all the televised sports you can absorb. Tennessee's (see Chapter 10, *Where to Eat*) is in the same building, if you want to spread towels all over the table in your room and have a BBQ picnic.

22. THE ELIOT, *370 Commonwealth Ave., Boston 02215. Tel. 267-1607, Fax 536-9114; Reservations, Tel. 800/443-5468. Rates: (all rooms are suites) single, $205-225; double, $245-265; two bedroom suites, $375-450. 91 rooms. Built in 1925. Amenities: Valet parking; all rooms have kitchenettes.*

Harvard University was feeling uncommonly good about itself in 1912, in the afterglow of the presidency of Charles W. Eliot, who had assumed the job while in his twenties and held it for forty years until 1909. Eliot was nationally famous for his writings, his judgment, and his leadership. In 1912, Harvard built a club on Commonwealth Avenue, so that alumni would have somewhere to dine and stay for short periods. It was a success, to the extent that it became hard to get a reservation to stay over.

In 1925, Charles Eliot's family took the opportunity to build a hotel next door, at the corner of Commonwealth and Mass. Ave., to catch the overflow of business, and to permanently align the names "Harvard" and "Eliot." For a long time it was a residential hotel, where Harvard old boys and Radcliffe old girls could live out their years comfortably. It is no longer the old slipper it was then.

In 1990, the family that owned the hotel (the Eliots having sold it in the 1930s) decided to turn it into a luxury "little hotel," a European-flavored hotel category of which Boston then had none. The whole place was renovated, inside and out. I thought the Eliot looked great to begin with; I thought it looked even better after the renovation, but the improvements keep coming: a new ironwork portico, worthy of Brussels; new uniforms for the doormen; better planters; new fur hats for the doormen in the winter. Some people look to the top of the old John Hancock building to see what the weather is going to be; some of us look to the headgear of the Eliot doormen.

The Eliot is located at the western end of the Back Bay, one block from the Hynes T-stop, three blocks from the Hynes Convention Center, and about four, in the other direction, from Fenway Park. Breakfast is served in a small dining area. Clio's is the Eliot's high-visibility bistro, serving an overly ambitious menu of nouvelle cuisine.

23. THE LENOX HOTEL, *710 Boylston Street, Boston 02116-2699 Tel: 536-5300, Fax 267-1237; Reservations, Tel. 800/996-3160; website, www.copleysquarehotel.com. Rates: $180-250; suite, $450. 214 rooms. Built in 1898. Main amenities: valet parking; small gym; room-service.*

The Lenox is a small but formal hotel, built in the last century, and renovated in 1996. It is in the midst of the Back Bay: across the street from the modern addition to the Public Library, two blocks from Copley Place, and about four blocks to the Pru and the Hynes centers. Perhaps it is the Lenox' combination of antiques and good reproductions – no, it is probably the way the wallpapers seem to have been handpressed in some cottage somewhere, that makes such an urbane hotel feel so much like a hillside inn once you're well inside. A glance at the brochure will tell you that it does not use fakey models in the pictures, but rather actual workers from the staff – the place definitely thinks it's in Vermont.

24. MARRIOTT COPLEY PLACE, *110 Huntington Avenue, Boston 02116. Tel. 236-5800, Fax 236-5885; Reservations, Tel. 800/228-9290; website, www.marriott.com/marriott/bosco. Rates: $225-235. 1,147 rooms. Opened in 1984 Main amenities: gym and indoor pool; good business services; 24-hour room service; babysitting.*

It isn't always clear where the Marriott begins and Copley Place ends. The two wings of the high-rise hotel dominate the shopping and office complex, which was the biggest development of its multi-use kind when it was built in the early 1980s. The Marriott's ground-floor lobby is as bustling as a town square, one with escalators reaching up into the mall itself.

The Marriott's restaurant, Gourmeli's, pops up in another part of Copley Place, as much a part of the mall as it is of the hotel. There is no feeling of retreat about the Marriott Copley Place, but it is well-connected: to the mall, to the Prudential Center, and to Hynes Convention Center.

25. MIDTOWN HOTEL, *220 Huntington Ave., Boston 02115. Tel. 262-1000, Fax 262-8739; Reservations, Tel. 800/343-1177. Rates: $79-159. 159 rooms. Built circa 1968. Main amenities: free indoor parking; outdoor swimming pool.*

The MidTown is a low, white building, both characteristics being rare for the Back Bay, even for the outer edge of it. The MidTown is more like a motel you'd find in a prosperous suburb, perhaps in California. The rooms are clean and comfortable, renovated in 1996, though I venture to doubt that you would borrow any of their decorating ideas for your own house. They are cheerfully ... basic. The hotel's public rooms, including the lobby, are more sleek, with an antique piece here and there.

Located almost next door to the Colonnade Hotel, the MidTown is across the street from the Christian Science church campus, and within a block or two of Symphony Hall, the Hynes Convention Center, the Pru, and the thick of the Back Bay. The MidTown's restaurant is called Tables of Content, serving all day.

26. SHERATON BOSTON, *39 Dalton Street, Boston 02199. Tel 236-2000, Fax 236-1702; Reservations, Tel. 800/325-3535. Rates: $159-260. 1,181 rooms. Built 1965. Main amenities: adjacent indoor parking; gym and indoor/outdoor swimming pool; 24-hour room service.*

The Sheraton rises right out of the Hynes Convention Center and marries it to the Prudential Center. It is the biggest hotel in Boston, surpassing the Marriott Copley Place only by a little. And both depend largely on conventions, those at the Hynes and the World Trade centers, as well as large-scale meetings that they stage on their own premises. At the Sheraton, the halls and public spaces are often lined with displays regarding some subject or other that you may never have known existed on this planet, except that 2,000 people at the hotel with you are talking about it in great depth. So it must exist. The rooms will not surprise you, but to make a couple of notes, they are fairly spacious with nice, heavy furniture. In addition to its proximity to the Hynes Convention Center and the Pru, the Sheraton is within four or five blocks of Symphony Hall, Copley Square, and the Esplanade.

The hotel, surrounded by the restaurants of the Prudential Center, features the Top of the Hub, which has a view from the 52nd floor. There is also a nightclub at the hotel itself and a standard American restaurant. The food court at the Pru is also around the corner, through the connected mall.

27. THE WESTIN, *Copley Place, 10 Huntington Ave., Boston 02116. Tel 262-9600, Fax 424-7483; Reservations, Tel. 800/937-8461. Rates: $285-345.*

800 rooms. Built 1985. Main amenities: valet parking; gym and indoor pool; 24-hour room service; business center.

The Marriott embraces Copley Place in a bear hug; the Westin is also part of Copley Place, but it stands by itself on a triangular block, connected to the rest of the complex by skybridges. The differences between the two hotels are not pronounced, except that the public areas of the Westin are less hectic. It is within five blocks of the Hynes Convention Center and the Prudential Center, by the street or through covered walkways. The hotel is about one block from the Back Bay train- and T-station, or the Copley T-stop, and it is adjacent to Copley Square.

The Palm, a New York steakhouse, opened in 1995 in the Westin, without overwhelming the city as yet for atmosphere or food. Turner Fisheries (see Chapter 10, *Where to Eat*) is more of a local tradition, with jazz every night at 8 pm in the lounge.

KENMORE SQUARE

28. THE BUCKMINSTER, *645 Beacon Street, Boston 02215-3201. Tel 236-7050, Fax 262-0068; Reservations, Tel. 800/727-2825. Rates: $55-119. 100 rooms. Built 1903. Main amenities: cooking and laundry facilities on premises.*

Homely on the outside, homey on the inside, the Buckminster is a quiet hotel, especially suited to longer stays since cooking facilities are available on each floor. Built at the turn-of-the-century, the hotel has been gently restored in 18th century English style. It is located just off Kenmore Square, over a traffic bridge to my favorite nest of restaurants at St. Mary's on Beacon Street in Brookline. Kenmore Square itself is not quite as delightful, though it is lined with take-away places and an improving roster of stores.

Kenmore Square is both a T-stop and a bus hub. Fenway Park is one block away; the Longwood Medical area about six long blocks away, or a short bus-ride. The Back Bay begins about four blocks down Commonwealth Ave.

29. HOWARD JOHNSON HOTEL, *575 Commonwealth Av., Boston 02215. Tel. 267-3100, Fax 424-1045; Reservations, Tel. 800/654-2000. Rates:*

$95-145, single; $105-175, double. 179 rooms. Built circa 1965. Main amenities: free parking. indoor pool.

The lobby decoration is outdated and the rooms are just plain, though some overlook the Charles River from the back of the hotel, yet the Commonwealth Avenue Howard Johnson Hotel is a reasonable and useful place, located on the far side of Kenmore Square from the Back Bay. It is two blocks from Fenway Park, one block from the Kenmore T-stop, and a block or two from the B.U. campus. Despite such widely known neighbors, the surroundings on Commonwealth are not quintessentially Bostonian; they are more frazzled than that. The area has many interesting restaurants, especially a quarter of mile away in the St. Mary's block of Beacon Street, but Kenmore Square has the reputation of becoming unraveled late at night. It is fine during the day and evening.

The dining room on the premises is a Chinese restaurant named the Hong Kong. There is a bar on the top (7th) floor overlooking the river that is rather coarsely decorated: a roadhouse with a view. It is popular with college students.

30. HOWARD JOHNSON LODGE, *1271 Boylston Street Boston 02215. Tel. 267-8300, Fax 267-2763; Reservations, Tel. 800/654-2000. Rates:$87-115; $97-135. 94 rooms. Built circa 1978. Main amenities: free parking; outdoor pool.*

With the same owners as the Howard Johnson Hotel on Commonwealth, the Lodge on Beacon is quite a different place. It is newer, smaller, and brighter. It is also located two blocks from Fenway Park, on the other side from the other hotel. The nearest T-stop is Kenmore Square, about three fairly long blocks away. The Lodge is located on a busy avenue, walking distance to the Museum of Fine Arts. The Back Bay begins about five blocks away.

A reasonably priced Italian restaurant called Pranzare is popular with families in the neighborhood.

AIRPORT

31. HARBORSIDE HYATT, *101 Harborside Dr., Boston 02128. Tel. 568-1234, Fax 374-9817; Reservations, Tel. 800/233-1234. Rates: $170-215, single; $190-240, double. 270 rooms; Built in 1993. Main amenities: Outdoor adjacent parking; gym and indoor swimming pool; 24-hour room service; business center.*

The Harborside Hyatt should be in the section above for waterfront hotels; no location in Boston has a better view of the water. But then, since Logan Airport is also a waterfront property, the Harborside can be that anomaly, the glamorous airport hotel. It is a glassy building, fourteen stories high, and it takes full advantage of its surroundings with careful landscaping, including a jogging trail along the harbor. The location is nextdoor to the M.B.T.A. Water Shuttle ($8) to downtown Boston, and the hotel operates a 24-hour courtesy bus to all airport terminals.

The Harborside Grill is the hotel's seafood restaurant, and when I mention the sparkling view from the tables overlooking the water, it will be redundant of every other note so far made about the Harborside Hyatt.

Other Airport Hotels

HOLIDAY INN BOSTON AIRPORT, *225 McClellan Hwy., Boston 02128. Tel. 569-5260, Fax 569-5169; Reservations, Tel. 800/465-4329.*

Located one mile north of the airport.

LOGAN AIRPORT RAMADA, *Logan Airport, Boston 02128. Tel. 569-9300, Fax 567-3725; Reservations, Tel. 800/272-6232.*

The hotel closest to the terminals.

CAMBRIDGE

32. THE CHARLES, *One Bennett Street, Cambridge 02138. Tel. 864-1200, Fax 864-5715; Reservations, Tel. 800/882-1818. 296 rooms. Built circa 1983. Main amenities: adjacent indoor parking; gym and spa.*

The Charles is part of a small, sophisticated complex that includes small stores and a patio, where a number of chic restaurants put out tables in fair weather. The hotel is about two blocks from the hub of Harvard Square, just far enough to turn the volume down a bit on the constant buzz there. It's a well-run hotel that acts smaller than it is, in service.

The best aspect of the Charles is its taste in restaurants. Henrietta's Table is folksy without being frumpy, serving homemade food, and selling it to take away, as well. The Rialto serves fine Southern European dishes, while the Regattabar (see Chapter 13, *Nightlife*) is one of the top spots for live music in the Boston area.

33. DOUBLETREE GUEST SUITES, *400 Soldiers Field Road. Tel. 783-0090, Fax 783-0897; Reservations, Tel. 800/222-8733. Rates: $189-209. 310 suites. Built in 1986. Main amenities: adjacent parking; gym and swimming pool.*

The Doubletree is an all-suite hotel on a main intersection just off the Harvard Campus. It is a comfortable hotel, but it really isn't walking distance from much. To compensate, the hotel runs a complimentary shuttle to points in Boston and Cambridge. The best thing about the hotel is its lively restaurant, Sculler's, which serves seafood and excellent jazz (see Chapter 13, *Nightlife*).

Other Cambridge Hotels

THE INN AT HARVARD, *1201 Massachusetts Ave., Cambridge 02138. Tel. 491-2222, Fax 491-6520; Reservations, Tel. 800/458-5886.*

Owned by Harvard University.

HARVARD SQUARE HOTEL, *110 Mt. Auburn Street, Cambridge 02138. Tel. 864-5200, Fax 864-2409; Reservations, Tel. 800/458-5886.*

Also owned by the university, but more reasonably priced.

UNIVERSITY PARK HOTEL, *20 Sidney Street, Cambridge 02139, Tel. 577-0200; Fax 494-8366; Reservations, 800/222-8733; website, www.universityparkhotel.com.*

A new 210-room hotel next to the MIT campus.

BED & BREAKFASTS IN TOWN

Boston has dozens of bed-and-breakfasts, or guesthouses as they are also called in the region. The adjoining town of Brookline is becoming rife with them. Here is a sampler, by section.

The Back Bay

34. NEWBURY GUEST HOUSE, *261 Newbury Street, Boston 02116. Tel. 437-7666. Rates: $100-130; winter, $85-115.*

A bank of 1882 townhouses in the thick of the street's shops and restaurants, the Newbury Guest house is rather large for a B&B, with 32 rooms. The atmosphere inside is Victorian, and guests can have breakfast outdoors in fair weather.

35. 463 BEACON STREET GUEST HOUSE, *463 Beacon Street 02115. Tel. 536-1302. Rates: $60 to 99. All major credit cards are accepted.*

The 463 is three blocks north of the Hynes Convention Center, toward the Charles River. It was built in 1887, and each of the 20 rooms has a kitchenette.

Beacon Hill

36. THE ELIOT & PICKETT HOUSES, *6 Mt. Vernon Place, Boston 02108. Tel. 248-8707, Fax 742-1364; website, www.uua.org/ep. The rate is $90 for a single room, and $105 for a double; all major credit cards are accepted.*

In the shadow of the State House, the Eliot and Pickett Houses date from 1832-34, and are attractively decorated with antiques. There are 20 rooms, none with TV, and guests have use of a kitchen where they can make their own breakfast.

Brookline

37. ANTHONY'S TOWN HOUSE, *1085 Beacon Street 566-3972. Rates: $38-78. No credit cards accepted.*

Anthony's is a restored brownstone that has been used as a guest house for several generations. It was built in the 1890s and there are ten rooms, simply furnished and quite small, rather like an eminently respectable boarding house. Guests have use of a kitchenette; bathrooms are semi-private.

38. BEACON INN, *1087 and 1750 Beacon Street, Brookline 02146. Tel. 566-0088, Fax 397-9267, website, www.publiconline.com/~beaconinn. Rates:*

$39-49 in winter and $89-99 in summer. Credit cards: all major. Limited free parking.

The Beacon Inn is actually two separate houses, built in 1900. There are 25 rooms, some with private bath. The rooms are large, with antiques or traditional furniture, complimented by original Victorian woodwork. The rates include continental breakfast.

Two other nice B&B's:

BEACON STREET GUEST HOUSE, *1047 Beacon Street, Brookline 02146. Tel. 232-0292; Reservations, Tel. 800/201-9692.*

BROOKLINE MANOR GUEST HOUSE, *32 Centre Street, Coolidge Corner, Brookline 02146. Tel. 232-0003; Reservations, Tel. 800/201-9676.*

Cambridge

39. **A FRIENDLY INN**, *1673 Cambridge Street, Cambridge. Tel. 547-7851, Fax 547-7851. Rates: $47-97.*

Located near Harvard Square. A meticulously restored home from the turn-of-the-century, the Inn is indeed as friendly as you want it to be, or as private, with rooms offering hotel-standard amenities, including air conditioning and telepehones. All rooms have private bathrooms.

40. **A BED & BREAKFAST IN CAMBRIDGE**, *1657 Cambridge Street, Cambridge. Tel. 868-7082, Fax 876-8991. Rates: $55-95.*

A domestic atmosphere prevails, with homebaked goods and the style of an 1897 house. All the rooms, freshly decorated with a flare for crisp colors, have shared bathrooms.

B&B SERVICES

If you are still up a tree for a good B & B, one of the following booking agencies may be able to help:

__Accommodations of Boston & Cambridge__, 335 Pearl Street, Cambridge 02139. Tel. 491-0274, Fax 547-5478; Toll-free 800/253-5542.

__Host Homes of Boston__, P.O. Box 117V, Waban Branch, Boston 02168. Tel. 244-1308, Fax 244-5156; Toll-free 800/600-1308. Free catalog available.

HOSTEL

41. HOSTELLING INTERNATIONAL, *12 Hemenway Street, Boston 02115. Tel 536-9455, Fax 424-6558. Rates: $15-17.*

The Boston hostel is like a college dorm without the specter of classes. It's a little institutional-looking, in a worn way, but a handwritten note on the front door says, "We're going to listen to folk music, meet at this door tonight at 7 pm." That is one touch that the Ritz-Carlton has yet to include. Some rooms are private. Main amenity: a computer in the lobby is available for use of guests in sending and receiving E-mail.

10. WHERE TO EAT

There aren't enough bad restaurants in Boston, that's the problem. In the olden days, a person found two or three dependable places and looked askance at all the rest. In the past few years, though, bright spots have opened up in nearly every neighborhood of the city. Now I look askance at my old reliables, knowing full well that there are better places out there. These days, it seems there are always better and yet better restaurants out there. I don't know what the world is coming to.

Overall, the easiest type of restaurant to find among the new ones is in the genre known, unappetizingly enough, as "fusion," which has brought all sorts of international influences to bear on angel-hair pasta. More and more, Japanese restaurants are everywhere in Boston, having replaced Chinese restaurants in sheer frequency among new places. As a matter of fact, Chinese restaurants are getting harder and harder to find outside of Chinatown. Perhaps because Boston's academic community draws people from every corner of the globe, most world cuisines, from Cambodian to Ethiopian, are represented by at least one restaurant.

Boston seems to have a natural resistance to the chain restaurant. Surprisingly few of them have survived against the competition of auteur restaurants, homegrown places that reflect ideas, not systems. **Starbucks** coffee-shops are profuse, as are Boston's own **Au Bon Pain** cafe-bakeries. As to those stalwarts of the shopping strip – hamburger, pizza, doughnut, or ice-cream franchises – they are relatively rare in this city. Bostonians, to generalize, tend to appreciate self-expression, even in ham-and-cheese.

The following list is organized by niche. About three choices are given for each, in various neighborhoods and, where possible, in different price categories. The hours listed are for dining; if there is a bar, it usually has longer hours (in Massachusetts, liquor can be served until 2 am). All will take major credit cards and reservations, except as noted.

The range in cost for a main dish is included as a point of comparison; the span doesn't include any unusually high- or low-priced dishes. If dishes and prices are notably different at lunch and dinner, they are noted separately. Hotel restaurants are fully described in Chapter 9, *Where To Stay*.

OPEN ANYTIME

Most hotels have at least one dining room that is open all day, and many lunch counters, such as **Charlie's** (see "Neighborhood Places" below) forge straight from breakfast to late night dinner. A few restaurants actually evolve through each day, though, changing in personality to suit each hour as it comes.

1. SONSIE, *327 Newbury St. near Hereford. Tel. 351-2500, website, www.avenue.com/sonsie. T-stop: Hynes. Hours: dining, Sunday-Tuesday, 7 am-11 pm; Wednesday-Saturday, 7 am-midnight. Main dishes: $7-11, lunch; $10-17, dinner. Typical: fettucini with wild mushroom ragout (lunch), $10.75; crisp fragrant duck with grilled chow foon noodles (dinner), $16.75.*

Sonsie seemed so avant-garde when it opened in 1994, and now I can't remember why. The front part of the restaurant looks like new Vienna, with wood paneling, tiny tables, newspapers within reach, and people puffing away, jabbering away, or reading away. Or brooding. Or eating, though they often just sip coffee there. The back of Sonsie, however, looks like old Vienna. It is more formal than the front, with ample tables and booths, fresh with white linen and tended by staff to match, in their white aprons. A bar glimmers and glints on one side of the room, completely separate from the dining room. Does that seem avant-garde to you? Probably not.

Perhaps what was most striking was that Sonsie was such an instant success when it opened. By the first week, everybody in the neighborhood seemed to have been going there for years. The wood-framed glass panels

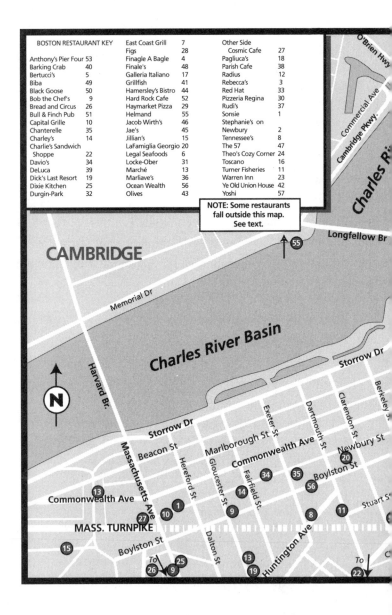

BOSTON RESTAURANT KEY	East Coast Grill	7	Other Side	
	Figs	28	Cosmic Cafe	27
Anthony's Pier Four 53	Finagle A Bagle	4	Pagliuca's	18
Barking Crab	40	Finale's	48	Parish Cafe	38
Bertucci's	5	Galleria Italiano	17	Radius	12
Biba	49	Grillfish	41	Rebecca's	3
Black Goose	50	Hamersley's Bistro	44	Red Hat	33
Bob the Chef's	9	Hard Rock Cafe	52	Pizzeria Regina	30
Bread and Circus	26	Haymarket Pizza	29	Rudi's	37
Bull & Finch Pub	51	Helmand	55	Sonsie	1
Capital Grille	10	Jacob Wirth's	46	Stephanie's on	
Chanterelle	35	Jae's	45	Newbury	2
Charley's	14	Jillian's	15	Tennessee's	8
Charlie's Sandwich		LaFamiglia Georgio 20	The 57	47
Shoppe	22	Legal Seafoods	6	Theo's Cozy Corner 24
Davio's	34	Locke-Ober	31	Toscano	16
DeLuca	39	Marché	13	Turner Fisheries	11
Dick's Last Resort	19	Marliave's	36	Warren Inn	23
Dixie Kitchen	25	Ocean Wealth	56	Ye Old Union House 42
Durgin-Park	32	Olives	43	Yoshi	57

NOTE: Some restaurants
fall outside this map.
See text.

BOSTON RESTAURANTS

that line the streetfront open completely in fair weather, for Newbury-watching – meanwhile, out along Newbury Street, artists perch their easels within the Sonsie aura and paint. Dining at Sonsie starts at breakfast, which consists mainly of muffins, granola, and other simple fare. Lunch, dinner, and brunch (on the weekends) can be quite formal.

To its credit, Sonsie changes the menu often, and uses seasonal ingredients. Generally, it offers simple favorites, double-crust spinach pie and pork loin with potato pancakes, for example, with a few, more eclectic plates, such as beef short ribs with soft polenta and spinach "agrodolce." Through the day and much of the night, Sonsie will be anything that you want it to be: quite a feat, when so many new restaurants are quite the opposite.

2. STEPHANIE'S ON NEWBURY, *190 Newbury St. Tel. 236-0990. T-stop: Copley. Hours: Monday-Saturday, bakery-cafe opens at 7 am; kitchen, 11:30 am-10 pm; Sunday: both, 10 am-9 pm. Main dishes: $6.95-11.95, lunch; $9.95-19.95, dinner. Typical: rotisserie chicken pasta (lunch), $13.95; salmon bouillabaisse (dinner), $17.95.*

There is a country pace about Stephanie's, even though it is a busy restaurant on a busy part of Newbury Street. It pauses over food, with that extra moment of care that can put any dish in the category of "comfort food." In the morning, a gentleman behind the bar serves up cordials of the baked variety: muffins, scones, bread and sticky buns. About half of the items are brought in from respectable bakeries around town, but I usually make a choice just by asking which are the contributions from the Stephanie's bakers, who know how to plump the flavor in any coffee cake or Irish soda bread.

Stephanie's is a well-dressed restaurant: carefully decorated in deep colors that refrain from upstaging any of the people within it. Perhaps that restraint is part of the reason Stephanie's is a popular spot for business lunches. Another part of the reason may be that its menu, which is not large, is nonetheless extensive, with macaroni & cheese side-by-side with far fancier creations.

LOCAL CHAINS

The national franchises need no explanation (which is part of their problem), but Boston has a few chains of its own that are not generally well known in the rest of the country. **Au Bon Pain**, the bakery-cafe, started in Boston, but it's all over the place now, and no longer counts as local.

3. REBECCA'S, *locations include: Prudential Center; 112 Newbury St., Back Bay; 290 Main St., Cambridge; 411 Brookline Av.; 560 Harrison Av.; 75 State St.; 75 Federal St., 56 High St.; 18 Tremont St. Hours: e.g. Prudential: Monday-Saturday, 7 am-9 pm; Sunday, 9 am-7 pm. Main dishes: $4.95-7.95. Typical: grilled chicken sandwich, $4.95; chicken salad plate, with grapes and walnuts, $7.95.*

Rebecca's is a cafe, open all day, that is especially popular for quick breakfasts and better-than-average lunches. In addition to sandwiches and salads, there are four daily entree specials, including a healthy choice and one vegetarian. Rebecca's has an earnest air about it that can make even a roast beef sandwich seem downright wholesome. (It could be on multi-grain bread, after all.)

Rebecca's recently signed a monumental international business deal – at least it seemed monumental to anyone who has been to Ireland in the past hundred years or so. Rebecca's now serves Bewley's tea and coffee. If all goes well, perhaps they will someday import Bewley's scones, as well, and Bewley's whipped cream, and Bewley's jam and also the view of Dublin from Bewley's Oriental Cafe.

4. FINAGLE A BAGLE, *locations include: 535 Boylston St., Copley Square, Tel. 266-2500; Government Center, Tel. 523-6500; Quincy Market, Tel. 367-9720; 70 Franklin St., Tel. 261-1900. Hours: Monday-Saturday, 6:30 am-8 pm; Sunday, 6:30 am-6 pm. Main dishes: $1.57-4.29. Typical: hommus bagel-sandwich, $3.10.*

Efficiency is all at Finagle A Bagle, and no bagle served is more than one hour old. They're usually warm, plump, and crusty, though personally I liked them better before they grew into "jumbo" bagles, back when they were more *crusty* than *plump*. Along the outer edge of the list of 17 varieties are wild-berry, triple chocolate-chip, jalapeno-cheddar, and energy-bar bagels. The name of the chain, Finagle A Bagel, is well chosen, because each shop has been finagled into what should be a perfect system: a line of bagels and a line of customers moving inevitably toward each other, along either side of a counter. In the system, the clerks seem well-trained to exhibit the same, officious manner toward each, be they bagels or customers.

For a little something to have a nightmare about, go to the Government Center location and see the whipsaw machine that guillotines each bagel into two halves; and be glad that you're in your line and the bagels are in theirs. The Copley Square location has a dining area on the second floor, overlooking Trinity Church.

5. BERTUCCI'S, *locations include: Copley, Tel. 247-6161; Faneuil Hall, Tel. 227-7889; Harvard Sq, Tel. 864-4748; Kendall Sq., Tel. 661-8356. Hours: i.e., Copley, Monday-Friday, 11 am-11pm; Saturday, 11 am-midnight; Sunday, Noon-11 pm. Main dishes: $6-9. Typical: small sausage-mushroom pizza, $8.25; linguini with clam sauce, $8.95.*

Bertucci's pizza restaurants have sprouted as far south as Georgia, but the chain started right outside Boston in Somerville's Davis Square, and it is still best represented in eastern Massachusetts. In Boston, each restaurant is quite different in decor, fitting itself into an airy, unusual space, rather than imposing a turnkey design onto just any storefront. A variety of Italian dishes are on the menu at lunch and dinner, but pizza is the mainstay, and it's definitely of the crispy, brick-oven style: wood-fired, in this case. As to what goes on above that very good crust, the choices loom endless, past 21 special toppings and 21 further combinations.

6. LEGAL SEAFOODS, *locations include: Park Plaza Hotel building, Tel. 426-4444; Copley Place, Tel. 266-7775; Prudential Center, Tel. 266-6800; Statler Office building, Tel. 426-5566, and Kendall Square, Cambridge, Tel. 864-3400. Hours: Monday-Thursday, 11 am-10 pm; Friday-Saturday, 11 am-11 pm; Sunday, Noon-10 pm. Main dishes: $8-20. Typical: smoked salmon sand-*

wich (lunch) $8.95; 1-1.25 lb. lobster, $25.95 (lobsters range up to the 2.5-pound size, which is $47.95.

High standards for meals and crisp service make Legal Seafoods an easy choice to make among seafood restaurants, though it is a shade expensive and liable to be crowded (those two factors must be related somehow), tempering the easy choice somewhat. It was a coup recently when the chain hired one of Boston's leading chefs, Jasper White, to make sure that the menu will not stand still on its baked-broiled-fried-raw selection of fish-shellfish-calamari. Now, long-running special menus inculcate the tastes and techniques of ethnic cuisines.

In fact, Legal Seafoods' newest experiment is a more casual little restaurant at Park Plaza, inspired by Caribbean ways with seafood. One favorite dish came in as a special and is now a mainstay by special demand: linguini with shrimp and broccoli in dijon-mustard sauce.

BARBECUE

7. EAST COAST GRILL, *1271 Cambridge St., Inman Square, Cambridge. Tel. 491-6568. T-stop: Central Square. Hours: Sunday-Thursday, 5:30 pm - 10 pm; Friday-Saturday, 5:30 - 10:30 pm; Sunday, 11 am-2:30 pm. Main dishes: $12-20.*

The East Coast Grill took the overalls out of barbecue, so to speak, treating it with the care of a more worldly cuisine. The portions bulge, as BBQ ought, and ribs are on the menu. But the owner searches the world for ingredients to bring back to the slabs of meat, chicken, or fish that are the staples. As a result, the dishes are as vivid as the informal decor, with its splashes of turquoise and yellow. Reservations are not taken, but the East Coast Grill recently expanded – now it's three storefronts wide. Anyway, there is often room at the counter, if the tables are all filled.

8. TENNESSEE'S, *Huntington Ave. at Exeter (in the Copley Square Hotel Building). Tel. 421-1400. T-stop: Copley Square. Hours: Sunday-Thur., 11:30 am - 10 pm; Friday-Saturday, 11:30 am - midnight Main dishes: $8-24.95. Typical: Memphis-style dry rubbed ribs platter, $14.95 (half), $24.95 (whole).*

Tennessee's tastes like a Fourth of July picnic. The meats – ribs, brisket, pulled pork, or chicken – are smoked in imported cookers

BESTING THE BEST

There is an estimable magazine in town that hands out so many awards, in such arcane categories, that a framed "Best of Boston," seems to be an adjunct to an operating license in the restaurant business. The best is always around the next corner, of course, but here are the results of our own research thus far, in categories limited to the essential five:

Best Ice Cream

Wai Wai Ice Cream, *26 Oxford St., Chinatown (downstairs), Tel. 338-9833.*

The way that Wai Wai makes it, it could be called ice cream-cream. Homemade on the premises, about five flavors are available at a time.

Best Apple Pie

Locke-Ober, *3-4 Winter St., Tel. 542-1340.*

Apple pie is a tricky balancing act, of tastes and texture, and of a fine pastry that must remain a homespun creation. Locke-Ober understands what I am talking about. Anyway, they understand apple pie.

Best French Fries

Dick's Last Resort, *55 Huntington Av., Tel. 267-8080.*

Some are crunchy, some are tender, some are intact, some broke apart along the way. But they all woke up in the morning as raw potatoes (not frozen things).

Best Cornbread

Tennessee's, *Huntington Av. at Exeter (in the Copley Square Hotel Building), Tel. 421-1400.*

In some cases, cornbread seems more like sustenance than food, if you see the difference. At Tennessee's, it is light; sweet (but not cakey); moist (but not oily), and it even tastes like corn.

Best Pot of Tea

Biba, *272 Boylston St., Tel. 426-7878.*

It is perplexing to order tea in the civilization known as the United States of America and receive a tepid cup of water, along with a teabag, somewhere else, by itself. At Biba, the pot arrives as tea, not as a lost opportunity to make tea. They use loose tea, no less, suspended in a strainer: lemon and sugar at the ready, utensils lined up with precision.

*Honorable mention: **Theo's Cozy Corner** (see "Neighborhood Places" below). No points for style, but at least they understand physics.*

(imported from Memphis), and the rest of the menu is just about what Ma or Pa would set down on the table. And like Ma or Pa, Tennessee's doesn't make everything, only what they do best. Don't order anything so urbane as french fries, perish the thought: baked sweet-potatoes, cucumber salad, and BBQ baked beans add up to a meal that is even greater than the sum of its parts. Glopped with homemade BBQ sauce, it's a mess that couldn't be better.

The portions are not especially big. That can be a plus, however, for some: too often, going for BBQ automatically equals stuffing yourself silly. It is mostly a takeaway restaurant. Surrounded by so many Back Bay hotels, it may be a good alternative to room service. If you do feel like sitting down in a civilized manner, though, with waiters and everything, the **Original Sports Saloon**, also in the Copley Square Hotel building, is a related rib joint, as well as a shrine to Boston sports stars.

9. BOB THE CHEF'S, *604 Columbus Avenue, near Massachusetts Avenue; Tel. 536-6204. T-stop: Massachusetts Ave. Hours: Tuesday-Wednesday, 11:30 am to 10 pm; Thursday-Saturday, 11:30 am-11 pm; Sunday, 2-9 pm (buffet brunch served). Main dishes: $6.95-13.95. Typical: Barbecued spare ribs, $12.95; mustard fried catfish, $11.95.*

One popular restaurant that I know of in Boston has seen fit to post little signs at the tables admonishing diners to please vacate the premises within twenty-five minutes of receiving their food. Surely there are more subtle ways of giving a paying customer the boot. However, none of them would be known at Bob the Chef's, as popular a restaurant as any, but one where relaxing – really taking it easy – is part of the menu.

In 1957, Bob the actual chef and his wife opened their restaurant and started offering the country cooking of South Carolina, just the way that African-American families there knew it. Their restaurant, which became something of a landmark, was sold in 1990 to a Digital Corp. engineer named Darryl Settles, who kept the recipes and the genuinely friendly spirit of the place, even while renovating it to a slick standard with modern art on exposed brick walls and room for a jazz band at the end of the room.

Creole dishes have jazzed up the menu at Bob's, but the star attractions are still the straightforward Southern ones, including the fried chicken known as "glorified chicken," served meaty and moist. The barbecued ribs are even better; they arrive sunken in sauce and fall apart on contact, they are so tender. Each entree carries a choice from a list of ten side dishes. I've noticed that a lot of the people – the Northerners – at Bob the Chef's order mashed potatoes and corn as their two side dishes. Both are good, but it is a shame to pass up the more unique tastes of black-eyed peas, red beans and rice, or candied yams. For all of Bob the Chef's efforts, a lot of people in Boston just don't know their way around one of the country's great cuisines.

BIG BUSINESS

A few of the places where you can flip your cravat over one shoulder and let the restaurant make a good impression.

10. CAPITAL GRILLE, *359 Newbury St. Tel. 262-8900. T-stop: Hynes. Hours: Monday-Thursday, 5-10 pm; Friday-Saturday, 5:30-11 pm. Main dishes: $15.95-27.95. Typical, lamb chops $25.95; steaks, $18.95-27.95. Everything is a la carte.*

The chefs are professional, the staff is professional, and the clientele is certainly professional. The Capital Grille is a blue-chip restaurant. Decorated to look like an Edwardian men's club, with a moose's head here and a picture of Theodore Roosevelt there, it has a streamlined, steakhouse menu of one choice in each basic category: veal, Delmonico steak, filet mignon, salmon filet, and so on. The potatoes – a creamy mashed called "Sam's" and cottage fries, mixed with onion strings – are especially good. (My own contribution to civilized living is putting some of each on one forkful.) Every vegetable to come out of the kitchen is cooked just right, and the wonder of the place is how little it varies from the same flawless standard, visit after visit.

11. TURNER FISHERIES, *The Westin Hotel, Dartmouth St. at Stuart St. Tel. 424-7425. T-stop: Copley. Hours: daily, 11 am-11pm. Cost: $8-16, lunch; $16-30, dinner. Main dishes: scallops, $13; salmon, $19.*

The decor is as subtle as fog rolling in from the harbor; it's the seafood that is supposed to stand out, and it does, on an extensive menu that appeals especially to serious connoisseurs of clams, oysters, and mussels. There are usually wide selections in each of those categories, depending on the season. And in a city cacophonous with boasts regarding clam chowder, Turner's is easily near the top, with a soup that is creamy without losing its heartiness, and crowded with the right kinds of clams. Most of the seating at the restaurant is in the form of high-backed booths, almost like little roomettes. Seafood is also served in the Lounge, where good, live jazz rings out every night at 8 p.m.

12. RADIUS, *8 High Street, across from One Financial Center. Tel. 426-1234. T-stop: South Station. Hours: lunch, Monday-Friday, 11:30 am- 2:30 pm; dinner, Monday-Saturday, 5:30 - 10 pm. Main dishes: $14-19, lunch; $25-34, dinner. Typical: lobster club sandwich, $19 (lunch); Potato-crusted halibut, $28 (dinner). Note: Radius has a table set aside at lunchtime for solo diners.*

The latest slang in replacement of the long-discarded "neato" and the rarely understood "tony" happens to be a word that suits Radius perfectly, because the place is, in every sense, "round." And round is the thing to be these days: as opposed to square, which most restaurants are by comparison to Radius. They'd have to be, for Radius has generally circular walls, in addition to a very tony understanding of what it means to be neato.

The design is stark in charcoal gray with red trim, and sleek like a new automobile. It apparently revs up the room, which is nearly always crowded and makes a buzz slightly more excited than might be expected. In fact, Radius sounds like a New York restaurant.

The cuisine can be described as new-neo-nouvelle, to coin a phrase, or to use any other expression that indicates the avant garde in dishes and the ingredients they combine. Gnocchi, for example, is filled with organic carrots and zucchini blossoms, among other things. The coriander and ginger-rubber chicken comes with caramelized endive, edamame, and pearl onions. Underneath it all, though, from the zucchini blossoms to the caramelized endive, the food at Radius is as smart as its customers: which is to say, fascinating... but never, ever high in fat.

CHILDREN, TOO

13. RESTAURANT MARCHÉ, *the Prudential Center (Huntington Avenue side), Tel. 578-0987. T-stop: Prudential. Hours: 9 am to 11 pm, daily. Main dishes: $3-8. Marché also has a wine bar, upstairs, and a foodstore, down.*

Restaurant Marché is the European response to an American industry: fast-food. And by comparison to Marché's village-fair atmosphere, industrial is just what America's fast-food joints seem to be. Located in a space about the size of a soccer field (to use European dimensions), the restaurant is composed of a dozen food bars, where various dishes are made from scratch and served. Having been issued with a tray and a check upon entering, guests simply roam around and get what they want, having the checks stamped along the way. They settle their duly stamped checks upon leaving.

Most of the stations serve American food – from pizzas to omelettes to hamburgers, soups and seafood. Each is a fair cut above the average, though, for being freshly prepared of fresh ingredients. Note that word "fresh" – it has been hard to come by in a quick lunch or dinner lately. Everybody can have what they want, which is a fine thing for many families traveling together and used to nothing less than that at home.

Marché is owned by the Swiss hospitality company Mövenpick, which betrays itself in the station devoted to rösti. A portion of lox or a grilled würst (sausage) and half-a-plate of browned potatoes, a rösti could possibly be an American meal. Possibly: but the spoonful of thick, Germanic sour cream gives it away as a taste of the old country, from Mövenpick's point-of-view.

14. CHARLEY'S EATING & DRINKING SALOON, *284 Newbury St. Tel. 266-3000. T-stop: Hynes. Hours: Sunday-Thursday, 11:30 am-11 pm; Friday-Saturday, 11:30 am-midnight. Main dishes: $8-17. Typical: chicken club sandwich (lunch) $7.99; broiled scrod (dinner) $13.99.*

Charley's is a bar – an "eating & drinking saloon." But everything about the place is big and honest, two qualities that children recognize in a snap. The food ranges from the simple to the sophisticated, depending on what kind of children you're with and what kind of adults *they're* with. The waiters and waitresses, for whatever reason, take their time with children and make them feel special. Like the Restaurant Marché, Charley's is a respectable choice for a date, for a meal alone, or for a business lunch – but both are in this category to emphasize that unlike many other places, they are each big hits with young people.

15. JILLIAN'S BOSTON, *145 Ipswich St. at Landsdowne, next to Fenway Park. Tel. 437-0300, website, www.jillian's.com. T-stop: Kenmore Square. Hours: Monday-Saturday, 11 am-2 am; Sunday, Noon-2 am. Main dishes: (bistro) hamburger, $5.95; (main restaurant) steak, $14.95. Note: Minors (under 18) aren't allowed without an adult after 7 pm.*

Nothing else in Boston is Jillian's. Not much, anywhere, is. Imagine being in a video arcade, walking up to a machine, putting a quarter in, and going inside of it, where, in between the lights and switches, and unworldly diversions, you sit down and order roast beef *au jus*. Jillian's has four floors, hundreds of video games, an array of virtual reality super-games, and fifty billiard tables. You can get American bistro food on two of the floors. A more serious restaurant is on the third floor. People flock around, slightly overwhelmed at the fact that any place could be so perfect for the 12-year-old within. And what is wrong with a place that is perfect for a 12-year-old? Not much, except the virtual expense, at a couple bucks a game.

ITALIAN

16. RISTORANTE TOSCANO, *41-47 Charles St., Beacon Hill. Tel. 723-4090. T-stop: Charles. Hours: daily, 11:30 am-2:30 pm; 5:30 pm-10 pm. Main dishes: $9-14, lunch; $19-25, dinner. Typical: risotto with mushrooms (lunch), $12; scaloppini Toscano (dinner), $24.*

Toscano is a classic Italian restaurant. There is nothing offbeat or gratuitously creative about its dishes. Their piquancy comes from expertise, not experiment. Pasta, chicken in butter-and-wine, veal: these are the dishes served for generations in Northern Italy, and so very well represented at Toscano. With soft peach walls, it is elegant the way that New York's vaunted French restaurants are: not in the sense of showstopping decor, but as a backdrop that makes the patrons feel comfortable and look good. Toscano knows just exactly what it is doing, and it stands at the top of Boston's long list of Italian restaurants.

17. GALLERIA ITALIANO, *177 Tremont St. Tel. 423-2092. T-stop: Boylston. Hours: Monday-Friday, 7 am - to "about" 10:30 pm; Friday-Saturday, open until 11 pm. Main dishes: $4-7, lunch; $16.50-22, dinner. Typical: seafood ravioli in cream sauce, $5.25; fish stew (dinner), $22. Note: credit cards accepted at dinner only.*

It is Italy inside the Galleria Italiano. The way they set the place up. The food they make. Most of the people who work there. Not Italian-American, mind you, like most of the North End, but an even purer form. The Galleria is open all day, starting with hot breakfasts and fresh breads. Lunch is not, I am beguiled to say, a smoothed-out system. You look over the food in big pans and then order, and then pay and then somebody heats up your food and adorns it with bread, and then you sit down and they bring the food over, and then you get up and go get a fork. Any American toddler of three could design a more efficient system for the Galleria, but then, that's the way American minds work.

At dinnertime, it becomes a more elegant place, candlelit and more conventional, with table service. The food is delicious, slightly surprising Italian food. Risotto is always cooked to order, and the pasta served at dinner is not only homemade but hand-rolled.

18. PAGLIUCA'S, *14 Parmenter St., off Hanover St., North End. Tel. 367-1504. T-stop: Aquarium, with quarter-mile walk. Hours: Monday-Thursday, noon-10 pm; Friday-Saturday, noon-11 pm; Sunday 11 am-10 pm. Main dishes: $3.75-7.50, lunch; $7.50-15, dinner. Typical: lasagna, $7.50; chicken Parmigiana with pasta, $11.95.*

The North End has been changing in the past few years; it now has an absurd number of restaurants, cheek-by-jowl on Hanover Street and its offshoots. Most are quite tiny, achingly sophisticated in appearance and cuisine, and something of a mystery to the local Italian-American population. Sometimes, they are a mystery to me, too. One vaunted place set the table with stale bread; that's not easy in a section of town pocked with family-owned bread bakeries. It shows a certain sense of planning, on the part of the restaurant, to age the bread so. Another chic little bistro served factory-made ravioli, frozen in Dayton or Camden or someplace like that. A hospital cafeteria can serve frozen ravioli, an Italian restaurant ... can not.

Pagliuca's is an Italian restaurant. The pasta is homemade, and cooked to order. The dishes are not astonishingly unique, but they are freshly made. Manicotti and lasagna are especially good. Owned by the same family for the past twenty years or so, Pagliuca's fills up with families and others from the North End. It's a small restaurant and unpretentious, with shiny chrome chairs, a linoleum floor and one, very nearly *quaint* brick wall, all canceling each other out, in terms of a decorating theme.

Once when I was there, I asked the waitress if she knew what team had won a certain ballgame; she didn't know, but walked around the restaurant asking at the other tables, until she found someone who knew the outcome. They wouldn't *do* that at the place with the stale bread. Lunch is a bargain at Pagliuca's, when most of the menu goes for half-price.

LOTS OF FOOD

Most people are hungry before a big meal. Some people are still hungry after one. These are places that might grant them peace, at least for a little while.

19. DICK'S LAST RESORT, *55 Huntington Av. bottom level of the Prudential Center. Tel. 267-8080. T-stop: Copley. Hours: daily, 11:30 am-2 am. Main dishes: $2.95-9.95. Typical: barbecued beef ribs, $10.95; BBQ pork ribs, 8.95/13.95; bucket of fries, $2.95.*

Dick's looks like the feeding station at a logging camp, with long tables and mismatched chairs. After you sit down, someone comes by to unroll some white paper at your place, tossing down a napkin twisted around some utensils. The table having been set with care, a waiter or waitress comes by – not to take the order, but to be obnoxious for a few minutes.

That is the way of it at Dick's: the serving staff is supposed to be smart-alecky. It's *schtick* as they say in entertainment, and entertaining is what it is supposed to be. Personally, I would go to Dick's more often if you could choose on the way in, as in "Smoking or non-smoking ... rabid or non-rabid?" However, having gone along with the fun (or not, in my grumpy case), the meal comes and all is forgiven. The food is delicious. A great hamburger for under three dollars, a big bucket of the city's best french fries, chicken, shrimp, or ribs: the food is much better than you would think in a place that has so much else to offer. There. I can be obnoxious, too.

20. LA FAMILIGLIA GIORGIO'S, *250 Newbury St. Tel. 247-1569. T-stop: Copley (also 112 Salem St., North End, Tel. 367-6711, T-stop: Haymarket). Hours: Sunday-Thursday, 11 a.m-10:30 p.m.; Friday and Saturday, 11 am-11 pm. Main dishes: $5.25-8, sandwiches; $9.50-17, pasta platters. Typical: tortellini in marinara sauce, $11.75.*

When you first see your dish of food at La Famiglia Georgio, you will either faint or burst out laughing. In the first place, it's not a dish, it's a platter, and in the second place, it's not food, it's a mountain. The idea, according to the family of Giorgios that operates the small string of La Famiglias around town, is that Italians are accustomed to bringing leftovers home from clan dinners. So, where you might order, say, dinner at an ordinary restaurant, you order your next couple of dinners, and at least a lunch-and-a-half, at La Famiglia.

The specialties are pasta dishes, combined with seafood, chicken, or veal. While it is not the best Italian food in Boston, it is a once-in-a-lifetime opportunity to eat like there is no tomorrow. There will be. (I know what you're thinking: no, you can't order one platter and share it; there's a rule about that.)

21. O'LEARY'S, *1010 Beacon St., Brookline; 734-0049. T-stop: St. Mary's (Green Line: outbound C-train, first stop after Kenmore). Hours: 11 am-1 am.*

Main dishes: $5-6, lunch; $9-14, dinner. Typical: beef stew: $5.75; surf and turf 13.95.

O'Leary's is a true pub, but not in the Georgian-Dublin sense of a place professionally Irish. It is a breezy, contemporary room, with a long bar along one wall and a line of tables opposite. More than some Irish pubs, O'Leary's tries to serve recipes from the old country. One is boxty, which is something like a potato pancake up in Ulster, though O'Leary's version is a little bit more of an omelette. Another is brown soda-bread, not often seen in this country. The food can be quite fine at O'Leary's, but it is always generous: order the beef stew, and you'll get a large bowl crammed with chunks of meat. A forkful in one hand, and a piece of soda-bread in the other: it's probably too much food for a city dweller, anyway.

NEIGHBORHOOD PLACES

22. CHARLIE'S SANDWICH SHOPPE, *429 Columbus Ave. Tel. 536-7669. T-stop:Back Bay Station. Hours: Monday-Friday, 6 am-2:30 am.; Saturday, 7:30 am-1 am. Main dishes: all meals are under $10.*

Charlie's is as plain and honest as its name. It's a dinette from another era – the late 1920s – and so the patina of times gone by is no put on. A counter, a couple of short-order cooks, a half-dozen tables, and waitresses who are friendly but never chirpy: those are the basic ingredients of Charlie's. The food itself may not be magnificent, exactly; sandwiches from the grill and a few daily specials make up the ambitious part of the lunch menu. But breakfast is always swell, and the ambiance is as comfortable as an old Cardigan.

23. THE WARREN INN, *2 Pleasant St., Charlestown. Tel. 241-8142. T-stop: Community College, with a quarter-mile walk. Hours: 11:15 am-10:30 pm Cost: $4.50-8.95, lunch; $9.95-15.95, dinner. Main dishes: Monument chicken salad (lunch), $7.95; lamb chops (dinner) $15.95*

Of all the many pubs in Boston, the Warren Inn may be the most authentic in essence. And it probably should be, because when it opened, in 1780 in the midst of the Revolution, it was practically in the British empire. Charlestown was then a separate town. Now Charlestown is part of Boston, the oldest and among the most charming sections of the city. Houses hundreds of years old line brick streets that wear antique street-lamps like necklaces. The Warren Inn is just down Pleasant Street from the Bunker Hill monument.

Small dining rooms, of different vintage, wrap around an open area before the bar. The reason that the Warren Inn is like an authentic pub is that it has none of the implications of a serious saloon: it's just the center of a restaurant that is a center for the town. Most of the food is American – club sandwiches, grilled chicken, onion soup – in addition to English fish 'n chips.

24. THEO'S COZY CORNER, *162 Salem St. in the North End. Tel. 367-2085. T-stop: Haymarket. Hours: Monday, 6:30 am-3 pm; Tuesday-Friday, 6:30-8:30 pm; Saturday, 6:30 am-4 pm; Sunday, 6:30 am-3 pm. Main dishes: $3-7. Typical: chicken cacciatore with pasta, $5.95.*

When a restaurant is wound up just right, the staff couldn't be busier, and the customers couldn't be more relaxed. That is the way of it at the Cozy Corner. And a little corner it is, with just six tables and two large windows on a quiet crossroad in the North End. The food is American, as oasis for that particular cuisine in the Italian section, with hamburgers, Philly steak-sandwiches, omelettes, and hot entrees that change daily.

Parmesans are a specialty: veal- and eggplant-parmesans, of course, but also broccoli and combo parmesans. Homemade soups are served with a big hunk of bread – and it is a quite a neighborhood for bread, with four family bakeries within earshot. There are fancier places in the North End, but not too many better places to sit and hear the latest.

OFF-BEAT, NEAR THE HYNES CONVENTION CENTER

The Hynes Convention Center is connected to the Prudential Center, a shopping mall and office complex, with a food court offering a better-than-average selection of take-away food. But, as you know, a food court is not a place – it is everyplace. Here are three suggestions for other lunch places within a few blocks of Hynes.

25. DIXIE KITCHEN, *182 Massachusetts Av. Tel. 536-3068. (Exit the convention center on Boylston, turn left up the street, one block to Massachusetts Av., turn left: the Dixie Kitchen is two blocks down on the left.). T-stop: Hynes. Hours: Monday-Saturday, 11 am-10 pm; Sunday, 3 pm-10 pm Main dishes: $4.75-7.95, lunch; $5.95-9.95, dinner. Typical: jambalaya (lunch), $4.95/ $5.95; crawfish and shrimp etouffee (dinner), $9.95.*

"Put some South in your mouth" is one of the mottos of the Dixie Kitchen, and there isn't much on the menu that isn't tinged with the hearty spicing of New Orleans cajun cooking or the downhome taste of the bayou. Fried alligator tail, in the Back Bay? You can order that, or fried okra, jambalaya, catfish or bourbon chocolate pecan pie. Just in case you haven't got the idea from the menu, the restaurant also has murals of the French Quarter on the walls and jazz music in the air. The Dixie Kitchen is open for supper, but it serves the city's perfect lunch for flagging walkers: Gumbo Ya-Ya, a rich seafood stew that is hearty enough to fill you up and spicy enough to revive your spirits.

26. BREAD AND CIRCUS, *15 Westland Av. Tel. 375-1010. (Follow the directions for the Dixie Kitchen and then continue on Massachusetts Ave., turning sharply right at Westland Av.; Bread & Circus will be almost immediately to your right.) T-stop: Symphony. Hours: daily, 9 am-10 pm Main dishes: $4-7. Typical sandwiches: sesame tofu, 3.99; grilled portobello mushrooms, 4.99.*

First of all: the name comes from an English expression, meaning the whole darn thing. Or something like that: the Bread and Circus in question is a supermarket, operated by an English company that is making a serious effort to sell organic, healthy, or environmentally responsible goods. It has produce (which is quite pricey, to use another English expression), a marvelous bakery, and an extensive dairy, among other things.

But the Bread & Circus delicatessen department is the most interesting place in the store, with fresh salads, chock full of the good stuff (the seafood salad, for example, is laden with shrimp), and robust sandwiches. Without wanting to worry upper management – which takes the store's mission so very much to heart – I don't think an overstuffed roast beef sandwich can be much of an organic creation, really. There are vegetarian selections, too, but the meats are smacking fresh, for a fine sandwich. There are tables in the front of the store where people can eat lunch purchased within.

27. THE OTHER SIDE COSMIC CAFE, *407 Newbury St., at Massachusetts Ave. Tel. 536-9477. T-stop: Hynes. Hours: Monday-Wednesday, 10 am-midnight; Thursday-Saturday, 10 am-1 am; Sunday, Noon to midnight. Main dishes: $3-6. Note: credit cards not accepted.*

The Other Side tries hard for the grungy look – of nineteen-year-olds who just don't care about anything (unless it came from Seattle). The restaurant is mostly gray inside, a generally undecorated warehouse space with a high ceiling, a small counter, haphazard tables, and a mezzanine section above. Pay no attention. It's all just a front. The Other Side Cosmic Cafe serves homemade food with such simplicity and care that the true name could be "Grandma's Little Cottage." The pies, cookies and cakes in the case near the door are made from scratch by the owner's sister, with help when her daughter gets home from school. There is nothing like home cooking, cosmic or otherwise.

PIZZA

28. FIGS, *67 Main St., Charlestown. Tel. 242-2229. Open Monday-Thursday, 5:30-10 pm; Friday, 5:30-10:30; Saturday, 5:30-11 pm Main dishes: $11.95-15.25, pasta; $10.95-16.95, pizza (serves two-three). Typical: butternut squash risotto, $14.24; spicy chicken-sausage pizza, $14.95.*

I have long maintained that the true test of a pizza parlor is a plain cheese pizza, a "tomato pie," as they used to call it before the name "pizza" was even known in this country. If I am right, then Figs is not in the top echelon: its traditional tomato-and-mozzarella pie is, as a matter fact, flat. If I am wrong, however, and a pizza is a just a launching pad for its toppings, then Figs is stupendous.

Figs makes thinny-thin crust pizza. It is rolled, not thrown, into shape, and baked in a brick oven, all within sight of the dining room. The restaurant, formerly the home of Olives (which is owned by the same couple), isn't much more than a storefront with about a dozen tables and a tiny bar, all dark brown and dusky. There are things other than pizza on the menu, including starters such as crab cakes and pasta dishes, leaning toward risotto and polenta, as opposed to anything pizza-parlor-ish, like ziti.

But there are thirteen pizzas on the menu and a few more on the specials board each night, including fried calamari and argula; fig, prosciutto and gorgonzola; kielbasa, potatoes, sauerkraut and mustard aeoli. One pizza, the size of a cookie sheet (on which it is presented), serves two or three people, and costs between $10.95 and $16.95. The gourmet pizza parlor, a field Figs is helping to pioneer, is akin to designer blue-jeans and old TV shows as big-time budget movies: the Old Brat market.

29. HAYMARKET PIZZA, *106 Blackstone St. Tel. 723-8585. T-stop: Haymarket. Hours: Monday-Friday, 9 am-8 pm; Saturday, 9 am-7 pm. Main dishes: $1 a slice.*

Haymarket is a space – I think we can call it that with accuracy – in the block that contains all the goat-butchers and down-cellar cheese shops at the Haymarket on Blackstone Street. If there were a pizza shop in colonial days, or medieval days, or cave days, it would be akin to Haymarket Pizza. I think that's the name; they didn't have signs in cave days.

But what good pizza. A gaggle of workers works the ovens on one side of the shop, but all they sell is pizza. If you want a drink to go with it, there are soda machines on the other side of the room, where the dining tables are made of boards resting upon barrels. As to chairs, there are a few; they seem to have been donated by sympathetic missionaries passing through a long time ago. But the fact that the tables can be dismantled is a practical matter on sunny days, when they are moved out on the sidewalk, and then the floorshow is made of the colors stroked into the Haymarket by bin after bin of fresh vegetables.

As to the pizza itself, we argue at our barrels over its best attribute: is it the tasty crust, thin but a little crispy, the sauce, sweet and snappy, or the cheeses, which maintain their character where so many pizza cheeses fade into mere white stuff. The field is open for research, and the pie among the least expensive in the city. I love to see the mix of people on a single board: workmen, kids, and always a number of well-dressed people who look like lawyers or stockbrokers. It's a fine broker who can find such an overlay, even at lunch.

30. PIZZERIA REGINA, *11 1/2 Thatcher St., North End Tel. 227-0765. T-stop: Haymarket. Hours: Monday-Thursday, 11 am-11:30 pm; Friday-Saturday, 11 am -midnight; Sunday, Noon-11 pm. Pizzas: $5.89-9.29, small; $9.59-15.99, large. Typical: spinaci e broccoli, $7.99/13.29.*

"Pizza; soda, wine or beer: that's our whole menu," said the waitress at Regina Pizza to someone who asked for coffee. Opened in 1926, in a rounded part of a building in the heart of the North End, Regina is the real thing: an adorable relic of the earliest days of the pizza fad in this country. About a dozen wooden booths provide the seating, along with a tiny counter. Through a window to the kitchen, the cook, or "pizzaiolo," can be seen throwing the dough in the classic way.

The aura of good times and Saturday nights is the best reason to find the way to 11 1/2 Thatcher Street, but the pizza is an awfully good runner-up. With a choice of 23 toppings for a bespoke pie, and ten "gourmet" concoctions, it's hard to complain, or even to notice, that there is only one foodstuff on the menu (pizza pie). Pizzeria Regina has spawned a chain of restaurants, including an outlet at Quincy Market, but the pizza elsewhere is not quite as interesting as it is at the home base, with sixty years of those Saturday nights standing behind it.

REAL BOSTON

31. LOCKE-OBER, *3-4 Winter Place (down a side walkway). Tel. 542-1340. T-stop: Park St. Hours: Monday-Friday, 11:30 am-10 pm; Saturday, 5:30 pm-10:30 pm; Sun, 5:30 pm-9:30 pm. Main dishes: $5-15, lunch; $18.75-27.50, dinner. Typical: chicken pot-pie (lunch), $10.25; roast rack-of-lamb Persillade, carved at table (dinner), $29. Note: Jacket and tie required.*

Locke-Ober sounds in some way German, but it started as the combination of two French restaurants, one of which dated to 1875. It's been at the forefront of the city's restaurants too long, though, to be considered anything but Bostonian through and through. Over the years, the restaurant's regular diners have howled at the slightest hint in a change of the decor, and so Locke-Ober is a Victorian castle against the years: beautifully paneled, gracefully appointed, and comfortable to a fault.

The preferred dining room is downstairs, though it is quieter and perhaps more private in the plainer upstairs room. It is harder to get a good table at the height of the lunch hour than at dinnertime. In general, you will receive a table eventually, even during a rush, as long as you are either: 1) a member of the ninth generation of a mighty good Boston family, or 2) patient. For the staff at Locke-Ober, waiting tables is a profession of fine points and attention to detail, so there is never anything unexpected about the service.

And the food that they serve is just as predictable: it is surpassing. Hearty roast-beef hash (made from an old recipe) or steak sandwiches are good at lunch. Sweetbreads; clams in pasta with a lobster sauce; crabcakes; chops and salmon are excellent dinner choices. And the desserts, including Baked Alaska, are as good as any to be found. Locke-Ober is not the most expensive of restaurants (though it is near the top); it is the most memorable, though, from any perspective.

32. DURGIN-PARK, *340 Faneuil Hall Marketplace, North Market. Tel. 227-2038. T-stop: State. Hours: Monday-Saturday, 11:30 am-10 pm.; Sunday, 11:30 am-9 pm. Main dishes: $4.95-16.95; chicken pot-pie (lunch), $4.95; lamb chops (dinner), $16.95.*

No place else is Durgin-Park. In fact, after well over a hundred years, it is amazing that Durgin-Park is still Durgin-Park: long tables, big portions, fresh food. Located on the second floor of one of the old warehouse buildings at Quincy Market, the restaurant has been there for at least a hundred and twenty-five years (its exact origins are murky). When Quincy was a real vegetable market, Durgin-Park was going strong ... when it was all but abandoned in the 1950s, Durgin-Park continued to pack customers in, all but alone in its stone fortress.

In the 1970s, Quincy Market came back to life as a colorful place to eat and shop, and Durgin-Park is still at the core of it all: three dining rooms (and one smaller one upstairs) where parties sit together at table, and hear what those around are saying, and see what they are eating. The place is famous for its prime rib: one portion hangs off both ends of a large platter. The mashed potatoes are soupy and delicate. Chicken pot-pie pops with plump pieces of chicken and bright vegetables under a thick crust. The seafood, across the board, must be the very freshest in the city – and Durgin-Park, where gourmands are known to cry "uncle" – serves my favorite diet lunch in Boston: broiled scrod with cabbage. Scant calories, plenty to eat.

For a long time, peppery waitresses were another hallmark of Durgin-Park, but they are replaced, more and more, by young people from Ireland. Tourists visit for the vintage atmosphere and the genuine Yankee menu, but they can rest assured that locals also go in droves; no where else is such good food so reasonably priced.

33. THE RED HAT, *9 Bowdoin St., Boston. Tel. 523-2175. T-stop: Government Center. Hours: daily, noon to 2 am. Cost: nothing is over $10. Main dishes: prime rib, $9.95; steak, $8.95; char-grilled pizza, $5.95-6.50.*

When the Red Hat was new, generations ago, its surroundings on Scollay Square were notorious. Burlesque houses were the cream of the neighborhood, which ranged downward from there to striptease joints, nefarious saloons, pool halls – and then downward from there a few more notches. It was the "bad" part of town, which was well known to a lot of otherwise good people. Scollay Square, it ain't what it used to be. The joints and the theaters were torn down about twenty years ago, replaced by Government Center and other, equally colorless buildings. Now, the Red Hat is all that is left, a cozy saloon with two small dining areas, the older one in the back lined with murals of old Boston.

The food is surprising, with plump, fresh fish and handmade pizza at the forefront. The Red Hat is getting more well known, and people are trudging over Beacon Hill to an otherwise fairly quiet part of town, in terms of nightlife. Now that the bulldozing is long over, it turns out that they didn't rub Scollay Square out, not completely. And wouldn't it be fun if it all came rushing back, through the portal at the Red Hat.

ROMANTIC

34. DAVIO'S, *269 Newbury St. Tel. 262-4810. T-stop: Hynes or Copley. Hours: daily, 11:30-11 pm. T-stop: Copley or Hynes. A second location is in the Royal Sonesta Hotel, 5 Cambridge Pkwy., Cambridge, Tel. 661-4810. T-stop: Lechmere. Hours: daily, 7 am to 10 pm. Main dishes: $6.50-$12, lunch; $16.50- 29, dinner. Typical: penne with applewood smoked chicken (lunch), $9.25; grilled veal chop (dinner), $28.95.*

A formal restaurant need not be stiff, as Davio's proves down the stairs at its Newbury Street address. Upstairs is a slightly more casual cafe, but in the cellarette, Davio's glows with warm light, crisp linen and some fairly good artwork on the walls. The staff takes good care in serving a meal, without trying to poke into an evening.

Davio's displays a respect for leisurely dining and estimable Northern Italian cuisine, re-interpreted with local ingredients. Roasted cod, in saffron-tomato brodo; homemade sausage; grilled salmon with "garlicky" spinach, and original pasta dishes are all specialties. With tiramasu at the top of the list, the desserts are especially good. On Newbury, Davio's is quietly festive. At the Royal Sonesta Hotel, it is more modern and spacious, depending for its atmosphere on the view of the Boston skyline across the Charles River.

35. CHANTERELLE , *226 Newbury St. Tel. 262-8988. T-stop: Copley. Hours: daily except Monday, 5:30 pm- about 10:30. Main dishes: $14-19. Typical: salmon Chanterelle ($16).*

Chanterelle was more *je ne sais crois* a year or so back, when all the waiters were young Frenchmen, like puppies trying to please. That was a bistro (!), with laughs and with charm. Then they disappeared for some reason and Americans took their places. The bistro (!) is more accurately a French restaurant nowadays, with delicious food, but no pups. Perhaps they'll be back. But the food at Chanterelle is very French, such as butter-soft filet mignon, in bordelaise sauce and fully surrounded, like every entree, by a hearty variety of practically perfect vegetables.

My own favorite dessert in town is the Crepes Maison at Chanterelle. Crepes folded in a bundle over a light cheese filling, a hint of almond, berries, whipped cream: out of all that emerges something of which I give people a taste and they abscond with most of what's left. I have to remember to stop offering. Dusky-red and neatly contemporary in decor, Chanterelle is hardly a large restaurant, though a gaping mirror (which I personally would like to spray paint) covers one wall and makes the place seem a little broader than it actually is.

36. MARLIAVE'S, *31 Bromfield. Tel. 423-6340. T-stop: Park St. Hours: Monday-Saturday, 11 am-10 pm; Sunday, Noon to 9 pm. Main dishes: $7-18. Typical: ravioli (lunch), $7; eggplant Parmesan (dinner), $15.*

Samuel Eliot Morrison's parents frequented Marliave's, back when it was known as the "Cafe Marliave." In case that bit of vital intelligence does not stand on its own: Morrison, an eminent nautical historian, grew up in one of Boston's most august families at the turn-of-the-century, and in his memoir, he made mention that Marliave was where his elders went when they went out to eat. I doubt that it's changed much since then, or since it opened in 1875.

Tucked into a walkway off of Bosworth Street, the ground floor is a little maze of wooden booths on a mosaic floor, with old paintings and borders of stained glass to harken back to the *refeened* elegance of a continental restaurant a century ago. Upstairs, Marliave is a garden room. I opt for the downstairs, if I can, but in either room, the place offers a unique atmosphere in the midst of downtown Boston. The menu is staunchly and plainly Italian, with good pasta and fish. (I have a weakness for vintage restaurants, though, and I would go to Marliave even if they didn't serve food; just to be there.)

SANDWICHES

37. RUDI'S, *30 Rowes Wharf, Atlantic Av. Tel. 330-7656. T-stop: Aquarium. Hours: Monday-Friday, 7:30-8 pm; Saturday, 8 am-6 pm. Also open*

Sundays in Summer. Main dishes: $4.50-$7.25. Typical: smoked salmon sandwich on croissant with boursin, $5.71.

Rudi's started out as a bakery, ambition enough, the way that Rudi's produced middle-European breads and pastries. Then it began to cook, as well as bake, and today Rudi's calls itself a bistro and offers more hot food, from baked haddock to veal piccata, danishes and brioches. Part of the reason for the transformation is that Rudi's moved from the Back Bay to Rowe's Wharf: a large and prosperous development of residences, offices, and a hotel. Trapped on the other side of a main drag (Atlantic Ave.), Rowe's Wharf is something of a captive audience for the take-away food that Rudi's offers. If you don't happen to have a penthouse overlooking the harbor at Rowe's Wharf, to which to take your meatloaf sandwich, there are some tables on hand at Rudi's. There are also places to sit outside at Rowe's Wharf, with a bag-lunch.

The sandwiches range from the gourmet, such as brie and sundried tomato, to the simple, such as egg salad, or an excellent rendition of that most difficult of sandwiches, chicken salad. Rudi's has five special sandwiches everyday, which are listed on a recorded message after 9 am (call Rudi's at the telephone number above).

38. THE PARISH CAFE, *361 Boylston St. Tel. 247-4777. T-stop: Arlington. Hours: Monday-Saturday 11:30 am-1 am; Sunday, Noon to midnight. Main dishes: $7.95-9.95.*

The rise of the chef-celebrity has been a resistible form of hero-worship, to me at least. Yet the Parish Cafe has a rather irresistible idea, in presenting 21 sandwiches, each one the special invention of a Bostonian chef-celebrity. Reading the menu is seeing some very mannered restaurants stripped of their guile. What do Lydia Shire and Susan Regis, co-chefs at Biba, like when they have a sandwich? Both like steak, according to the Parish Cafe: Shire's design is for tenderloin on blue-cheese bread with Roquefort butter; Regis' is for flank steak on flat bread, with mushrooms and marinade. Chris Schlesinger, of the East Coast Grill, puts his name to a smokehouse ham, chutney, and monterey-jack cheese sandwich on – this is out of the East Coast Grill, remember – banana bread. For those who are entirely immune to the appeal of chef-celebrities, as well as their sandwiches, the Parish Cafe also offers unsigned salads and entrees, such as fishcakes, meatloaf, and pasta.

39. DE LUCA, *11 Charles St. Tel. 523-4343. Hours: daily, 7 am-10:30 pm. Cost of sandwiches: $3.99-5.99. Typical: ham, $4.99; meatloaf, $3.99.*

In an era when supermarkets are the size of small countries, it is amazing to see that a market the size of the DeLuca store can have everything any person could need, from mops to biscotti. The DeLuca market on Charles Street dates back to the mid-1920s – and it probably was considered a supermarket in its day. Now its overstuffed shelves, its profusion of cottage-made goods, and its idiosyncratic ways – why is there a piano in the corner? – amount to a charming stop for visitors and a necessary storehouse for people who live on Beacon Hill. The deli in the back of the store makes excellent sandwiches, with hot entrees and good cold salads too. The Charles St. DeLuca's is about 20 paces from the Common, and combines with it to make for a perfect picnic.

SEAFOOD

40. THE BARKING CRAB, *88 Sleeper St., at the Northern Ave. Bridge. Tel. 426-2722. T-stop: Aquarium. Hours: daily, 11:30am to 11pm, Sunday brunch, noon to 3pm. Main dishes: $6-10. Typical: crab-burger (lunch), $9.25; fish 'n chips (dinner), $8.95.*

Let's say there was a great restaurant on Cape Cod that was basically a lobster tent that the owners finally got around to winterizing (sort of), with a view of the water and tables for families, and an attractive, gregarious crowd spilling all the way from the bar to the wood-burning stove to the piano in the corner. It would be worth a drive, wouldn't it? The Barking Crab is just a such a beach-bum of a restaurant, practically in downtown Boston, off Northern Avenue on the Fort Point Channel.

The fish-and-chips are batter-dipped, and excellent; clams, lobster, and other fresh fish are also very good. In fair weather, the tent-flaps open to a patio and a wide-angle view of the city of Boston. But let me tell you what the Barking Crab is like in Boston's other kind of weather, just so you know. It's noisy: the listeners are far outnumbered in the typical crowd. It's warm enough, but drafty, because the tent-flaps wiggle. And it's not always easy to get a seat, because families swoop down on the two long tables, and there aren't many others. Gossipy – drafty – families marching around, as if they were one ... Cape Cod is such fun.

41. GRILLFISH, *162 Columbus Ave. Tel. 357-1620. T-stop: Boylston. Hours: Sun-Monday, 5:30 pm-10 pm, Tuesday-Saturday, 5:30pm-11pm. Main dishes: $7.95-14.95. Typical: swordfish with pasta, $14.95; Mediterranean calamari over pasta, $7.95.*

Grillfish is decorated as a cavern, a post-modern cavern. The facade is a bank of windows and so you can look in first to see if the decor, looming all around in stony grey, will agree with your digestion. It seems to attract a hip crowd to the bar, but it's still a bit silly looking. The cuisine at Grillfish is, on the other hand, a very good idea, a wide selection of fresh fish served with pasta at reasonable prices. Sauces, sometimes one each for the pasta and the fish, compliment every dish: among them are marsala, piccata, and a sweet onion recipe.

A blackboard at the back of the restaurant is crammed with the day's choices, from mako shark to catfish to the more typical salmon, scallops, and calamari.

42. YE OLDE UNION OYSTER HOUSE, *41 Union St.; 227-2750. T-stop: Haymarket. Hours: Sunday-Thursday, 11 am-11 pm; Friday-Saturday, 11 am-midnight. Main dishes: $9-18. Typical: fish 'n chips, $9.50; broiled scrod $15.*

In the years around 1826, oysters were a staple food along the American coast. They were the ultimate fast food – even scooping them out of the water wasn't too hard in earlier days – but scooping them off an oyster bar was even easier. Ye Old Union House has a marvelous oyster bar, and if you like oysters, it's altogether one of the best seats in the city: gleaming old wood, cracking fresh shellfish, and a lot of activity on both sides of the counter.

Beyond that oyster bar, the Union House is a very Yankee fish-restaurant, but it is no bargain. The prices are perhaps fifteen percent higher than might be expected elsewhere. That is the price of admission, if you want to join a parade dating back hundreds of years and go at least once to the Union Oyster House to plow through a platter in one of the old wooden booths.

SERIOUS ABOUT FOOD

43. OLIVES, *10 City Square, Charlestown; 242-1999. T-stop: Community College (with ten-minute walk). Hours: Tuesday-Friday, 5:30 pm-10:15 pm; Saturday, 5 pm-10:30 pm. Main dishes: $15-25. Menu varies daily. Note: no reservations.*

People who love Olives love it a lot – and they had better, because it's going to be a trying affair. No reservations are taken and the wait, even on a rainy Tuesday, can be rather long. The food is unimpeachable: modern and eclectic, with an Italian sensibility, though it would be wrong to call Olives an Italian restaurant per se. The name is derived from the foodstuff, olives, not from a person's name. A selection of rarely seen varieties of olives helps to set the table.

The menu changes daily, which is part of the appeal of the place for the chefs and the diners, but a typical entree is pan-sauteed native sole, with artichoke hearts, silk, and white noodles with a sherry glaze, and warm crab salad. Olives moved from the storefront now occupied by Figs (see "Pizza" above) to a swanky new location on Charlestown Square. The drawbacks to the new location are that it's an unattractive hike from the nearest T-stop and there is scant hope of finding a parking place, though valet service is available.

The only drawback to the restaurant itself is that it is, alas, a high-class version of Dick's (see "Lots of Food" above), in terms of the prevailing degree of respect paid to the diner. But at Olives, it's no act. It's the marketplace at work. Customers are in supply and Olives is in demand. Easy to love, but so trying.

44. HAMERSLEY'S BISTRO, *553 Tremont St. Tel. 423-2700. T-stop: Back Bay Station, with quarter-mile walk. Hours: Hours: Monday-Friday, 6 pm-10 pm; Saturday, 5:30 pm-10:30 pm; Sun, 5:30 pm-9:30 pm. Main dishes: $18-27.*

A meal at Hamersley's Bistro is not just a meal, it is an education. And I think they expect you to pay attention. The dishes are exquisite, and presented in spare surroundings, with a distinct seriousness of purpose. The chefs search out new ingredients, as though they were painters finding new colors for their palette. The result is that the restaurant is well-respected throughout Boston, if only because no city can be stodgy that has venison au poivre on the menu: venison au poivre with figs and ginger.

THEATER DISTRICT

45. JAE'S, *212 Stuart St., Tel. 451-5237. T-stop: Boylston Hours: 11:30 am - 10 pm. Main dishes: $10.95-17.95. Typical: Thai noodle soup, $10.95; Yook Kae Jang (spicy shredded beef and noodles), $12.95.*

Jae's is part of a small chain in the Boston area, with other locations in Cambridge and on Columbus Avenue in the South End. It has managed to present what seems like a fresh idea in the realm of Oriental cuisines: a choice among them, under the same roof.

Predominantly a Japanese restaurant, Jae's has an extensive a la carte sushi menu. For fun, in a mischievous way, about one dozen sushi platters are directed toward different types of customers, with different selections for vegetarians, Californians and Bostonians. For the beginner, Jae's offers a cucumber roll and a california roll. For the advanced sushi eater: salmon roe, mackerel, uni with quail egg, giant clam and octopus.

Chinese dishes such as lo mein are also on the menu, as are several dozen Korean entrees, which are the most interesting of all, although they can be overwhelmingly spicy. One of the most distinctive is Bibim Bab, marinated, seasoned raw meats or seafoods that are served over vegetables and rice. The best is Tuna Tartar Bibim Bab, which is hearty, but not heavy, as a pre-theater dinner.

It is impossible to be bored in any restaurant – or any world – in which you get to say Tuna Tartar Bibim Bab.

46. JACOB WIRTH'S, *31 Stuart St. Tel. 338-8586. T-stop: Boylston. Hours: Monday, 11:30 am-8 pm; Tuesday, 11:30 am-9 pm; Wednesday-Friday, 11:30 am-10 pm; Saturday-Sunday, Noon to 10 pm. Typical: baked scrod (lunch), $8; wiener schnitzel (dinner), $13.50; all other dishes under $15.*

Jacob Wirth's has a motto that defines any truly historic restaurant: "We haven't changed for the better. We haven't changed for the worse. We haven't changed at all." It probably hasn't since it opened in 1868. It's a bar and further down, a kitchen on one side of a large room. The rest of the room unrolls across a wooden floor, with wooden chairs and tables, and a paint scheme (cream-yellow) and prints that go back to the last century. If you think you know a lot about baseball, see if you can identify the Red Sox players whose pictures hang near the bar. They were playing before Ted Williams was born.

Jake's was a German restaurant when it opened, and good wursts and kraut are still staples of the menu, which keeps up with other basic trends in sandwiches, soups, and salads. Too plain for some people, perhaps, Jacob Wirth's is an intact example of a type otherwise nearly extinct: a restaurant that doesn't think, it just is.

47. THE 57, *in the Radisson Boston Hotel, 200 Stuart St. Tel. 423-5700. T-stop: Boyston. Hours: daily, 11:30 am-10:30 pm. Main dishes: $7-14, lunch; $13-25, dinner.*

The 57 is part of the Radisson Hotel now, but for a generation centered on the 1960s it was an independent restaurant of the same name, with a broad local following. The specialty is beef and New England cooking, served in dignified surroundings. The portions are generous and, for those without a curtain to make, the pace is never rushed. Less colorful than many restaurants in the theater district, the 57 is a calm in the minor storm that naturally swirls in the neighborhood.

48. FINALE, *1 Columbus Avenue in the Statler Building, next to the Park Plaza Hotel. T-Stop: Boylston. Hours: 11:30 am-3 pm, lunch; 5 pm-midnight, dinner.*

Finale is at its best after the theater, when elaborate pastries accompany a babble of theater reviews and other assorted gossip. The golden-hued decor, by the same designer responsible for Radius (see entry under *Big Business*, above), is itself reminiscent of a Viennese bakery, in a post-modern way. Finale serves light lunches and dinners, but no matter where you take your nourishment, you can stop on the way home for dessert and coffee.

2 COOL 4 U

It's not al*ways* fun to enter this particular lane, whizzing as it is. I was put out of a place called Les Zygomates one bitter, windy, winter day, when the maitre d' looked over a mid-afternoon dining room awash in empty tables; looked at me, adorned in a habille intended only to keep me warm, and then observed that there were no tables available. I protested mildly and then walked out in the middle of her next sentence. It's not always fun, I repeat. There was only one thing for me to do, that day. With my nose even redder from another walk in the wind, I showed up at Biba a half-hour later. Biba: the *arbiter elegantae* of Boston, nationally famous as a place-to-be. If Biba would not have me, then I would I would do as Les Zygomates liked, and disappear, mid-sentence.

49. BIBA, *272 Boylston St. Tel. 426-7878. T-stop: Arlington. Hours: (lunch) Monday-Friday, 11:30 am- 2:30 pm.; (dinner) Sunday-Thursday, 5:30-10:30 pm; Friday-Saturday, 5:30-11 pm.; (Sunday brunch) 11:30 am- 3 pm. Main dishes: $14-25.*

"It doesn't look cold out, but it is," said the maitre d' who showed me to a table overlooking the Public Garden. The cold: a subject upon which I might discourse with my former flair. I soon recovered, not just my equanimity, but the feeling on the tip of my nose. Biba is a *moderne* restaurant, a bar and cafe on the first floor, and a dining room upstairs, where the view of the Public Garden is all the decor needed at the best tables by the window.

The menu is not only creative, but downright courageous in offering gourmet dishes rarely seen elsewhere: rare tuna with a risotto of marrow and truffle, for example, or calf's liver with onions and raw apple. At the same time, Biba serves dishes seen everywhere, such as steak or lobster, but on its own standard. It's expensive, and lunch, alone, can add up to $50 per person quite easily. To place Biba among just a couple of Boston's other leading restaurants, it is more festive in atmosphere than Hamersley's Bistro; more adventurous in culinary ways than Locke-Ober, and more of a showplace for locals on the hoof than Aujourd'hui. Many people consider it the best restaurant in Boston, and it gives no evidence of being anything else.

50. THE BLACK GOOSE BAR & BISTRO, *21 Beacon St. Tel. 720-4500. T-stop: Park St. Hours: Monday-Wednesday 11:30 am-10 pm; Thursday & Friday, 11:30 am-11 pm; Saturday, 5 pm-11pm; Sunday 10 am-10 pm. Main dishes: $7.50-9.95, lunch; $9.50-15.95, dinner. Typical: chicken pesto salad (lunch) $8.75; grilled stuffed pork loin (dinner) $15.25.*

In a room that was a bank, built when banks liked to look like Greek temples, the Black Goose restaurant has taken residence and retained just enough marble details, separated by golden-yellow walls, to seem exactly like ... a former temple.

The Black Goose is in an area between Beacon Hill and downtown that doesn't have many up-tempo places, and so the bar in the middle of the room is usually swarming with professionals and government workers from the State House nearby. It's a smart place and the kitchen is quick about its business at lunchtime, with delicious sandwiches on focaccia bread and large Caesar salads. The food is quite serious at dinnertime, when that bar is still rolling along.

TOURIST PLACES

51. THE BULL & FINCH PUB, *84 Beacon St near Arlington. Tel. 227-9605, website, www.cheersbos.com. T-stop: Arlington. Hours: daily, 11 am-midnight. Main dishes: $6-13. Note: minors are only accommodated in the company of an adult.*

According to the legend, three Hollywood television producers were in Boston, visiting neighborhood bars to find one on which to base a new show they were creating. The one they liked was the Bull & Finch Pub. It was not especially old, the interior having been designed and built in England in 1969. What it was, though, was friendly, and the bartender at the time treated the trio with just the jocular amiability that they saw as a theme of the show. They based their new show, "Cheers," on the Bull & Finch and, in effect, left the place the biggest tip ever proffered: lasting fame as a television shrine. The food is good, though that doesn't matter. It is expensive, though that doesn't matter. What matters is only that it seems so much like the place on the show.

52. THE HARD ROCK CAFE, *131 Clarenden Av. Tel. 424-7625. T-stop: Back Bay Station. Hours: Sunday-Thursday, 11:30 am-11:30 pm; Friday-Saturday, 11:30-1 am Main dishes: $5.99-14.99. Typical: T-bone steak, $14.99.*

Good music, good hamburgers, and fairly predictable memorabilia speak to a far-flung generation. The restaurant-tribute to a state of youthful rebellion, Hard Rock Cafe works hard for a certain glamour and it succeeds, especially for teen-agers, and anyone else who sees the spiritual connection between an electric guitar and a Harley-Davidson motorcycle. A relatively new wrinkle is the Cavern Club downstairs, where the music is live.

53. ANTHONY'S PIER FOUR, *140 Northern Ave. Tel. 482-6262. T-stop: Aquarium, then a one mile walk; taxi suggested. Free parking available. Hours: daily, 11:30 am-11 pm. Main dishes: $9.95-14-95, lunch; $16.95-29.95, dinner; lobster bisque (lunch) $6.95; seafood combination, including shrimp, scallops, salmon, and swordfish (dinner ($21.95) Note: Jacket required.*

South Boston, which is surrounded on almost all sides by at least a little bit of water, is gathering a lot of momentum these days, with the World Trade Center hosting major expositions and the new Federal Courthouse anchoring the harbor. Nonetheless, Anthony's Pier Four remains the busiest spot on the main drag, Northern Avenue: a glassy and extensive restaurant right on the water's edge.

Anthony's is something of a machine, into which the customers fit like cogs. Every meal starts with hot popovers and other complimentary tidbits – that can't be bad. No one knows how to prepare salmon as well as Anthony's and the food can be expertly prepared, though it is sadly uneven. In summer, customers can dine outdoors on a deck. Indoors or out, a good table on the left (west-facing) side of the restaurant takes the cityscape in gulping eyefuls. Even better, perhaps, the tables on the other side face the airport, which entertains Anthony's with a continual airshow of planes taking off and landing.

WORLD CUISINES

54. OCEAN WEALTH, *8 Tyler St. Tel. 423-1338. T-stop: Essex. Hours: daily, 11 am- 4 am. Main dishes: average plate, $10.*

There are two menus in most of Chinatown's restaurants. As you might suspect, one is in English and one is in Chinese. The English version will list the chow meins and mu shu porks familiar to Americans, while the Chinese menu is likely to list completely different dishes, exotic outside of Chinatown, but closer to the core of the cuisine.

At Ocean Wealth, a Chinatown restaurant popular with the families in the neighborhood, the specialty on both menus is fish – it may be wealth, but it is not necessarily from the ocean. The restaurant literally gurgles with aquariums stocked with many of the fish doomed to become entrees before the day is through. It's discomfiting to me to see my dinner in a good mood, or any mood, while its fate is in my hands, but the style at Ocean Wealth is that of the islands, including Hong Kong, along the China coast. That is, the fish are stored alive. Seafood is the thing to order at Ocean Wealth, and many tables will share a lobster as one course, a practical idea that the Yankee restaurants ought to pick up.

The cheapest Chinese food around, and good in a gruff way, comes from a tiny shop at 68 Winter St. It is called **68 Chinese Fast Food**. You can spot it from a great distance at mealtimes by the line on the sidewalk: mind, it only takes about three people to make a line go out the door at 68, but at about two bucks for a mounded plate of food, your time may well be worth the wait. Eight entrees, with salad and fried rice, are priced at $2.25, including beef with broccoli and chicken pepper with black bean sauce.

55. SOL AZTECA, *914A Beacon St., Brookline. Tel. 262-0909. T-stop: St. Mary's (Green Line: outbound C-Train, first stop after Kendall) Hours: Monday-Thursday, 5 pm-10:30 pm; Friday-Saturday, 5 pm-11 pm; Sun, 5 pm-10 pm. Cost: average entree price, $10. Main dishes: enchiladas, $10.50.*

Sol Azteca has reigned for over 20 years as the leading Mexican restaurant in Boston (it is actually just over the line in Brookline). Everytime you think it would be nice to find a friendly cantina, with just a little class about it, and a taste of its own from the kitchen – you end up back at Sol Azteca. While there is a list of more formal entrees, different types of enchiladas, burritos, and tacos can be ordered in combination plates that are far above average. More important, they come with rice and beans – humble rice and beans that are exalted in Sol Azteca's rendition. It's a very popular restaurant, consisting of two intimate and well-appointed dining rooms, down a few steps.

56. THE HELMAND, *143 First Street, Cambridge. Tel. 492-4646. Hours: Sunday through Thursday, 5 pm- 10pm; Friday and Saturday, 5 pm-11 pm. Main dishes: $9.95-$15.95. Typical: Mantwo (homemade pastry filled with onions and beef, served with yoghurt, carrots, yellow split-peas, and sauce), $10.95.*

Not very much is generally known about Afghanistan, a country of violent discontent in Central Asia. Part of its problem, in geopolitical terms, is that it is a crossroads trying to maintain its autonomy, even at the cost of self-destruction. In culinary terms, however, that very inclination is the glory of Afghanistan: it is a crossroads that has insisted upon having a distinctive identity all its own.

So you can't say Afghan food is like Middle Eastern food, or Indian food, or any other food. As served at the Helmand, it's not a cuisine of unusual ingredients, but of seasoning that resonates without overpowering. A tenderloin of beef, prepared with a snappy marinade and then grilled, is served with lentils and rice. Lentils and rice may not be exciting side dishes in just any hands, but flavored just so, they are irresistible. The lamb chops are excellent, thick cuts, served rare on the inside with a charbroiled crust: the meat retaining all of its flavor with a tender texture, too.

The Helmand is a sophisticated restaurant in a high-ceilinged room softly yellow in hue. The crowd that frequents the place looks worldly. They don't necessarily look Afghani, it isn't that, but there is the aura of people who have been to at least a couple different corners of the world in the past, say, week.

57. YOSHI, *725 Boyston St. Tel. 859-8181. T-stop: Copley. Hours: Sunday-Thursday, 11:30 am-midnight; Friday-Saturday, 11:30-1 am. Main dishes: $8.50-13, lunch; $12-25, dinner. Typical: Fish katsu, $16.*

Neither ultra-glamorous nor slouchy like a noodle shop, Yoshi is a fairly large and certainly a versatile restaurant with an extensive menu. There is a sushi bar, and some booths toward the front, but most of the tables are at the back, served by waitresses trained to do their scurrying at a fast trot. The prices are high, as at nearly all the Japanese restaurants in town, and there is almost nothing on the menu that isn't strictly Japanese – no California influence or vice-versa. In fact, Yoshi concedes little to the fact that it is such a long, long way from the nearest stop on the Keisei Line.

Also in the Back Bay, the **Men Tei Noodle House** *(66 Hereford, at Newbury; Tel. 425-0066)* has big bowls of good soup, starting at about $7.

BAKERIES

"I break for bakeries," to coin a bumper-sticker:

LMNOP, *79 Park Plaza, across from the main entrance to the Park Plaza Hotel. Tel. 338-4220.*

The *raison d'etre* for LMNOP is to produce phenomenal bread for the restaurant called **Pignoli**, next door. Walk inside the door and you will see bakers busily doing just that, and trying to keep up with demand. Every so often, they let a tray of hot rolls drop into a basket at the front, or they slide a few loaves onto the rack at the counter, and then LMNOP is in business for itself. There are pastries and tortes, too, sandwiches, and even one or two hot entrees as lunchtime selections.

RESTAURANT ROWS

For those who would like to window-shop for a place to eat before choosing one:

The North End - *Hancock Street between Cross St. and Tileston (but don't ignore the sidestreets). Italian restaurants, from six-table, ultra-chic storefronts to rambling restaurants operated by the same family for generations.*

The Back Bay - *Newbury and Boylston Sts., especially between Exeter and Hereford Sts. All types of restaurants, many with patios.*

Harvard Square - *Cambridge, especially down John F. Kennedy St. to Eliot St. An eclectic mix of many, mostly smaller places. Rather a carnival atmosphere on summer nights.*

The South End - *Tremont Street, between W. Canton St. and E. Berkeley. The newest conclave, it is led by some of the trendiest of the trendy.*

Beacon Street, Brookline - *around Arundel St., just past Kenmore Square (and close enough to Fenway Park to walk to a game after a meal). A little United Nations of restaurants and bakeries, all small and all different.*

But the reason to hope that LMNOP is on your way someplace is the selection of scones. Crusty, plump, tasty: all that I was told once, when I complimented them extravagantly, is that they are made "by the girls downstairs." I don't know who the girls are, but I imagine that they are deeply Irish and that they have been downstairs for the past one-hundred-and-fifty years, perfecting the recipe.

JAPONAISE, *1020 Beacon St., Brookline. Tel. 566-4963. Also: 1815 Massachusetts Ave, Cambridge, Tel. 547-5531; and 10 Muzzey St., Lexington. Tel. 674-2233.*

Japan is devoted to its many bakeries, a fact that comes as a surprise to some Americans, who do not associate that country with bread and pastry. The favorite bread is a thick cut, perfectly square white bread that is rather dense without being heavy. The cakes, across the board, are slightly richer – egg-ier – than American cakes. With an acknowledged French influence (hence the name, which is French for "Japanese"), Japonaise carries both bread and a sprightly display of pastry: cream buns, tarts, cake squares, and bon bons. In addition, it sells sandwiches, made in advance, cut and packaged, as is common in Japan. The place is immaculate and well-ordered; it is a pleasure just to look and conjecture.

SAVOY FRENCH BAKERY, *1003 Beacon St., Brookline. Tel. 734-0214.*
Note: Savoy is across the street from Japonaise.

Savoy usually has a small, exquisitely executed selection of chiffons, napoleons, and other pastries. The place is better known for its croissants, which are very good, though not on the same level as , say, the mocha tart. Most of the time, the selection of bread is somewhat limited: there are long loaves of French bread and short loaves of French bread.

ELDO CAKE HOUSE, *36 Harrison Av., Chinatown. Tel. 350-7977.*

Eldo is a Chinese bakery, specializing in advance-order cakes, some of which, like Black Forest, seem familiar, but some of which, like chestnut-filled, are more obscure. It is a hectic store, with one large case of pastries. To generalize, the offering at a Chinese bakery is more distant from the usual American selection than that of a Japanese bakery, such as Japonaise. A lotus-seed paste roll, a honeydew flower cake (each about 80 cents): it's all good. The Eldo Cake House is one of at least a half-dozen bakeries in Chinatown. It is the one I know of where fresh pastries come out from the ovens quite often all day long. I just stand there at Eldo Cake House until the next tray comes out, and snap up something from it.

A. PARZIALE & SONS, *78 Prince St., North End. Tel. 523-6368.*

Italian bread: at Parziale, the question is only how much you want. By the window, there is usually a loaf the size of a footstool, but the handheld rolls and regular sized breads keep coming out all day, so you have a good chance of landing something still warm, steamy and crusty.

MIKE'S PASTRY, *300 Hanover St., North End. Tel. 742-3050.*

Mike's is profuse with cases and shelves that are filled with goodies. Biscotti by the yard, pies, and pastries: *sfogliatella* with infinite layers; the local favorite "lobster tail," which is a bigger version of the same thing; napoleons, cheese *pastaciotti, paragina,* and so on until you find that you are completely surrounded by cheese filling. There is so much for sale, though, that it doesn't all move out as quickly as say, that one kind of bread at A. Parziale. In other words, some of the aging pastries only *look* good, so you have to remember to ask the clerk what's fresh (albeit, a question that shouldn't have to be asked). Mike's has a couple of tiny tables, usually taken up by high-schoolers.

If you want to sit down in a more old-fashioned Italian cafe for a bit of dessert, go to **Caffe Vittoria**, *296 Hanover St., Tel. 227-7606,* just down the street, or to the cavernous **Caffe dello Sport**, *308 Hanover St., Tel. 523-5063.* The trio of Hanover Street bakeries is so popular that many restaurants in the North End have given up serving dessert at all.

HOTEL SWEETS & SPECIALS

*On Sunday afternoons, **Le Meridien Hotel's Cafe Fleuri** offers a chocolate buffet, from pies to cakes to mousses to fondues and crepes: all-you-can-eat at $15.50 (adults) and $7.75 (children); Tel. 451-1900, ext. 7125. On Friday and Saturday evenings from 9 pm to midnight, the **Four Seasons**, Tel. 338-4400, has a Viennese dessert buffet, with a choice from about 20 platters; two desserts are $8.75; four cost $17.50. Every evening but Monday, the **Ritz-Carlton** hosts a Degustation table, a prix-fixe dinner for fourteen, like a party at which most of the guests did not know each other before sitting down ($85 per person; Tel. 536-5700, ext. 6286).*

11. SEEING THE SIGHTS

"Boston has so much physically unique. Its personality derives from hills and harbors. Its streets are scaled to the six-foot man and three-foot child. People here are still on intimate terms with grass and water. They still find sky. It is a city free of rigid grid. The fact that Boston's past touches us daily is the most modern thing about the city."
– **Ben Thompson**, architect of the Faneuil Hall Marketplace, 1975

THE MUST-SEES

Boston is not only where much of American history occurred, but, more importantly, it is why. A city of aspiration and considerable righteousness: its outrage became America's rebellion, and its patriotism has been the country's backbone since the very beginning.

There are handsome, delightful diversions in the city, but the ones at the top of the list show Boston at its best: reaching up, and up a bit further. The following list of eight "Must Sees" is in an order of priority, starting with the heart of the city, the **Public Garden**. A city with a heart has also had a voice, at **Faneuil Hall**, and some remarkable people have breathed its air since the 1740s. Its influence will never end, yet not all of Boston is so ancient, and the **John F. Kennedy Library** still rings with words that have shaped our own time. The **Museum of Fine Arts** is itself a masterpiece, continuing to prove one of Boston's oldest tenets, that art is for everybody.

Like Stockholm and Hong Kong, and some other cities around the world, water is as important to Boston as land, and the **New England Aquarium** gives an eyeful of a perspective on that. The **USS Constitution**

GOING HALFIES

*The **Boston Citypass** offers half-price admission at six of the most highly recommended sights in Boston, listed in this chapter. It is good for nine days, and is purchased in booklet form, complete with the tickets ready for use (thus saving time waiting in lines). The cost is $27.50, adults; $20.50, senior citizens, $14, children under 18. The tickets are good at: the New England Aquarium; John F. Kennedy Library; Museum of Science; Isabella Stewart Gardner Museum, John Hancock Observatory, and the Museum of Fine Arts.*

is not just a relic of war on the water, circa 1800, it is a registered vessel in the current fleet: many a fight, never a loss. It was built in Boston, and has always called it home.

Isabella Stewart Gardner was a quintessential Bostonian, in her love of arts and letters. She was one of a kind, however, in spending the last half of her life and a massive fortune, building a palazzo and a collection, to declare it her greatest love. The very settlement of Boston was only six years-old when **Harvard University** was founded in 1636. The **Museum of Cultural and Natural History** there is not only an astounding museum of natural history, but of the endeavor to study that farflung subject from a base in the shadow of Boston.

1. PUBLIC GARDEN, *located in the square formed by the following streets: Arlington, Boylston, Charles, and Beacon. T: Arlington.*

Some people who don't know any better shrug impatiently when corrected on the difference between the Common and the Public Garden. "The Ritz-Carlton Hotel and the Four Seasons are kitty-corner from each other on the Common," they will explain in the midst of another point. "The Public Garden –" you interject quickly. Though it's impolite to make trivial corrections, it is every Bostonian's duty to make the important ones. The Common and the Public Garden are right next to each other and they're both parks of a sort. They may be a couple, in

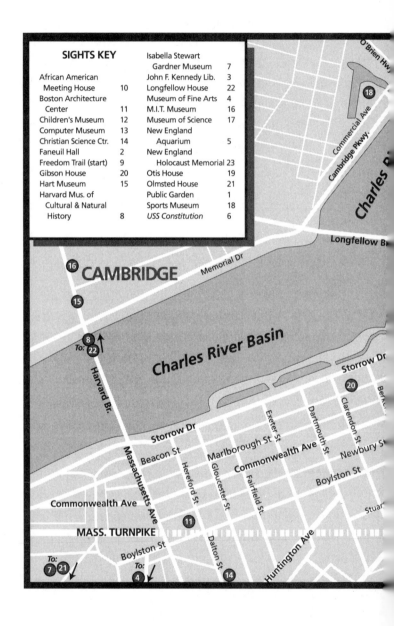

SIGHTS KEY

African American	
Meeting House	10
Boston Architecture	
Center	11
Children's Museum	12
Computer Museum	13
Christian Science Ctr.	14
Faneuil Hall	2
Freedom Trail (start)	9
Gibson House	20
Hart Museum	15
Harvard Mus. of	
Cultural & Natural	
History	8
Isabella Stewart	
Gardner Museum	7
John F. Kennedy Lib.	3
Longfellow House	22
Museum of Fine Arts	4
M.I.T. Museum	16
Museum of Science	17
New England	
Aquarium	5
New England	
Holocaust Memorial	23
Otis House	19
Olmsted House	21
Public Garden	1
Sports Museum	18
USS Constitution	6

O'Brien Hwy

Commercial Ave

Cambridge Pkwy.

Charles R

Longfellow Br

CAMBRIDGE

Memorial Dr

Charles River Basin

Storrow Dr

To: Harvard Br.

Storrow Dr

Massachusetts Ave

Beacon St

Marlborough St

Commonwealth Ave

Hereford St

Gloucester St

Fairfield St

Exeter St

Dartmouth St

Clarendon St

Newbury St

Boylston St

Stuar

Commonwealth Ave

MASS. TURNPIKE

Boylston St

Dalton St

Huntington Ave

To:

To:

a sense. But just as it's cloddish to confuse a husband with a wife, it's important to remember that a public garden is not a common, and vive la difference.

The Public Garden is two hundred years younger than its neighbor. When Ben Franklin was a boy, he fished off the bank at the end of the Common, sitting where Charles Street is today, and plunking his line down where the Public Garden is. In 1794, the city filled in the marsh that Franklin had used as a fishing hole. Many an alderman wanted to build houses on the new land, but in 1839, a self-appointed committee from Beacon Hill insisted that what the city needed was a botanical garden. The committee was led by an amateur horticulturist named Horace Gray, who was known in the city for growing camellia trees in his small, private greenhouse ... before long, Boston had the beginning of its Garden, in the form of a very large, public greenhouse, filled to the brim with thousands of camellia trees. It stood near the corner of Beacon and Charles streets.

Some of the Public Garden was still being used as a dump, however, and so, in the late 1850s, the whole parcel of about 20 acres was formally – very formally – laid out. Formidable trees and complex flower plantings gave texture and color to the land. With the addition of a **Swan Pond** in 1861, the landscape was finished largely the way it remains today, though the flower beds have been simplified over the past generation. The littlest suspension bridge in America spans the pond, into which **swan-boats** were launched in 1877. The distinctive swan-boats are open-air flatboats, each with a large swan molded into the back. They carry about 20 people, and are propelled by the peddlework of a guide who sits at the back. Spied from the bridge, the people onboard nearly all carry the same expression of dumb contentment, out on the water, that calm water, peddled in a swan-boat (and the word "dumb" is used, as it is observed from the bridge, with a smart pang of envy).

Not much will ever be built on the Public Garden that isn't already in place. The last big construction project, painstakingly considered, was the installation of a lifesize statue of a mother duck and her young, in honor of Robert McCloskey's book, *Make Way for Ducklings*. The place does not require further improvement. The Public Garden is a graceful moment in Boston's day, a place of curves, not angles, and quiet, not silence.

2. FANEUIL HALL, *Congress St., Quincy Market. Tel. 635-3105. T: Government Center. Hours: daily, 9 am-5 pm. Free.*

The unspoken capital of Boston is Faneuil Hall – "unspoken" being, of course, the exactly wrong word to use in conjunction with a place where torrents of words have been flying around since 1742. It was built by Peter Faneuil – generally pronounced as "Fannel" today (though his grave-marker at the Granary Burial Grounds spelled the name, perhaps phonetically, "Funel.") Faneuil had inherited one of the city's great fortunes from his uncle, who stipulated that he could keep the money only as long as he didn't get married. Peter didn't. He was a conspicuous bachelor in Boston society, entertaining in his mansion across from King's Chapel, which was another landmark to which he donated generously. Against the tide of conservative sentiment, he wanted to build a big, new marketplace for his city, and he ultimately added the meeting hall on the upper floor, only as a ploy to help sell his plan to civic leaders.

Enlarged once, by Charles Bulfinch, Faneuil Hall has been a truly public building since before the Revolutionary War – anyone could use it for a speech, and the likes of Samuel Adams did so, fashioning the arguments that would lead the whole country to independence. Like a church without a bible, Faneuil Hall has been rebuilt many times over by words alone. Before the Civil War, it sounded out for liberty once again, as a primary meeting-place for the abolition movement.

Faneuil Hall was meticulously restored in 1993. The main floor is an elegant assembly hall, with rows of seating, a stage, and a gallery on three sides. The appointments are worthy of a Virginia mansion, and the National Park Service, which administers the hall and gives informal talks about it, has collected paintings of its history, without turning the hall into a museum. The most impressive aspect of the whole place is that it can still be used for speeches or meetings.

BOSTON'S MR. BULFINCH

Charles Bulfinch was born in 1763 and raised in Boston, the son of a physician. After he graduated from Harvard in 1781, he traveled through Europe on behalf of a Boston trading firm. During a lull in Paris, he looked at architecture in the company of none other than Thomas Jefferson. Upon his return, he gave what he later recalled as "gratuitous advice in architecture." In 1788, however, he took a serious commission, and a church (no longer standing) was built according to his plans. Boston was not a grand looking place at the time, but after Charles Bulfinch entered the profession, his buildings stood as a challenge to which the rest of the city began to rise.

Bulfinch incorporated neoclassical details common to the Federal era, but his work is best recognized by subtler qualities of proportion and restraint. Through activities as a developer, he was nearly always broke, and he was jailed for bankruptcy once. In 1818, he left all of that, and Boston, behind, accepting the invitation of President James Monroe to work in Washington as the capital's official architect. Bulfinch's primary assignment was the Capitol, for which he designed the East Portico. Charles Bulfinch died in 1844.

Bulfinch sights are discussed throughout this chapter: Faneuil Hall; St. Stephen's Church; Old North Church (Bulfinch replaced the steeple in 1804); Nichols House Museum; and the State House. The Otis House, 141 Cambridge Street, was only the first of three homes designed by Bulfinch for that same family; neither of the others is open to the public, but they can be seen at: 85 Mount Vernon Street (1800-02) and 45 Beacon Street (1805-1808). Other selected Bulfinch sites (these are not open to the public, except as noted):

- *72 Broad Street; 1805-07, commercial building*
- *13, 15, and 17 Chestnut Street, Beacon Hill; 1804-5, residences*
- *29A Chestnut Street; residence*
- *Beacon Hill Memorial Column; Mt. Vernon Street behind the State House, 1790-1*
- *Bulfinch Pavilion and Ether Dome; Massachusetts General Hospital, 1818-23. Limited access.*

3. JOHN F. KENNEDY LIBRARY, *Columbia Point, Dorchester. Tel. 929-4523, TTY 929-1221, website, www.cs.umb.edu/jfklibrary//. T: JFK/ UMass Hours: daily, 9 am-5 pm. Cost: adults, $8; senior citizens and students, $6; children, $4. Other Facts: Documentary, RFK Remembered, Saturday-Sunday, 2:30 pm. Children's Programs, certain Saturday mornings at 10:30 am, Tel. 929-4523 for reservations. Boston Harbor Cruises operates a water-shuttle to the Library from Long Wharf, Tel. 227-4321 for information.*

The John F. Kennedy Library sits on the edge of the land, almost a part of the ocean, which was so much a part of the man. You can see Kennedy in a flag whipping in wind off the water, and in the light of an ocean sky. Unfortunately, the building itself, a typical I.M. Pei block of ... block, has nothing to do with the warmth or vitality, or wit, of John Kennedy, though the exhibits inside make up for all that.

During its first twenty years or so, the Kennedy Library was much different than it is now. The Kennedy family is closely associated with the institution and many of the exhibits looked like the emptied contents of drawers, trunks, and extra boxes. The more nosy you are, by nature, the more intriguing it was. In 1995, however, a stronger hand reorganized the museum. After seeing a little movie about John F. Kennedy, visitors walk through rooms recreating the Kennedy presidency, from the nominating convention of the 1960 election, forth. Displays show the campaign from the perspective of the voter, or the average reporter, or the petty politician. There are clever touches, like newspaper machines from around the country, displaying actual papers of the day. With the election, the route through the museum enters a section suggesting the White House, with rooms focusing on the crises and the achievements of the Kennedy years: the Space Program, the Cuban Missile Crisis, the Peace Corps, and so on.

Dozens of videotapes play Kennedy speeches in conjunction with various displays. When I first saw them, I balked: going to museums, on the whole, is supposed to pry people away from TV. As it turns out, though, if you want to remember what was great about John Kennedy, it is quite simple to do. You can watch one of his speeches. You can watch a whole bunch of them – they are not tiresome, whatever the subject – but if you watch just one, you can see the optimism, the strength, and patriotism that gave so many people of both parties a new attitude during those "Camelot Years." There is an extra price of admission to this particular exhibit, however, and it is that you have to walk through the short, perfectly dignified section regarding the killing of Kennedy in 1963.

As to history, the John F. Kennedy Library is utterly unique. The President was so trained with dreams, and so often peering into the future, that you will discover something remarkable when you listen to John Kennedy make a speech. It is you that he is talking about.

4. MUSEUM OF FINE ARTS, *465 Huntington Ave, the Fenway. Tel. 267-9300; TTY/TDD, 267-9703, website, www.mfa.org. T: Museum. Hours: Tuesday and Thursday-Saturday, 10am-4:45pm; Sunday, 10am-5:45pm; Wednesday, 10am-9:45pm. West Wing only: open extended hours on Thursday and Friday, 5pm-9:45pm. Musical instruments collection hours, Tuesday-Friday, 2-4 pm; Saturday-Sunday, 1-4:45 pm. Japanese Garden, spring to early fall, daily, 10 am-4 pm. Cost: adults, $10; senior citizens and students, $8; under 17, free.*

The name is wrong. The Museum in question embraces all of the arts: not merely painting and sculpture, but decorative arts, ancient arts, visual and performing arts, and even architectural arts. The name is correct, however, in that the collections are indeed Fine, in each category. At least, it is, in those categories about which I am qualified to form an opinion. My own experience in going to the MFA is that I love two-thirds of what I see so much that I need a special room, somewhere in the basement, with cots and warm milk for people profoundly depressed because they can neither have nor make any of the extraordinary items in the cases.

Wobbling into other exhibitions, I find that about a sixth of the things on display are interesting enough, without making an impression one way or the other. And past that, about one-sixth infuriate me, and insult the rest the of the collection, and make me wish for another special room at the Museum for people profoundly depressed because they could very easily make the stuff on the walls of certain galleries. It's a perfect proportion, for a roller-coaster or a fine-arts museum.

The Museum is known for its collection of Impressionist paintings, which take over one compact gallery on the second floor. They are major works by artists including Renoir, Degas, Monet, Cassatt and Van Gogh, and the effect is exciting. Either go out to Suffolk Downs for the day, or go to the MFA and just look and look and look into Paul Degas' painting of a racetrack in Paris. A gallery lined with examples of early American silverwork features the work of Paul Revere, and even his father. Boston was a vibrant market for Chinese export porcelain in the 18th and 19th centuries, and hundreds of examples are displayed, near a gallery of French and other European porcelain.

The newer West Wing is largely devoted to modern art, with major new exhibits staged in the Gund Gallery. MFA archaeologists worked on excavations in Egypt and Greece over many years around the turn-of-the-century. Displays of art and other items from an array of ancient civilizations takes up much of the museum. Two important interiors have been installed, in tact: one from a Federal-era mansion near Boston, and one from a 15th century house in England. The Museum building itself is worth looking at, as well, especially since the murals in the rotunda are by John Singer Sargent.

5. NEW ENGLAND AQUARIUM, *Central Wharf, off Atlantic Av., Boston. Tel. 973-5200, website, www.neaq.org. T: Aquarium. Hours: July 1 to Labor Day, Monday, Tuesday, Friday, 9am-6pm; Wednesday and Thursday, 9am-8pm; Saturday-Sunday and holidays, 9am-6pm. Winter, Monday-Friday, 9am-5pm; Thursday, 9am-5pm; Saturday-Sunday and holidays, 9am- 6pm. Cost: Ages 12 and up, $12; ages 3-11, $6; under 3, free; senior citizens, $10. Recorded information, Tel. 973-5200 (voice), TTY/TTD 973-0223. Special programs, each given at least five times daily: Sea Lion Presentation; Giant Ocean Tank Divers; Auditorium shows, and animal interviews. Whale Watch, 5-hour excursion, Tel. 973-5206. Boston harbor tours, about one-and-a-half hours, Tel. 973-5207.*

Penguins may look like headwaiters when they are waddling around on land, but underwater, they look like fat fish. That is the first observation to be made at the New England Aquarium, where the ground floor is designed as a penguin tray. The second observation is that there is no such thing as a fat fish. If one learns anything by looking at the 10,000 fishes there, it is that they are each of them too masterfully well-adapted and beautifully designed to do anything groundless, such as get fat.

And that frivolous example is the on-going experience at the Aquarium: the scattershot observations that one makes are continuously organized by the exhibits themselves into something like knowledge. That is the measure of success for any museum. You should neither spend the whole time reading placards, nor should you leave the place carrying nothing weightier than the stuff you bought at the gift shop.

The New England Aquarium is on the harbor, and it is a door right into it, with outdoor exhibitions and cruises for whale-watching. The building is arranged vertically over three floors, a double-spiral winding around a central "Giant Ocean Tank." On the way up, you look at small tanks along the outer wall, displaying fishes of specific characteristics. Staring is allowed. The tank showing fishes that have developed definite colorations as camouflage is an outright fashion show: razor-thin red lines against a black background; brash orange with a splotch of turquoise; Mayfair stripes of pink and gold. I would order a robe in any one of them.

Fishes that school have a special sensory perception: as a matter of fact, a lot of fishes have senses that are non-existent or undeveloped in humans. It's a fact, and I would call it a sixth sense, except that some of them don't have all of the first five, as humans do. Fish that dart, as though they were one, have organs on the sides of their bodies that gauge water movement so sensitively that they know instantly which way to turn, to stay with the group. Electric eels have an aura of electricity – they can't hear and can barely see, but they can "see" the most minutely charged body moving into that aura. Sharks can sense the bio-electrical heart pulses of a fish, even if it buries itself in the mud. There are other senses than the human five, and other ways of finding out things.

Piranha, those South American fish famous for attacking en masse and decimating a cow or occasional human, only go on such feeding frenzies during one month per year, according to the Aquarium. Yet to see them all hanging absolutely motionless in the water, waiting ... waiting

... waiting, is the most frightening sight at the Aquarium, moreso than sharks or giant octopi. Patience taken to perfection must be the scariest weapon of all. If you don't think so, then you probably won't care to know which month it is, in which piranha get so peckish. (July.)

After walking around seeing how fishes have adapted to the beautiful and terrible world of the waters (beautifully and terribly), the downward spiral leads right past the Giant Ocean Tank, 40 feet across and 23 feet high. Bigger fishes seem to be at the top, leading down to the smaller types at lower depths. Since the fishes are nearly always swimming, in order to breathe the way that they do, a visitor has the museum-luxury of standing still in front of the one of the windows and letting the exhibits move by. Apparently, everybody wonders why the sharks don't eat all the other fishes in the tank. They are never hungry; the staff makes sure of that.

The New England Aquarium's whale watch excursions, offered from April to October, last about five hours. Shorter harbor cruises are open to the general public during July and August.

6. USS CONSTITUTION, *Charlestown Navy Yard. Tel. 426-1812. T: North Station, with one-half-mile walk. Water Shuttle direct to Navy Yard from Long Wharf, near Aquarium, Tel. 227-4320 for schedule. Hours: Spring to Fall, open daily 10am-5pm, summer, 9am-6pm; Winter, Monday to Friday, 10am-4pm, Saturday and Sunday, 9am-5pm. Cost: free.*

USS CONSTITUTION MUSEUM, *same as above. Website, www.ussconstitutionmuseum.org. Cost: ages 16 up, $4; ages 6-16, $3; senior citizens, $3; active military, children under 6, free.*

USS CASSIN YOUNG, *same as above. Cost: free.*

America had no navy when the *Constitution* was commissioned in 1794, but as a fighting ship, it saw forty battles without ever giving way to a single boarder, let alone a defeat. That the nation is grateful has been proven since, both in the response by private citizens to appeals for money with which to maintain "Old Ironsides," as it is known, and in the fact that the officials of the U.S. Navy have yet to de-commission the ship. It is now the oldest warship in any fleet around the world.

The *USS Constitution* is moored in the Charleston Navy Yard, once a great center for building and servicing ships. It was born and built across the Charles River in Boston, and was the tallest structure there at the time. Now it stands out starkly against the skyline of Boston's new buildings and skyscrapers. The *Constitution* is a graceful giant, painted black and white, with three masts and a complement of nets and rigging. It is 200 feet long, and displaces about 2,200 tons, but under full sail, it could move. With the equivalent of about 600 horsepower, it had a topspeed of 13 knots, or about 15 mph, which is good time at sea. Once or twice a year, usually on and around the Fourth of July, it goes out into open water, to fulfill its description as an active Navy ship.

In Old Ironsides' days of fighting the Barbary Pirates off the shores of Tripoli (in the Tripolitan Wars of 1801-1805), 450 men sailed onboard. Now the ship is manned by a dozen sailors and two officers, often dressed in US Navy uniforms of 1812. The greatest fights the ship had were during the War of 1812, in which it won exciting battles against British ships off Brazil, Canada, and Spain. The goal, as the young sailors explain today, was not to sink the enemy ship, but to render it helpless, forcing it to surrender. The weaponry with which to do so is still at hand on the gun deck – including Starshot, a type of cannonfire that slashed into rigging like a spinning star, and canisters filled with broken bone and glass. Since sailors didn't wear shoes, a spray of sharp objects on the deck would stop each man in his tracks. Some of the 55 cannons have names, carved into signs just above each one. Read straight across in a line, they sound like the voice of the men of 1812, explaining why they were fighting: "Raging Eagle," "Liberty Forever," "Yankee Protection."

Ninety percent of the ship has been replaced through several major restorations over the years. What remains, other than a design from a distant era, is the feeling of strength, and true invincibility, which is what makes the ship mean more than its age, or its size. "Old Ironsides" helped set a whole Navy on course.

Another Navy veteran is docked across a parking lot from the *Constitution*. It is the World War Two destroyer *USS Cassin Young*: grey, where the *Constitution* is crisply black-and-white, metal where the earlier ship is wood, and guns form its silhouette, not sails. Perhaps for these reasons, it seemed even more like a machine of war, into which men were fit, yet neither ship was built for anything but hard action.

Launched in 1943, the *Cassin Young* joined the Pacific fleet the following year, and moved north in the island-hopping that closed the Pacific Theater. Only one type of attack was at all successful against the ship: kamikazes. Near Okinawa in the last month of the war, a suicide pilot crashed his plane (more of a one-seat missile, really) into the middle of the *Cassin Young*. Twenty-two American sailors were killed, but the ship recovered for duty within twenty minutes.

Decommissioned in 1960, the *Cassin Young* has been a museum ship since 1985. One million people visit the *Constitution* each year, and about one-third that number also board the *Cassin Young*.

One of the old brick buildings at the Navy Yard houses a natty museum devoted to the *Constitution* and its adventures in battle and on world cruises over the course of about a hundred years, or most of the 19th century. There are also some hands-on exhibits; in one, you are supposed to press buttons, representing the basic actions and the sequence necessary to fire a cannon like those on the ship. If they added a lurching, jerking motion underfoot; thick smoke and steam; made the buttons red-hot, with painfully loud noises, the exhibit might be even more accurate, but even as it is, it's harder than you think. The Museum schedules many demonstrations and talks, both indoors and out. Serious nautical issues are covered, as well as topics of interest to children, making a three-cornered hat, for example.

Until recently, the quiet embarrassment of the *Constitution* was that it hadn't moved under its own power since 1881. It was towed everywhere it went. In time for its 200th birthday in 1997, the ship emerged from a successful effort to make it seaworthy again. It can sail under its own power and usually does so on the Fourth of July.

7. ISABELLA STEWART GARDNER MUSEUM, *280 The Fenway. Tel. 566-1401, website, www.boston.com/gardner. T: Museum. Hours: Tuesday-Sunday, 11am-5pm. Cost: adults, $10 ($11 on weekends), senior citizens, $7; college students $5; under 12, free.*

They say that Isabella Stewart Gardner's house was turned into a museum. The fact is that Isabella Stewart Gardner didn't have a house. She built a museum from scratch and so happened to live in it, but the place was never a house in the sense of leaving a newspaper and an apple core by the sofa, or playing cards by a sunny window. Mrs. Gardner built a museum.

Isabella Stewart Gardner was born to a rich family in 1840 and married a very rich man twenty years later. She was spoiled by all concerned. More generally, she was not very well liked in Boston, though she could certainly make friends where she wanted to. Within weeks of being widowed in 1898, Mrs. Gardner already knew what she wanted next and she purchased land near the Boston city limits for a brand new 15th century Venetian villa. With workmen sworn to secrecy, no one in Boston could tell what Mrs. Gardner's new place was going to be like inside, rising four stories in plain blond brick on the outside.

Meanwhile, Mrs. Gardner herself was in Europe, making purchases of art and antiques under the guidance of experts like Bernard Berenson (whom she had befriended when he was a student at Harvard). On February 23, 1903, the house, called **Fenway Court**, was opened to guests for the first time. It is largely the same today as it was that day. To walk through the Isabella Stewart Gardner Museum is to go to Europe, to visit a favorite marchioness.

The house is built around an immaculate garden court, covered four stories up at the top by a greenhouse roof. Glimpses of the garden are a part of every floor, not by way of glass, but through open-air windows facing the court. It's always a nice day in the garden.

Certain rooms in the house reflect a specific flowering, but overall, the Gardner collection is eclectic, with paintings by masters of all eras, including works by Rembrandt, Titian, and Sargent. No one piece or artist dominates. What is best about the Gardner Museum is the chance to see works of art in the settings in which they belong. It is a shame to see a fine, old painting in the harsh white light of the typical museum gallery, surrounded by nothing but other works demanding the exact same attention.

At the Gardner, the light is gentle, and sometimes downright dim, but the paintings bask in it. And the works are surrounded by furniture and antique furnishings that allow powerful artwork some friendly breathing room. Rembrandt's *Self-Portrait* looks down on the dining room. Even more than the art (several important canvases were stolen in 1988, a crime which is still unsolved), I like the fabrics: Italian and Flemish lace, so fine that it would embarrass a spider, or cut-velvets and brocades from the Renaissance. Some pieces are just remnants, but they are the sort of textile that doesn't often last in any form. And they contribute, along with everything else, to the richness of the rooms.

Many people have suggested that Fenway Court was planned and built to give its only occupant a measure of immortality. It does speaks for her. And she for it, when she wrote to a friend two years before her death in 1924: "I have music, and both young and old friends." As in Mrs. Gardner's day, the courtly Tapestry Room is the setting for music recitals; they take place at 1:30 p.m. on Saturdays and Sundays from September to April. For concert information, call 278-5102; reservations are advised. In fair weather, the museum's regular cafe serves outdoors, not in the vaunted Garden Court, but in a delightful outer garden.

8. HARVARD MUSEUM OF CULTURAL AND NATURAL HISTORY, *26 Oxford St., Cambridge; 495-3045. T: Harvard. Hours: Monday-Saturday, 9 am-5 pm; Sunday, 1-5 pm. Cost: Adults, $5; senior citizens and students, $4; ages 3-12, $3. Free every Saturday 9 am-Noon.*

Many museums obviously hold that "interactive" equals learning, and you can't have one without the other. It seems a bit insecure – which is one thing that the Harvard University Museum assuredly is not. By design, the only thing interactive in the whole, old-fashioned place is that you look at an exhibit, and suddenly hear yourself say, "I can't believe it." That happens automatically, pretty much.

Boston's finest display of dinosaur bones is at the Harvard Museum, and it includes a full-sized kronosaurus, along with the head of a triceratops. Another display is of a fish known to have gone extinct ninety million years ago, until someone caught one off of the coast of Africa. A few more were caught in the same area, and Harvard managed to gain possession of one, a shapeless green little guy that proves to us all: you're not extinct until you say you are. Another exhibit is an ant farm, and there are enough stuffed birds to make Audubon dizzy, though they are displayed with a certain serenity. In the geology rooms, a diamond as big as the Ritz – or at least, an aquamarine as big as the Copley Plaza – and thousands of other gems, rocks, and minerals, line the cases. They show not merely how the earth may have developed, but how the science of geology did, as the collection began early in the 19th century and is still in flux today.

For those who like science, as well as those who do not, however, the star of the museum is the **Ware Collection of Brushka Glass Flowers**. Have you ever been told that only God can make a tree? Well, the news from Harvard is that so could Leopold Blaschka. So could his son, Rudolph. They could make any kind of plant or flower, accurate down to the last speck of pollen, the last swaying stamen. The story of the collection is that of a father and son, and of a mother and daughter. It also spans the worlds of art and botany. Leopold and Rudolph were from Bohemia (now a part of the Czech Republic), where they taught themselves to make exact recreations of plants out of glass. A professor at Harvard heard about them near the end of the 19th century, and asked Elizabeth and Mary Lee Ware, mother and daughter, to fully sponsor their output, on behalf of the school. The result is the collection now on display: 3,000 plants, unwilting and unbelievable.

BOSTON BY BOAT

The MBTA operates a summertime shuttle-boat called **Boston By Boat** *on a loop to the following sights, at or near the harborside: The New England Aquarium; The USS Constitution Ship and Museum; the North End/Old North Church; and the Children's and Computer museums. A single leg costs $3, while all-day, on-and-off passes are $5 for adults and $4 for children. If you want to arrange tickets before you leave home, call 800/ 235-6426.*

THE FREEDOM TRAIL

Any map of Boston is veritably dotted with historical landmarks, a fact that must have given the city the idea of connecting at least some of those dots, sixteen of them, as the **Freedom Trail**. For anyone from the most expert map-reader on down, the Freedom Trail makes exploring the sites only as demanding as following a broad red line painted right onto the sidewalk. About three miles long altogether, the Trail can be shortened into clusters of buildings and monuments just a few hundred yards apart from each other. That is how it is organized below, though some of the sites are described even more fully elsewhere in this book.

The city notes that the whole Trail can be covered in three hours, though it can easily fill a full day, depending on the length of the stops. None of the stops charge admission, except where noted below.

The Freedom Trail: Boston Proper

The **Boston Common** (See Chapter 12, *Walking Tours*) is the first designated site, and the Freedom Trail officially starts at the Information kiosk on Tremont Street, at West Street near the Park Street T-stop. The Information kiosk offers 150 free brochures, including *The Boston Freedom Trail* brochure; even with the red line running down the sidewalk, it isn't a bad idea to have a map in hand.

Overlooking the Common from Beacon Hill, the **State House** is in use today as the seat of Massachusetts government, just as it has been since it was built in 1798. The architect was **Charles Bulfinch**, who designed most of Boston's important buildings in the first part of the 19th century and gave Boston a tradition in architecture of warm and effortless grace. The dome was copper in the early days – and it was Paul Revere & Sons that received the job to lay the copper. The gold of the current dome belongs to another era: the Gilded Era, in fact, since it was installed in 1872. At least a glint of the State House dome can be seen from all over the city.

Two expansions, started in 1889 and 1917, respectively, did little to interfere with the exterior of Bulfinch's original building. The interior decorations date from all different eras over the past 200 years. Vivid murals on the third floor depict Massachusetts regiments in various conflicts, including the Civil War (when Baltimore civilians attacked one such regiment marching south, in a very early case of bloodshed in the war). Mosaic floors, stained glass windows, and intricate ironwork make the State House much more than an office building, but something less than a museum. A display of original regimental battle flags was replaced a few years ago with a set of garish transparency pictures of the same items. Remarkable, how unstirring transparency pictures can be. A couple of other overly modern changes also intrude, as in the case of the Great Hall, a harsh space carved out of the soft open court formerly in the back of the building.

Out on the lawn, statues of some brilliant Massachusetts orators remind you, however, that a State House is not a question of decoration, but of voices rising. Daniel Webster, John Kennedy, and Horace Mann are among them, as are Anne Hutchinson and Mary Dyer.

Mary Dyer was burned as a witch in 1660, because she would not change her religious views. Her body was buried without much ceremony in the **Granary Burying Grounds**, the next stop on the Freedom Trail. Her grave wasn't even marked, but starting in 1667, others were, with inscriptions delicately carved in slate that has weathered the years since. The dark gray headstones, shaded by tall trees, constitute a somber place in the city, almost like a room, braced on three sides by tall buildings. One of the reasons that the Burial Ground has remained unmolested is that so many famous people were among the 1,600 Bostonians buried there. Three signers of the Declaration of Independence are interred there: John Hancock, Robert Paine, and Samuel Adams. Paul Revere was, too.

The Granary Burying Ground was named for the Town Granary building, which stood where the massive **Park Street Church** is today. The church is part of the Freedom Trail, having been built in 1809, after the Revolution but in time for the War of 1812, when it was a hotbed. Or at least a cool dry one, for gunpowder was stashed in the church basement during the war. Nineteen years later, the Rev. Samuel F. Smith needed a patriotic song for a special program at the church, so he lifted a tune from a German music book, and wrote the anthem *America* ("My country 'tis of thee, sweet land of liberty ...") in about a half-hour. It was sung for the first time on July 4th, 1831, at the Park Street Church. He was only trying to plug a hole in the program. How was Rev. Smith supposed to know that the little tune would become immortal? Doubly immortal, unfortunately – how was he supposed to know that it was also *God Save Our Gracious Queen,* the British national anthem?

King's Chapel is not much to see from the outside – the builders ran out of money before they could add finishing touches, such as a spire. But on the inside, it is magnificent, rich with gifts sent from Britain's royal family and serene with the aura of a city of peace and great prosperity. King's Chapel was built in 1754, but it incorporates many details from its predecessor, a building dating from 1668. Both filled the same role, leading the Church of England in colonial America. King's Chapel looked like an English building, standing grey in granite amid Boston's wooden or brick buildings, and it sounded like one, too, with music from an imported organ, surrounded by the solemnity of Puritan meeting houses that regarded music as a sin.

The Chapel still has that organ, and still has the bell that Paul Revere's foundry cast in 1816. The only thing that it doesn't have anymore is the fine silver that various monarchs sent over, to be used in services. The vicar at the time of the Revolution took it all to Canada for safe-keeping – and neither he nor it was ever seen again. A Church of England chapel was not required in Boston after the Revolution, and the King's Chapel was turned over to the Unitarian Church, a sect deeply rooted in the New World. Unitarian services are conducted on Sundays at 11 a.m. and Wednesdays at 12:15. Organ recitals are held on Tuesdays at 12:15 pm, with a $2 charge.

A few of the next sites on the Freedom Trail are more like pauses than stops. In front of the **Old City Hall**, now an office building, a statue commemorates Benjamin Franklin, as well as the fact that his alma mater once stood on the same spot. It was **Boston Latin School**, or the "Free Writing School," as it was also called. Founded in 1635, it is still going strong, but in another location. The **Old Corner Bookstore**, built in 1718, was a hundred years old before it came into its own, as the home of Ticknor & Fields, the publishing company that nurtured a great flowering in New England literature, bringing out books by Nathaniel Hawthorne, Ralph Waldo Emerson, Henry David Longfellow and Henry Thoreau. Nothing is left inside to evoke those days, but the building is still earning its keep, housing a bookstore.

Each of these first stops on the Freedom Trail is surrounded by the city at its busiest. In the midst of it all, the old sites and buildings begin to take hold, in relation to each other. You can see that Boston was a small city, close and convenient, one that held far more than its share of vibrant minds.

The **Old South Church** is a museum today, an austere building in counterpoint to King's Chapel. During the Revolutionary War, when the British occupied Boston, the church was ignominiously transformed into an indoor riding ring. British officers burned anything they could rip out and then brought in dirt to ride on, and refreshments too, along with the horses. As a museum, the Old South Church has wisely focused itself on an earlier, more gallant day, when patriots meeting at the Church riled themselves into action over Britain's latest tea tax, and ended up staging the **Boston Tea Party**. The interior of the Old South Church, renovated in 1997, is a beautiful Colonial room, white and airy, with dainty arched windows and a full mezzanine, supported by pillars and a balcony above that. It is still used for meetings and for one church service per year, at

Thanksgiving, under the auspices of the same congregation that used it after the Revolution.

Don't mix up the State House and the **Old State House** (though everybody else does). Like the King's Chapel, the Old State House was an all-too prominent symbol of British presence in colonial Boston. When it was built in 1718, it was known as the "Town House." The governor and his officers operated upstairs, while a market filled the lower floor.

One cold day in 1770, a mob just outside grew unruly, and a detachment of British grenadiers emerged from the Town House to quell it. Mostly, they just stood around with their guns on their shoulders, while the colonists taunted them, shouting, among other things, "Fire! Go on and fire!" In the growing confusion, some of the soldiers mistook the command for a real one, and they killed five civilians. Known even at the time as the **Boston Massacre**, it made the Town House a symbol of British disregard for colonists, though it may well be that the martyrs were nothing more than thugs who landed on the right side of a Revolution.

After the Revolutionary War, the Town House was used by John Hancock, the first governor of the Commonwealth of Massachusetts, and the name was immediately changed to the State House. After Bulfinch's hilltop State House (see above) opened, the Old State House took on its prefix. A long, narrow building, set like a peninsula in the flow of Washington Street, it is now a privately operated museum of Boston history. Next to it, at 15 State Street, the National Park Service has a full-service visitor center, with a bookstore, as well as free information on the Freedom Trail and other sites in greater Boston. The next stop on the Freedom Trail is the centerpiece of it, Faneuil Hall (see *Must-Sees* above).

The Freedom Trail: The North End

Some stops on the Freedom Trail recall the great heroes of the fight for independence. At the **Revere House**, it is a minor figure who is remembered: a hero only inasmuch as he represents the others who looked for ways to help, and found them. Revere House is one of the oldest houses left in Boston, and it is doubtful that it would have been saved if not for an unlikely surge of interest in its late tenant.

FREEDOM TRAIL TOURS & EVENTS

*The National Park Service conducts free walking tours of part of the Freedom Trail, starting at the **Boston National Historical Park Visitor Center** (the corner of Devonshire and State streets, Tel. 242-5642). The tours last an hour-and-a-half, and leave every day between the hours of 10 am and 3 pm.*

*For a daily roster of special happenings, call the **Freedom Trail Events Hotline**, Tel. 242-5695.*

The house was 90 years old when Paul Revere bought it in 1770. It was old-fashioned even then, with an overhanging front, reminiscent of the English style of the 17th century. Revere, a silversmith, hustled to make money in related businesses, and needed the sturdy house for his large family. Despite his activities before the Revolutionary War, he would be remembered today only as a silversmith, inasmuch as silversmiths are remembered, if **Henry Wadsworth Longfellow** had not heard the local legend of Paul Revere and written it as a rousing poem in 1861, one that began, "Listen children and you shall hear, Of the midnight ride of Paul Revere." And it is an injustice, considering that another patriot made approximately the same ride (his name was William Dawes). Revere represents him, and all the other comfortable people who risked every-thing for American independence. It was a unique Revolution in that respect, and Paul Revere – and his house – are reminders of it.

The house was at the end of its days, in use as a tenement, when a private group saved it in 1905. They restored it, and it has been renovated periodically ever since, to the point that only ten percent of the original materials are left. Most of those are in the underlying structure, though.

One of over 100 bells that Revere cast at his foundry is encased in a display in the yard. One like it, only bigger, is still ringing out at King's Chapel. Revere's copper-rolling mill covered the State House dome. Revere's own silver work is on display at the Museum of Fine Arts. Forget the fact that Revere was a hero of the nation's first war: he remains in the city of Boston through his own hands, and without need of poetry.

St. Stephen's Church is next on the Freedom Trail: rather chunky for a Bulfinch building. A marker in front notes its lasting claim to fame: Rose Kennedy, the mother of President John F. Kennedy, was baptized there in 1890, and a Mass of Resurrection was said for her at the same place in 1995.

The **Old North Church** is a bona fide tourist attraction, by virtue of its own role in the Revolutionary effort, but it wears that mantle without the callouses expected of a place so famous for so long. Visitors are warmly welcomed at services (highly recommended), at which time they are assigned a box-pew, and enjoy, at the very least, a lovely choir. Even at other times, visitors are handled with a greeting that seems fresh, and makes the Old North Church seem like a country parish.

It isn't. Its official name is "Christ Church," and it is not only the oldest church building in Boston, having been raised in 1723, but by far the one with the longest continuous affiliation with one denomination (Episcopal). According to Longfellow, which is to say according to local tradition, the colonists used the steeple to warn distant camps of the approach of British troops, "One, if by land, and two, if by sea." On April 18, 1775, two lanterns swung in the window of the steeple.

On the highest point in the North End is another burial ground, **Copp's Hill**. The views from the hill are spectacular, of the Charleston Navy Yard, across the Inner Harbor and the boat traffic in and out. The most famous of those people buried on Copp's Hill, "secure from sorrow or alarms," in the words of one epitaph, are the ministers, Cotton Mather and his father, Increase Mather (whose house was on the site of Revere's house, a long time before).

The Freedom Trail: Charlestown

The last two stops on the Freedom Trail, the *USS Constitution* and the Bunker Hill Monument, are both in Charlestown, across the Charles River (which becomes the Inner Harbor at the Charlestown Bridge). Charlestown is the kindliest walking neighborhood in Boston, though it will not look like it at first, on the highway-strewn walk from the Charlestown Bridge to the Navy Yard and the *Constitution* (for a description of which, see *Must-Sees* above).

The **Bunker Hill Pavilion**, a small multi-media museum regarding the battle, is next to the Navy Yard. I suspect that many people visit it and skip the extra twenty-minute walk to the **Monument**. There are reasons not to give in to that temptation. First, you should always take any excuse to take a stroll through Charlestown, so that you can wonder with the rest of us: how come some people get to live like this? Charming old well-kept houses, with the occasional crooked street and tiny bakery: that's what Charlestown looks like. Second, the Monument is on the battlefield, and there are sounds left in all battlefields, if you can listen the right way. And third, the Bunker Hill Monument is a marvel, all by itself.

It's interesting to ponder, when American history, as history, started. The fact of the matter is that America didn't yet have any other monuments when the Bunker Hill Monument Association came into being in 1823. The Association was plying new waters when it purchased the Battle of Bunker Hill fields and commissioned drawings for a 221-foot obelisk. As with many ventures that ply new waters, the Association went bankrupt numerous times along the way, after the cornerstone was laid in 1825 (by no less than the Marquis de Lafayette). The granite for the Monument had to be transported from a great distance. A genius named Gridley Bryant finally solved the problem, laying out the world's first railway to move the blocks. Mind, it was just a railway – Bryant didn't invent the locomotive to go with it. But on rails fitted with special cars, tons of stone could be moved by a three-year-old (horse).

The Bunker Hill Monument opened in 1843. The "Lodge" next door has a diorama to show how the untested Americans repelled their crack British foes two times on June 17, 1775, before finally capitulating. That initial resistance changed strategies throughout the balance of the Revolutionary War. The footnote to the whole Monument is that the **Battle of Bunker Hill** was actually fought on **Breed's Hill**: the British general was the first to mix them up, and so they have remained ever since. The climb to the top of the Monument is almost 300 steps.

The Freedom Trail ends with the Bunker Hill Monument. One pleasant way to return to downtown Boston is by the water-shuttle, *Tel. 227-4320*, from the Navy Yard to the Long Wharf near the Aquarium. If you have walked the entire Freedom Trail, you can proceed to Durgin-Park and have "double-mash," as they call two bowls of mashed potatoes. Actually, if you have walked the entire Freedom Trail, you can have anything you want.

THE FREEDOM TRAIL:
INFORMATION FOR MAJOR STOPS

· *The State House. Tours, Monday-Friday, 10 am-4 pm. Free.*
· *King's Chapel. Hours: daily in summer, 10am-4 pm; Monday, Friday and Saturday in winter, 10am-4 pm; donations accepted.*
· *Old South Meeting House. Hours: April 1, October 31, daily, 9:30 am-5 pm; November 1-March 31, Monday-Friday, 10 am-4 pm; weekends, 10 am-5 pm. Special events line, Tel. 482-6439, modest admission.*
· *Paul Revere House. Hours, daily: 9:30 am-4:15 pm; closed Mondays, January-March. Modest admission.*
· *Bunker Hill Monument. Hours: daily, 9 am-5 pm. Free.*

OTHER SIGHTS

THE BLACK HERITAGE TRAIL, *starts at the Boston African National Historic Site, 46 Joy St., Beacon Hill. Tel. 742-5415. Hours: daily, 10 am-4 pm Free.*

The Freedom Trail gives a strong impression of 18th century life and the mood in Boston at the time. The Black Heritage Trail gives a glimpse into a time and mood just as important, as it turned out: the 19th century and the community that inspired and helped instigate the nation's most fervent abolitionist, or anti-slavery, movement.

The section of Beacon Hill known as the **North Slope**, near Cambridge Street, was the center of Boston's African-American community a century ago. The residents were free citizens; no slaves had lived in Boston since before 1790. Many worked effectively with both white abolitionists and with the Underground Railroad that gave hope to runaways from the South. The activists of the North Slope area were remarkable people at a crucial time, because the abolitionist movement that emanated out of Boston was a factor leading to the Civil War.

The Black Heritage Trail is a collection of fourteen sites on a route of about twenty blocks on Beacon Hill, through the city's most picturesque streets. You can only go into two of the sites; the rest are private homes. Even so, you can see the community and the way people lived there, and you can hear or read stories about ordinary-extraordinary people, the types upon whom history turns.

The **Abiel Smith School**, the first public school in Boston for black children, is now the **Boston African-American National Historic Site**. Due to be restored in the coming years, it is now taken up largely by administrative offices, but it is the starting point for guided tours of the Black Heritage Trail. If you would rather explore by yourself, the Park Service offers a comprehensive brochure, with a map.

Next door to the Abiel Smith School is the **African Meeting House**, built in 1806 as the home of the **First African Baptist Church**. It is a brick building, with tall, arched windows, and a sober intent about it. The ground floor is now a gallery.

BOSTON ARCHITECTURAL CENTER, *320 Newbury Street. Tel. 536-3170. T: Hynes. Monday-Thursday, 9 am-9 pm; Friday-Saturday, 9 am-5pm; Sunday, Noon-5 pm. Free.*

The lobby of the Boston Architectural Center, just off the street at the corner of Newbury and Hereford, stages exhibits pertaining to buildings, interiors, or landscapes. Often consisting of actual sketches or mock-ups used in the planning stages of projects, the displays are always a glimpse into the mind of the architect, the way the world looks when it is just a gleam in somebody's eye.

THE CHILDREN'S MUSEUM, *300 Congress Street, Tel. 426-8855, website, www. tcmboston.org. T: South Station. September to June, open Tuesday-Sunday, 10am-5pm, Friday, 10 am-9 pm; July and August, daily, 10 am-5 pm, Friday, 10 am- 9 pm. Cost: adults, $7; seniors and children 2-16, $6; one-year-olds, $2, babies up to one year, free.*

The Children's Museum is expensive. The tally for a family of four is about $25, depending on the exact ages. Granted, a children's museum can't very well give a reduced rate to kids, as other museums do. (But it could give one to grown-ups.)

Children aged three to six are the most likely to enjoy the Children's Museum. The exhibits are lightly structured and very colorful, spread over four floors in a former warehouse. Most are consistent with the observation we have all made of kids that age: that their favorite toy of all is likely to be the cardboard box that a new toy came in. And so many of the most popular exhibits involve climbing on simple things, like a giant plastic tire, or through things, like a plastic tunnel. At other popular displays, kids can work a handpump, or make big soap bubbles. You can weave with big strips of cloth, as part of an exhibit on Native American crafts, or go on TV, in a closed-circuit television set. The most extensive exhibit, on daily life in Tokyo (underwritten by several Japanese corporations), has never been crowded when I've been at the Museum: nothing to climb on.

Throughout the day, staff members bring out little animals to show the young patrons, and short plays are presented in a special theater. One ill-advised exhibit is called the Recycle Shop: it is supposed to sell a variety of items made through recycling programs. But many of the bins are filled with flea-market goods, such as photo-albums, vinyl camera-cases, or surplus game pieces. One would think that there are sound reasons to confine the merchandising at a museum to the gift-shop.

THE COMPUTER MUSEUM, *300 Congress Street. Tel. 423-6758, website, www.tcm.org. T: South Station. June to Labor Day, open daily 10 am-6 pm; September to May: 10am-5pm, closed Mondays. Cost: adults, $7, children 5 and up, senior citizens, $5; children 4 and under, free.*

The Computer Museum is generously sponsored by a long list of high-tech companies. Perhaps too generously, because the result seems, at its best, like a Pavilion at a World's Fair. At times, it bears down even harder than that. Taking up two floors in the same building as the Children's Museum (with a separate entrance), the Computer Museum is one of the few institutions in the world devoted to the short history and long future of the smartest of machines.

Two displays cover the development of the computer, and the basic way that it works, but most exhibits consist of working computers, to be used by visitors. One of the first is a lab, where you take a card printed with a "UPC" code. Logging in with it at the first station, you type in four lines of information about yourself. After that, a proviso comes onto the screen to the effect that if you choose the option to keep this very basic information (name, age, and zip code) private, you will not be allowed to see the overall records on other visitors. It seems gratuitous to punish people, a bit, for being inclined to protect their privacy. It's a mystery why the museum feels it has to put its patrons in that position, and I don't think it's a minor point.

However, putting thoughts of old Salem aside, you go to the next station, and swipe your coded card at another computer, expecting to do something really cool – only to sit through a soft-sell video on how constant telephone accessibility is essential to modern life. The next station pertains to e-mail: how you can write to your Congressman as often as need be, with e-mail. Another station, another video. Those in the know skip them.

Down the line, there are computers that do engage visitors, first-hand. At different stations, you can create a greeting card; let a computer with a voice read text that you type in; make up a cartoon; make up a song; or look at a three-dimensional screen. You can go on-line. These computers and others that play games or solve specific types of problems are the first to become crowded. Standing around just looking at the screens, flashing, you are likely to overhear parents killing time with their children, and amazing them with stories of how slow computers were, way back when, when they were all so young.

In the Spring of 1999, the Museum of Science absorbed the Computer Museum, with plans to relocate and enhance it. Those interested are advised to call first, as the Computer Museum is now reflecting the computer age even better than ever: it's on the move and waits for no one.

FREE FOR ALL

Special times, when admission fees are waived:

· **Museum of Fine Arts** – *Wednesdays, 4 pm-9:45 pm, pay what you wish*

· **Suffolk Downs** – *no charge after the seventh race (a typical card is ten or eleven races)*

· **Harvard University Art Museums** – *no charge. Saturday mornings 10 am -Noon*

· **USS Constitution Museum** – *on weekends, kids under 16 admitted free*

· **The New England Conservatory of Music** – *classical music concerts, Monday evenings*

THE FIRST CHURCH OF CHRIST, SCIENTIST, *250 Massachusetts Ave., near Huntington Ave. Tel. 450-3790. T: Symphony. Hours: Cost: free.*

Mary Baker Eddy founded the Christian Science in Boston over the course of many years at the turn-of-the-century, and the world headquarters are still located within the city limits. The Mother Church is a Byzantine building in the manner of a small cathedral, surrounded by a modern campus of buildings as well as an attractive reflecting pond.

Several types of tours are available. The Church makes non-adherents welcome at the fantastic and non-religious **Mapparium** (see *Only in Boston* below), and at an exhibit on the history of the Bible, which includes a short film.

HART NAUTICAL COLLECTIONS, *MIT Campus, 55 Massachusetts Ave., Cambridge. Tel. 253-5942. T: Kendall. Hours: daily, 9 am to 8 pm. Free.*

If I had a nickel for every model ship in Boston ... I'd buy the Red Sox, just for starters. The lobbies of the Boston Harbor Hotel and the Bostonian Hotel each have small fleets of them, worth stopping in to see. Most of the models on display these days are of sailing ships: picturesque clippers, mostly. The Hart Nautical Collection has some of those in its three dignified gallery-rooms on Mass. Ave. near the river. There are also displays of hard-working steamships, and even diesel-powered ones.

What's more, it has models of ships the likes of which no salt around today ever saw – the *Turtle*, for example. It was designed and commissioned by a Korean admiral in 1591 and could be completely covered during battles with an enclosed deck, heavily spiked to maim boarders. Somewhere underneath, sailors would row and fire cannons. And just in case all else was not intimidating enough, the carving at the front was supposed to make the ship look like a giant turtle – a giant turtle in a bad mood.

The Hart Collection certainly goes beyond mere clippers. Since MIT was long the leading center in the country for the study of ship architecture, revolving exhibits often honor the contributions of graduates, such as those who responded to the immediate need for new types of ships during World War Two.

MIT MUSEUM, *265 Massachusetts Ave., Cambridge. Tel. 253-4444. T: Kendall. Hours: Tuesday-Friday, 9am-5 pm, Saturday-Sunday, Noon-5pm. Cost: adults: $3; $1 for students, senior citizens, and children 12 and under.*

Across Massachusetts Avenue from the New England Candy Co. (Necco, as in wafers), and upstairs in an old warehouse, the Massachusetts Institute of Technology displays work that straddles the border between science and art.

The major permanent exhibit is called **Holography: Artists and Inventions**. Greeting-card stores may sell holographs of seagulls, and the waiting room at the doctor's office might have a table-top holograph of a geometric blur, but the holographs at the MIT museum are in some other category. They are very scary, without trying to be. A holograph is a technique for making an image using laser light. The portraits of people made through the process are as truly three-dimensional as real life is – moreso than sculpture, because the subject of a holograph can move as you move. You peer all the way into it, as though it were a room. Or a bottle: "They look like pickled people," is what my mother once said of them, though the subjects are all smiling and hale, suspended not in liquid but in light. It's art and it's science, and it's sorcery.

Another permanent exhibit at the MIT Museum pays tribute to the college's long, proud history of "hacking," or playing pranks on campus. That faux police car is there, the one that was placed on top of the dome on campus, complete with trooper and doughnuts. So is a complete explanation of the "smoot," that unit of measure unique to the Harvard Bridge, a span which is precisely 364.4 smoots long, plus one ear. In the words of Mr. Oliver Smoot, Class of '62: "In October, 1958, (classmate) O'Connor devised the idea of marking the bridge in Lamda Chi Alpha pledge-lengths. Scanning the assembled class, he determined I had the short end of the stick." Mr. Smoot did a lot of laying down for the measurements, which were painted plainly on the pavement. Go and see for yourself. To this day, Boston Police use smoots when describing the exact location of accidents on the Harvard Bridge.

My own favorite MIT hack, however, was an addition made to the opening of a modern-art show on campus. Slipped in among the sculptures, it was a cafeteria tray with a plate, a glass, and a few utensils. A placard explained the piece, called "No Fork," in a perfect lather of artsy jargon. No art critic or curator ever suspected that "No Fork" was no art. And so it is still on exhibit, this time as a perfect hack.

MIT has other museums, as well. The Hart Nautical Collection is described above. The **Compton Gallery**, *Building 10, 77 Massachusetts Ave., Cambridge, Tel. 258-9106,* concentrates on architectural exhibits. The **List Visual Arts Center**, *The Cube, Ames Street Cambridge, Tel. 253-4680,* is an art museum specializing in modern work. To take a stroll through the MIT campus, with an eye on notable sculpture and architecture at the school, purchase a copy of the book *Art and Architecture at MIT: A Walking Tour of the Campus.* It costs $8 and is available at either the main MIT Museum or the List Visual Arts Center.

MUSEUM OF SCIENCE, *Science Park, Boston. Tel. 723-2500, TTY 589-0417, website, www.mos.org. T: Science Park. Hours: Saturday-Thursday, 9am-5pm (to 7pm in summer); Friday, 9am-9pm. Cost: adults, $9; senior citizens and children, $7.*

MUGAR OMNI THEATER and **CHARLES HAYDEN PLAN-ETARIUM**, *Educational shows daily; laser shows with rock and roll music, Thursday to Sunday evenings. Cost: adults, $7.50; senior citizens and children, $5.50.*

They call it the Museum of Science. It's "The Playground of Amazin' Phenomenon." No sooner do you walk into the first gallery than you are staring into a cross-section of a wave in motion, commanding a three-dimensional multiplication machine to cipher five times four times three, or setting up a sand pendulum. The museum asks visitors to work with most of the exhibits in one way or another, and so you have to hunt around to find something as simple-minded or old-fashioned as a glass case filled with specimens. Looking is allowed at the Museum of Science, but the favorite word around the galleries is "Investigate," exclamation point, and that is what most of the visitors set about doing.

A primary complaint with the Museum of Science would also be its strong suit: it seems to be aimed squarely at the fourth-grader. Science embraces an exuberantly wide variety of subjects, from traffic management to color composition, handed over in little bites. Since most adults know little more about such subjects that the average fourth-grader, that's still a strong suit. But the exhibits don't go much further than to explain one isolated facet of nature. Only rarely are the little exhibits pulled together with any broader implication. The Museum of Science may be Boston's best museum for children; but it really need not stop there.

Originally, it was the Boston Society for Natural History, founded in 1830. The Museum of Science evolved out of it and moved into its current home, square in the middle of the Charles River, in 1972. The building is part of a dam, jutting right into the water alongside a bridge: three big squares of granite that make the galleries big enough for anything, from a life-size model of a Tyrannusaurus Rex, to the great metal balls in the Van de Graff generator, used to demonstrate some of the properties of electricity. Some of the general topics covered are, for example, the human body, greenhouse plants, water, and mathematics.

My two favorite exhibits test one's own mettle. The first is called "Hip Operation," and it includes a video-tape that asks, part-way through, whether you would like to continue by seeing the operation as rendered on a plastic dummy, or a real-live person. I always opt for the real operation and then never get past the first incision before I run away. The second is called "Skin Sensor," in which you place two fingers on a piece of metal, and watch your nervous reactions plotted across a screen: tell a lie – just think one – and it jumps. While I am sitting quietly at the Skin Tester (Investigating! my mendacity), I hear gales of laughter coming from other exhibits: whole families flapping their arms against a screen are playing Virtual Volleyball, while another family is convulsed exploring Deferential Geometry, in the form of a curved mirror.

Demonstrations on electricity are given on the Van de Graff generator; the show, called "Lightning!" crackles in its ear-splitting way about three times a day. Other, smaller theaters are used throughout the day for introductions to live animals, participations in various scientific investigations, and "Science Magic." Busting science completely out of that glass case, the Museum even puts on short theatrical plays: a recent dramatic production was, for example, *UFO's Over Massachusetts?* Casts are professional actors, and the subject matter is intended to be thought provoking. Purveying science as entertainment, the Museum has two major attractions in the **Charles Hayden Planetarium** and the **Omni Theater**. They are located across from each other in one wing, and each requires a separate admission.

Individuals and families can also take classes at the Museum. Many of them only consist of one session, and would be appropriate even for visitors. Among the dozen or so single-session offerings are Water Works; Animal Survival in the Desert; and The Sun and the Stars. Classes last about two hours, and cost about $30. For schedule and registration information, call Courses and Travel at the museum, *Tel. 589-0300.*

THE NEW ENGLAND HOLOCAUST MEMORIAL, *Union Street, Tel. 457-0755; website, www.nehm.org. T-stop: Government Center or Haymarket. The Memorial is an outdoor exhibit that is always open and carries no admission charge.*

The New England Holocaust Memorial is an exceptionally well-conceived monument, not only to the mass murders committed by the Nazis during World War Two, and the violence rendered to all humanity because of them, but to the individual people who suffered in the Holocaust, their courage and their stories. That is what is written into this Memorial.

"Ilse, a childhood friend of mine, once found a raspberry in the camp and carried it in her pocket all day to present to me that night on a leaf," said a survivor named Gerda Weissman Klein, "Imagine a world in which your entire possession is one raspberry and you give it to your friend." Klein's is one of the intimate recollections chosen for the Memorial, instead of the ponderous words of some statesman or philosopher.

The New England Holocaust Memorial consists of six tall glass towers, each representing a different concentration camp, and etched with the serial numbers of each of its victims. Visitors walk beneath towers rife with details to be noticed; the walk can take two minutes or twenty, or even more. However, the effect of the Memorial is neither heavy-handed or pre-ordained; everyone responds to different things. The only goal of the New England Holocaust Memorial is its final word, chiseled into the walk ... Remember.

SPORTS MUSEUM OF NEW ENGLAND, *Cambridgeside Galleria, 100 Cambridgeside Pl., Cambridge. Tel. 577-7678. T: Lechmere. Hours: Monday-Saturday, 10 am-9:30 pm; Sunday, 11 am-7 pm. Cost: ages 12 and over, $6; senior citizens and ages 5-11, $4.50, children under 4, free.*

The Red Sox, the Celtics, the Bruins, the Patriots – the Sports Museum only starts with the bigs. It goes from there into every nook and cranny of winning, losing, and playing to a tie in all of New England: BC, UConn, Dartmouth, Amherst, Yale, Harvard; the high schools, and the people who played with nothing at all written on their jerseys. The subjects covered range through every column in the sports section, from racing to skating to candle-pin bowling. To heroes of the moment and heroes of all time. They didn't miss much in putting this museum together in a large hall at the Cambridgeside Galleria shopping mall.

My only real complaint is that the attention within the big sports seems to catch on the very, very biggest star in each. There are so many pictures of baseball's Ted Williams, for example, that it might be hard to keep in mind that he put his pants on one leg at a time, just like everybody else – except that there is a picture of him putting his pants on, one leg at a time. Larry Bird is the Celtic. Bobby Orr, the Bruin. I admire these players, but after a point, you can come to resent your own heroes. And what of Joe Cronin?

One "little person" represented at the Museum certainly didn't stay little: there is a picture of future president George Bush as the captain of the Yale baseball team in 1947, shaking hands with Babe Ruth. For fun, you can look through a catcher's mask and let Roger Clemens (that lousy New York Yankees pitcher) demonstrate four of his best pitches. There are four other interactive exhibits and tens of thousands of items in all, recalling all the great playing days in New England.

RUNNING IN

In earlier days in Boston society, mornings were open houses for visiting. It was called "running in," and it is still welcomed at the following homes.

HARRISON GRAY OTIS HOUSE, *141 Cambridge Street. Tel. 227-3956, website, www.spnea.org. T: Bowdoin. Hours: Tuesday-Friday, Noon-5pm; Saturday, 10am-5pm. Tours on the hour (last tour at 4 pm). Cost: $4; senior citizens, $3.50; children 6-12, $2.*

Special fact: Walking tours of Beacon Hill ($10) leave from Otis House on Saturdays, Mid-May to October. Call for reservations.

Whom We Are Visiting: Harrison Gray Otis was a lawyer and politician, a very public figure who made numerous speeches at Faneuil Hall and other locales. Moreover, his wife, Sally Otis, was a leading literary

figure in the 1840s and 1850s, respected and quite loved, for books like
The Barclays of Boston. They had a large family.

What We Are Visiting: Charles Bulfinch designed a new home for the
growing Otis family in 1796. A handsome brick house, it is now the last
free-standing mansion in the city. The restoration, by the Society for the
Preservation of New England Antiquities (SPNEA), varies from stupen-
dously accurate, as in the wallpaper and carpets (specially recreated) to
rather threadbare, as in the motley prints lining the grand hall. Note:
SPNEA oversees 33 historic properties in the region; the *SPNEA Guide*,
a booklet describing each, is available at the Otis House.

THE GIBSON HOUSE, *137 Beacon Street. Tel. 267-6338. T: Arlington.
Hours: May 1-October 31, Wednesday-Sunday and November 1-April 30, with
tours starting at 1, 2 and 3 pm. Cost: $5.*

Whom We Are Visiting: The Gibson family made a tidy fortune in
trade with Cuba. In 1859, the matriarch built a narrow brick house on
Beacon Street for her son, who later married a woman with an even better
lineage and considerable money of her own.

What We Are Visiting: The last of the Gibsons devoted the years
before his death in 1956 to retaining the house as a monument to what
he considered a better era, the late 19th century. The house is largely as
he left it, original wallpaper, crank telephone, black walnut paneling,
furniture in its place: the Gibsons lived well, and their house looks like it
expects them back any moment.

FREDERICK LAW OLMSTED NATIONAL HISTORIC SITE, *99
Warren Street, Brookline 02146. Tel. 566-1689. Hours: Friday-Sunday, 10 am-
4:30 pm. Cost: free.*

Whom We Are Visiting: In 1857, Olmsted took his very first job as a
landscape architect (a term that had not yet been coined): no less than
Central Park in New York. He went on to change the urban look of
America, completing 5,000 projects in the course of his career. In 1883,
he moved to Brookline, near Boston. The firm remained in the same place

for almost a century, until the National Park Service accepted the property in 1980.

What We Are Visiting: The house was an 1810 farmhouse, and still looks like one, in natural clapboard and green trim. Olmsted, however, soon expanded it into an office large enough for dozens of employees. The Olmsted house is not a home any longer. It represents a rare opportunity to tour a hundred-year-old workspace, with original equipment and in original condition. Outdoors, the property is only an acre or two, but Olmsted landscaped it, of course, and separate tours show it in fair weather.

LONGFELLOW NATIONAL HISTORIC SITE, *105 Brattle Street, Cambridge. Tel. 876-4491. T: Harvard Square. Hours: Wednesday-Sunday, 10 am-4:45 pm. Cost: $2, under 17, free.*

Whom We Are Visiting: The house was already historic when a certain Mr. Henry Wadsworth Longfellow starting writing his poems there in the 19th century. During the Revolutionary War, George Washington stayed at 105 Brattle, when he arrived in Cambridge to accept command of the Continental Army.

What We Are Visiting: A huge, yellow clapboard house dating from 1859, the Longfellow House is filled with memorabilia pertaining to the famous poet's way of life and work. The house was his from 1837 to 1882.

Brattle Street is rich with old homes, and you should include time for a leisurely stroll to look them over. Another house that is open for tours is just a short distance away: **Hooper-Lee-Nichols House**, *159 Brattle Street, Tel. 547-4252; limited hours: Tuesday and Thursday, 2-5 pm.* A late 17th-century home, it includes domestic details dating from the subsequent years, including a fetching doll collection.

Other Historic Homes Open to the Public

• **Blake House** (c. 1648, the oldest house in Boston); **William Clapp House** (1806); **Captain Lemuel Clapp House** (1710). All three are administered by the Dorchester Historical Society, *195 Boston Street, Dorchester, Tel. 265-7802,* and are open for tours on the 2nd and 4th Saturday of each month.

- **John F. Kennedy National Historic Site**, *83 Beals Street, Brookline. Tel. 566-7937. Hours: Wednesday-Sunday, 10 am-4:30 pm. Closed Winter.* Family home of the president.
- **Nichols House**, *55 Mt. Vernon Street Beacon Hill. Tel. 227-6993.* Built in 1804; home of peace activist and landscape gardener. Designed by Bulfinch.
- **Orchard House**, *399 Lexington Rod., Concord. Tel. 508/369-4118. Hours: Monday-Friday, 11 am-3 pm; Saturday, 10 am-4:30 pm. Sunday, 1-4:30 pm. Cost: general, $5.50; $4.50, students, senior citizens; $3.50, ages 6-17.* Louisa May Alcott's family home.
- **Shirley Place**, *33 Shirley Street; Tel. 442-2275. Hours: Thursday-Sunday, Noon-4 pm. Cost: $5. House: 1747-51.* This was the home of a military hero of the mid-18th century.

ONLY IN BOSTON

*These are some of the things that people made with their own hands,
sometimes with a good reason, and sometimes ... only a pretty good reason.*

• **Mapparium**, *250 Massachusetts Ave., near Huntington. Tel.
450-3790. T: Symphony. Hours: Monday-Saturday, 10 am-4 pm Free.
Boston has called itself the "Hub of the Universe," since Pilgrim days, but
anyone standing in the Mapparium really is at the hub, of a marvelous glass
universe. It's a great stained-glass globe, 30 feet in diameter, and visitors
walk right into the center of it, a sensation unlike anything else. The
Mapparium was completed in 1935. It's geography. It's art. And it's
acoustics: sound does peculiar things, bouncing and sliding around the
Mapparium.*

• **The Ware Collection of Blaschka Glass Flowers** - *see the Harvard
Museum (Must Sees, above). Leopold Blaschka started out making glass
jewelry in the shape of flowers. Soon, however, botanists discovered that they
could study one of his imitations, as though it were an actual specimen.
Blaschka may have been trained as a craftsman, but he became a serious
scientist. From 1886 to 1936, he and his son, Rudolph, made about 3,000
models of 830 species. "Many people think that we have some secret
apparatus by which we can squeeze glass suddenly into these forms,"
Leopold Blaschka wrote, "but it is not so. We have tact."*

• **The Steaming Kettle**, *located high over 63-65 Court Street near
Government Center. In 1873, the owner of the Oriental Tea Company got
a brilliant idea, gratis from a customer. Put a giant copper tea-kettle over
the store. Improve business. The 200-gallon kettle is still there, puffing its
steam. But what would the Oriental Tea Company think of the fact that the
kettle is now puffing over a Starbucks Coffee Shop?*

12. WALKING TOURS

"The Back Bay has been filled up,
and a section of Paris dumped down into it."
*– **Mrs. A.D.T. Whitney**, Hitherto*

THREE WALKING TOURS

Harvard University

Harvard points with pride to the fact that it has built fewer new buildings over the past 15 years than at any time since the mid-nineteenth century. It's not a question of money, heaven knows – the university squeaks by somehow on a $9 billion endowment – it's the spirit of renewal. Harvard has undertaken a major program to find ways to use existing buildings, rather than build new ones, with the result that the campus is in better repair than ever before, and the overall look remains traditional.

Tradition is important to greater Boston's oldest family: the Harvard community. The campus is held together by a lot of tradition and a little mortar, by comparison. It is not a snobby place, in actuality, though there are undoubtedly some pretty steep heights within it, in that regard. The campus itself is easy to see and to tour, either by yourself or with a group led by a Harvard student. Either way, start your walk at the **Harvard Information Center**, *in the pedestrian mall at the Holyoke Center, 1350 Massachusetts Ave., Harvard Square, Cambridge, Tel. 495-1573.*

For a quarter, you can buy a campus map, containing directions for a self-guided tour. It's even cheaper to be led by a student-guide: that hour-long tour is free. The tours go out on schedule, except during school vacations: Monday-Friday, at 10 am and 2 pm, Saturday at 2 pm; June to

August, Monday-Saturday, 10 am and 11:15 am, and 2 and 3:15 pm, Sunday at 1:30 and 3 pm.

When you're at the Holyoke Center, you're already at Harvard, since the 10-story building is used for non-academic offices. However, facing away from the Holyoke Center across Massachusetts Ave., you will be looking Harvard in the face, the Harvard of John Hancock, Henry Thoreau, Leonard Bernstein, and Bill Gates. And the Radcliffe of Helen Keller, Gertrude Stein, Elizabeth Dole, and Bonnie Raitt. Radcliffe is the umbrella under which females go through the university, though there is not a completely separate campus.

A brick wall surrounds the core of the campus, the **Harvard Yard**, a block measuring 22 acres. But where another school might have called a mason to build such a wall, Harvard called McKim, Mead & White, the leading architectural firm at the turn of the century. The wall was finished in 1899. Most buildings on the campus are brick, but the first building on the other side of the gate, **Wadsworth House** (1727), was built of wood, in a roomy colonial style. George Washington slept there when he was in Cambridge at the outbreak of the Revolutionary War in 1775.

Freshmen, of whom there are about 1,500 each year, use residences in the oldest part of the campus, where the sense of *Harvard* reigns thickest. Walking straight ahead into the Old Harvard Yard, two freshman dorms, **Matthews** and **Grays** will be on either side, making a turn in the corner. The oldest building on the campus is the rather delicate pile of bricks that comes up next on the left. **Massachusetts Hall** dates from 1720 and **Harvard Hall** is next to it. According to university lore, a previous incarnation of Harvard Hall housed the university's most treasured possession: Rev. John Harvard's library of books. It was largely the donation of that library to the fledgling school that influenced its overseeers to proclaim in 1639 that "the colledge agreed upon formerly to bee built at Cambridg shal bee called Harvard Colledge."

Harvard built itself around the Reverend's books, and forbade students from taking them out, until a fire at Harvard Hall wiped out the whole library. The school was in shock, until one student stepped forward with a single volume that he had saved from destruction, having slipped it out of the library on the night before the fire. The president of the school, Edward Holyoke, was deeply grateful. He thanked the student sincerely, and then expelled him.

The next building past Harvard Hall is **Hollis Hall** where Ralph Waldo Emerson and Henry David Thoreau once roughed it, as students residing there. Having seen a gaggle of quaint old living quarters, you might, by this time, be wondering where the all the learning goes on. Walk straight out of the Old Harvard Yard, through a gate in the wall – the world does feel a bit different, for better or worse, outside the wall – and look straight ahead at a big slice of a building, the **Science Center**. Rest assured that somebody in there is cramming. Fade off to the right toward a red brick monastery. That's no monastery, it's a dining hall, built in memory of the 136 Harvard students, teachers, and alumni who died in the Civil War. Their names are inscribed on the walls. But here's the sad and wrenching part: the men memorialized were all Union soldiers. The several dozen Harvard men who fell on the Confederate side are not a part of the air of remorse that quite naturally hangs over the building. That is how the builders wanted it, and so the building is in that worst category of memorial. It is a perpetuation.

Turning left before that building, Memorial Hall, follow Oxford Street a half-block to see the **Harvard Museum of Cultural and Natural History** on the right, *26 Oxford Street, Tel. 495-3045; Hours: Monday-Saturday, 9 am-5 pm; Sunday, 1-5 pm; Cost: Adults, $5; senior citizens and students, $4; ages 3-12, $3; Free every Saturday 9 am-Noon*. You'll want to go in there now or later. It houses the university collections, which are all of them exciting, being neither overbearing nor obtuse. Listed in a rush of enthusiasm, they are: awe-inspiring glass flowers and plants (and the occasional bee); stuffed birds by the flock, perfect for bird-watchers born with an iota of patience; arresting dinosaur and mammal bones; rocks and minerals as far as the eye can see (in one big room), and dioramas of early Native American dwellings in the Northwest, along with artifacts including totem poles.

Returning on Oxford Street, and following it around the turn to the left, take your first right on Quincy Street and you will find the **Sackler**

Museum taking up much of the streetfront between Cambridge Street and Broadway (where the entrance is). The Sackler is considered one of Harvard's Art Museums, but the collections inside are as much historical or archaeological as strictly artistic. It contains fine representations of ancient art from Greece, Rome, India, and China. Special exhibits usually highlight world art, in some aspect, modern or historic.

The **Fogg Museum** is just across the street, though you'll have to wend your way around the building to find the entrance. The Fogg, opened to the public in 1895, is Harvard's full-service art museum, with paintings and a few sculpture pieces, dating from the Renaissance to the post-Impressionists. The great names in painting are at the Fogg, though the work represented is not typically up to the level seen, for example, at the Museum of Fine Arts. It is a remarkable university museum, and a good art museum in the open division.

Information on the **Harvard University Art Museums**: *Fogg (32 Quincy Street), Sackler (485 Broadway), which includes access to the Busch-Reisinger Museum of German-related art, Tel. 495-9400. Hours: Monday-Saturday, 10 am-5 pm; Sunday, 1-5 pm. Cost: adults, $5; senior citizens, $4, students, $3; under 18, free. Saturday mornings free, 10 am to Noon. Tours, Monday-Friday: Fogg, 11 am; Sackler, noon; Busch-Reisinger, 2 pm.*

Back on the walking tour, and continuing on Quincy Street, the building next to the Fogg is a projection of the artistic spirit called the **Carpenter Center for the Visual Arts**. Designed by the renowned French architect Le Corbusier, it is so angular that the self-guided tour suggests that you look at it from the across the street. If you do, you will have the following question: who's that guy? Stretched across the middle of the building (if there is a middle to such a structure), there is a gigantic, close-up photograph of what looks suspiciously like an aging French architect. And so it is.

Waving good-bye to him, you can proceed on Quincy Street and find the next gate through the wall, on the right. It will come along just before the next intersection, at Harvard Street. Back in the confines of the Yard, you will be generally surrounded by libraries, on all sides, including underfoot. John Harvard's last surviving volume rebounded and today, the university's library system encompasses 12 million books. There are 90 Harvard libraries.

Just for a taste of the worlds within them, pop into the **Houghton Library**, a tidy brick building straight ahead from the gate. The august room to the left, inside, exhibits displays from various literature collections. If you go outside and around to the back, and down a little hillock, you will find the entrance to the **Pusey Library** built into the base of the hillock. Just inside that non-building (it's a cellar), there is always an exhibit of original material from the theater collection: letters from irate vaudeville actresses and original manuscripts of famous plays. Come out of the Pusey, look up and you will see the **Widener**, the main library at the university. Walk to the right, and then left around the Widener and take in the quadrangle before you, presided over by the **Memorial Church**, at the opposite end. Or, don't look at anything in particular; look at everything at once and what you'll see is pure Harvard.

Continue on your way past the Widener Library, turning left and then right again, to face the back of **Wadsworth House** (George Washington slept here), where your Harvard walking tour ends.

GUIDED TOURS

Walking is one of Boston's leading industries. Guided tours last between one hour and two hours, typically, and cost about five to ten dollars. Tour organizations, and a few of their itineraries, include:

*• **Historic Neighborhoods**, Tel. 426-1885. A non-profit organization with volunteer guides, HN offers such walks as: "Make Way For Ducklings," Thursday-Saturday, at 11 am and "Beacon Hill Sunset Strolls," Thursday, 5:30 pm. The tours last 90 minutes and cost $5.*

*• **City of Boston Park Rangers**, Tel. 635-7383. Free walks include: "Boston's Black Heritage," "Pond Explorations," "Women's Herstory," and "Make Way for Ducklings." The tours are free.*

*• **Boston By Foot**, Tel. 367-2345. Started in 1976, Boston By Foot is a non-profit group that gives a roster of standard walking tours and imaginative "Tours of the Month," such as Beacon Hill with a Boo, for Halloween.*

The Back Bay

You can start out in the **Back Bay** feeling veddy uppah closs, shopping on Newbury Street, then become even more uppah closs and disdain shopping (you already own everything), by shifting one block north to Commonwealth. If you feel too peppy for a residential street, zig south two blocks back to Boylston. Should you want to be all alone as far as the eye can see, move back over south to quiet Marlborough Street; on the next street, Beacon Street, the view of the Charles River pokes its face through the brownstones every chance it gets. They're not streets, they're different planets – and that is one way that the Back Bay differs from Beacon Hill, which is more homogeneous.

This walking tour pauses over some of the noteworthy buildings, with the admonishment that in this particular case, the delight is in the details. No encyclopedia could point out all the thousands and thousands of ideas that have been placed on public view in the Back Bay, especially along Commonwealth Avenue. I have tried to favor places that are open to the public, even for a peek. Keep in mind that the Back Bay is a triumph of unstilted planning – and that the cross streets are coded alphabetically, from Arlington-Berkeley-Clarendon, and so on to Hereford.

According to the plans laid out by the dreamers who filled in the city's back bay starting in the 1850's, the Back Bay begins at the **Public Garden**. Standing at the corner of Arlington Street, the view looking up Commonwealth is a city-borne vista and it is the Back Bay at its grandest. On the opposite corner, to the left, is the **Ritz-Carlton Hotel**, with its condominium-wing facing Commonwealth. On the righthand corner, **Hurbridge House**, *12 Arlington*, is one of the Back Bay's early mansions, built in 1859 in that French-inspired style of stone and austerity that was to become a mark of the district. Walk past it to the corner of Beacon Street, and turn left. **The Gibson House**, *137 Arlington*, occupied by the same family from 1860 to 1956, has been a museum ever since the last Mr. Gibson died. Tours are given in the afternoon, but you can go inside for a look at a wholly Victorian sensibility, even without the tour.

Almost across the street, 150 Beacon is a later mansion, owned by Alvin Fuller, a former governor, still known in the antique-car world as an important Packard dealer in his day. His house, built on the site of Mr. and Mrs. Isabella Stewart Gardner's first mansion, is a determinedly timeless building, which so happened to have been built in 1904. You can step inside; it's a college library today. An even more evocative interior is at the former residence at 170 Beacon, now the **Goethe Institute**. Cross the street and return to make a right turn at Berkeley.

The French Library is at the corner of Berkeley and Marlborough behind a wrought-iron fence. It was a private home when it was built, but now welcomes the public as a center for French culture in Boston. You can read a book or magazine, and look at the schedules for special activities. Both the Goethe Institute and the French Library sponsor free films and concerts. Not that the original owners of the French Library had delusions of grandeur, but the salon is said to be copied from Empress Josephine's.

Turning right at Commonwealth, you can either saunter up the sidewalk or the grass mall in the middle. The former **Hotel Vendome**, *160 Commonwealth*, on the corner of Dartmouth Street, was a relatively small hotel when it was built in 1881, but the height of luxury nonetheless. Today, the interior is wiped clean of its past, having been transformed into new offices and condominiums in the early 1970s, yet the exterior remains a landmark, still known as the Hotel Vendome long after the last guest checked out. The rather amorphous red brick building at the corner of Hereford (number 40) and Commonwealth housed the **Fanny Farmer Cooking School** after 1902. The building itself is about 20 years older than that. The extraordinary **Burrage Mansion**, dating from 1889 and bordering on the fantastic, is directly across Hereford Street It is an adult home today.

Turning to the left on Hereford, cross Newbury and meet Boylston at the **Hynes Convention Center**. Turning left and looking right, you will see the "Pru," the tower that changed the Back Bay so dramatically when it was completed in 1965. In the first place, it was approximately fifteen times taller that the buildings all around it. In the second place, it replaced a trainyard which formed a natural border between the Back Bay, where standards were upheld, and the South End, where they had not been discussed in decades. In terms of the Back Bay, the **Prudential Center** is still a border between the Back Bay and the rest of the city on the other side, but it is also a bridge, when need be, a connection to other neighborhoods. Adjacent to the Hynes Convention Center, the Pru underwent a major renovation in 1994, installing an expanded shopping mall on the first floor.

Following Boylston Street past the Pru, you will arrive at the modern (1971) addition to the **Boston Public Library** at the corner of Boylston and Exeter. Enter the library, pass through the turnstiles and go immediately to the left, following the halls around a zig-zig to emerge in the garden court. All year-round, the garden court is an open and hushed place for a break – from study or from the city beyond the walls. A garden club tends the flowers and plants in the middle, and the library leaves Windsor chairs around the surrounding portico for people who take books, or books and a light lunch, to the garden court.

Continuing through it to the other side, you will go into the library's old wing, the one opened in 1895. It is a landmark of architecture, a full representation of the architecture firm of McKim, Mead & White, and a landmark of art – John Singer Sargent painted the mural decoration on the third floor – but over all, the Boston Public Library is a landmark of public spirit. Starting from its first quarters in 1854, it was the first great public library in the country. When the English writer Arnold Bennett toured the Boston Public Library soon after it opened, he appreciated all of its aesthetic qualities, but said that the most impressive thing he had seen was the sight of a scruffy newsboy studying at one of the tables in the great reading room, Bates Hall. *The library gives free tours of both buildings, Tel. 536-5400.*

Outside, standing on the steps of the library, you will see **Copley Square** in all of its disparate glory. The buildings do not go together ... except that they do. The square itself is dotted with trees and benches, plantings and a big patch of grass, and if that seems an obvious furnishing to make for a plaza, go look at the absurd tundra in front of the Government Center. Peeking from the right is Copley Place, the complex of shops, offices, and hotels that has given the Prudential Center competition as the very most upscale place in the Back Bay.

The presiding dowager of the place, the **Copley Plaza Hotel**, is right on the square. It is where Louis XV would stay, if he ever stopped in Boston and wanted to feel at home, because it is a 1906 Bostonian tribute to the golden-hued glamor of 18th century France. Next to it, all of a sudden, is the **John Hancock Tower**, a mid-1970s skyscraper clad in reflective blue glass. It is gigantic, a full city block at a height of 790 feet, but the glass and its shape make it less bulky than it could be.

Its greatest fame came during construction, when the windows – weighing 500 pounds a piece – kept popping out and shattering on the streets and sidewalks below. On one night, January 20, 1973, sixty-five of them fell. No one was hurt, but the building seemed to be an impossibility. People called it the "Plywood Palace" because of the ersatz repairs that were made. The architects and engineers who worked to salvage the situation have been sworn to secrecy ever since, but the latest rumor, printed in a story in the *Globe* a few years ago, is that the falling windows were only the half of it. A German architectural engineer who flew in to consult on the problem reported that if the wind were just so (in a city of all winds), the whole tower would fall over. That would change the cityscape, somewhat. Vitally important shock-absorbing material was introduced into the core of the building, after which the windows stopped falling out. And the building didn't tip over.

That is good, because hefty film sales in Boston depend on the reflection of the old and little **Trinity Church** in the new and mammoth Hancock Tower. The Trinity Church is Boston's own unofficial cathedral, designed by Henry Richardson in a European style, yes, but one that suits Boston uniquely. The church was consecrated in February 1877, under the words above the altar, "Blessing and Honour and Glory." You are invited to go inside, where the interior is warm with a close, intimate feeling, for such a big church. Music is a vital part of the atmosphere at Trinity. Half-hour organ concerts begin every Friday at 12:15 pm. *For current information about other choir and instrumental programs, call 536-0944, ext. 311.*

From the library steps, look to your left, to the corner of Clarenden and Boylston. The way that the newsstand there spills outdoors, all of its neat little piles of good reading have to lie under stones or plastic, depending on the skies. The name, handwritten over the stand, is **Copley Square News**, and that describes just where it has been since the 1920s. Copley Square is not just the buildings, but the space between. It is the Hancock Tower *and* Trinity Church. It is the glorious Public Library *and* the ignoble Copley Square News. Lovably ignoble.

At the corner of Boylston and Berkeley, you will see a free-standing building of dark brownstone, looking like an embassy. Actually, it was built in 1862 as the Museum of Natural History and it was an anchor for the Back Bay at the time, a great institution throwing in its lot with the new neighborhood. The original occupant eventually grew into the Museum of Science, which is now located on (or in) the Charles River. The building later housed the Bonwit Teller department store, and when that company vacated, the neighbors worried. The land is so valuable. But so, fortunately, are good clothes: **Louis, Boston**, one of the nation's finest clothing stores, moved in, treating both the building and the interior with respect. Take a look inside. And if you have a few hundred dollars lying loose – pick up a tie. With a right on Newbury, it is only another block to the Public Garden, where the Back Bay starts – or ends.

A Half-Hour On Beacon Hill, & A Couple Hundred Years

John Singleton Copley was a painter, who left behind exquisite pictures of American personalities, including Samuel Adams, when he quit the colonies at the age of 36 in 1774 to extend his reputation to England. Copley was also an important landowner in Boston. Most of his property was undeveloped pastureland along the Charles River, but the city grew in his absence and eventually a group of intrepid businessmen decided to move Boston; the rich people therein, further to the west toward the Charles.

In 1795, they bought the 18-acre Copley tract. It was the Louisiana Purchase of Boston history, not only because the new owners all but stole it from the old owner, over in Europe, but because it changed the shape of the city, in social terms. The new owners called themselves the Mount Vernon Proprietors, and they were led by a lawyer named Harrison Otis, a young man who was determined to recoup the fortune that his family had lost when he was boy.

Once the Mount Vernon Proprietors took possession of their pastureland, they had to think how to transform it into the best address in Boston. They did what they could: they engaged Charles Bulfinch (himself a part-time Proprietor) to design the first house there, and in 1800, Harry and Sally Otis moved in, making as grand an appearance as they could. It was a free-standing house, a true mansion, but since the new neighborhood did become Boston's best address in the first third of the nineteenth century, the houses were afterward built in blocks, in order to use every inch of Copley's old fields to advantage.

There were no more free-standing mansions, but the overall style of **Beacon Hill** has remained intact ever since: upstanding brick houses and quiet cobblestone streets. And an old neighborhood, made new with light: sunlight plays with Beacon Hill, finding its way around the hill itself and into the narrow streets, so that it can paint different details and tints at its whim. A walk through Beacon Hill need not take in anything more than that, since the sun certainly knows Beacon Hill better than any guide.

Geographically, a good place to start a walk through Beacon Hill is at the corner of Charles and Beacon streets. **Charles Street**, lively without ever being brash, is the shopping street of the neighborhood. Stroll down it for two blocks and turn right at Mount Vernon Place, stopping at **Number 85 Mount Vernon**, which is still a private residence. Number 85 was the very house that Bulfinch built for Mr. and Mrs. Otis in 1800: it may be smack in the middle, but it is the beginning of Beacon Hill. With little extraneous adornment, the house is squarely built, in bricks, of course. The windows, which are grand on the first floor, practical on the second, and arrested on the third, are handled with Bulfinch's fine eye for proportion, and it is the windows that give sweep to the square facade. You have to let your eyes "read" the windows in a Bulfinch building; they were a major part of his language.

Up the hill, the Nichols House Museum, *55 Mount Vernon Street*, is another Bulfinch-designed house, and it is open to the public. Commissioned by Jonathan Mason, one of the Proprietors, the house was finished in 1804, quite early for Beacon Hill. Inside, it reflects both the Federal era in which it was built and the roving interests of Rose Nichols, the last occupant. Returning toward Charles Street, turn right as you go down the hill into Louisburg Square. Louisbourg was a battle in which troops from Boston helped the English defeat the French in Nova Scotia in 1745; Louisburg Square was named after it about 80 years later. The square was a new idea at the time it was built in the 1830s and 1840s: a joint ownership community, by which anyone who owned one of the twenty-two lots on the perimeter also owned a one-twenty-secondth share of the green in the middle.

Those who lived in Louisburg Square had both a house and a very big yard. The houses are not ostentatious, yet possession of one has always made a personage out of a mere person in Boston, as Louisa May Alcott knew as well as anyone. The minute she had her first fortune from writing, she bought **Number 10** on Louisburg Square. The townhouses have remained in private hands, and have not been broken up into apartments.

Going to the other end of Louisburg Square, turn left on Pinckney Street. Notice, if I can be diplomatic about it, that not every ancient townhouse on Beacon Hill is in perfect repair. Once, when I was looking for a very inexpensive apartment in Boston, the agent started by showing a lot of flats on Beacon Hill. In Santa Monica, they have to legislate mixed-income housing, but on Beacon Hill, you can be poor or you can be rich, and it's entirely up to you.

Lope down the hill to **Cedar Lane Way**, and turn left. It is a mews that would be at home in some gentle town along the Thames in England, except that the hous-ettes of Cedar Way Lane, so often decked out in flowers, were obviously built in the shadow of Charles Bulfinch and have that Boston look about them. Following the Way across Mount Vernon Street, turn left when you come to the end, on **Chestnut Street**. It is another of the hallmark streets of Beacon Hill. The three matching houses at numbers 13, 15, and 17 were commissioned by a rich woman who gave one to each of her daughters, as soon they were married. Designed by Bulfinch, they stand with his best work. Known as the **Swan Houses**, after the mother, Hepzibah Swan, they are brick townhouses accented by

PICTURES FOR YOUR MIND

Wherever you start out, these destinations will provide a good look at Boston.

The Harvard Bridge looking northeast toward the city from the Cambridge side. *The city skyline and the river pose against each other in soft colors, especially at sunrise or sunset.*

The Memorial to Robert Gould Shaw and the 54th Regiment. *The bas-relief itself is as close as Saint-Gaudens could come to making a moving picture in cast bronze. Around the Memorial, there are vivid pictures of Boston on three sides. The first is the view down sloping Beacon Street, where Federal-era townhouses face the Common and the Public Garden further down. The second, from beside the Memorial, is of the Common rolling out in lawns and walks. The third is the steep view of the State House, directly across Beacon Street.*

Just to the left as you walk over the Northern Ave. Bridge to South Boston, the **Fan Pier** *(Pier No. 1) gives a powerful perspective in the skyline, and the wharves poking out into the Harbor, before the hill of bricks on the North End. Looking straight out, on the other hand, you can interest yourself in the harbor itself and the airport on the other shore. The pier is considerably built up, with a new Federal Courthouse, but there is still room to walk.*

pillared white doorways and black shutters. The houses were all built in 1806, though the last of the daughters was not married until 12 years later, at which time she finally took possession of her house (obviously in no hurry, she must have had either very good character or very bad taste in architecture).

If you return down Chestnut Street and turn left at Spruce Street, you will find yourself facing the Common. Nip up the hill a few steps, and you can see the third and last home that Charles Bulfinch built for Harry and Sally Otis, at **Number 45 Beacon Street**. By turning right on Beacon Street, though, you will be heading for home, at the corner of Beacon and Charles. Along the way, you can see one of the dopey, but popular, tourist attractions of Beacon Hill – the **purple windows**. They are set into the King's Chapel Parish House at 63-64 Beacon Street. Symbolically, they demonstrate the eccentric and/or frugal Bostonian mind at work: in 1818, the window glass imported from a certain English company was found to have turned purple in transit, due to its chemical composition. The glass certainly did not go to waste, however and several houses on Beacon Hill still have it – 175 years later.

If you will consult your map, now that the walking tour is finished, you will note that it was a rather inefficient route. That was entirely on purpose.

VIEWS

The Prudential Center and the John Hancock Building are only four or five blocks from each other in the Back Bay. The Pru is 759 feet high; the Hancock is 740. Each has an observation floor, and you might think that they would have approximately the same views. Yet the experience in each is different, and so is the view.

The **Hancock Observatory** has more exhibits and features to enrich the view than the Pru. The best of them is a bank of seats facing downtown. While you sit there, trying to figure out what you are looking at, the overview recorded by the historian Walter Muir Whitehall explains precisely what you are looking at. As in his book, *Boston, A Topographical History*, Whitehall on the tape is witty, relaxed, and madly in love with the city of Boston. He was associated for many years with the Atheneaum. His audio aerial-tour takes about twenty minutes. Another feature that is supposed to be helpful – but I don't like it – is marking on the windows to highlight certain landmarks. I wouldn't put anything on the windows: it just gets in the way.

The Hancock Observatory has a clear view of Logan Airport, across the harbor in East Boston, accompanied by a transmission of the radio-communication through the control tower there. If you are interested in hearing a lot of activity, stop in before 10 am or after 4:30 pm. Mr. John Hancock himself, Massachusetts' first governor and a notably crotchety patriot, is the subject of another display, breathtaking in its own way. Among the old family baubles on exhibit is a bracelet owned by Dorothy Hancock, John's wife, featuring a picture of her husband's uncle and benefactor, Thomas Hancock. The portrait on the bracelet was painted by no less than John Singleton Copley, and the gold bracelet itself was made by Paul Revere. The Hancock collection also includes fairly engaging letters written by George Washington, Thomas Jefferson, Paul Revere, and the old Signature, himself, John Hancock.

John Hancock Observatory, 60th floor, Hancock Building, Copley Square, Tel. 572-6420, website, www.cityviewboston.com. Monday-Saturday, 9 am to 11 pm. Open Sundays, May to October at 10 am; November to April, at noon. Cost: adults, $4.25; ages 5 to 17, and senior citizens, $3.25.

The Prudential Center has a simpler observation floor, called the **Skywalk**. The Pru-view (to be expedient about it), is at its best looking toward the Charles River. The Charles is a nice river, treated very kindly through Boston, but I never thought of it as romanticized, almost idyllic, almost – *English*, until I saw it from the Prudential Center. If you can, take both views, for the dimension.

Skywalk, 50th floor, Prudential Center, Tel. 236-3318. Hours: daily, 10 am to 10 pm. Cost: adults, $4; ages 2-10, and senior citizens, $3.

WALKS TO NOWHERE

The **Boston Common** has been set aside as a place to walk since 1634. Or, as Edward Everett Hale remembered it from his youth in the 1820s:

1. A pasture for cows.
2. A play-ground for children.
3. A place for beating carpets.
4. A training ground for the militia.

Or, as I remember it from my own youthful days in the 1970s:

1. A place for three-card monte games.

The Common was starting to become part of the street in those days, with panhandlers and slicksters dotting the walks, but now it has been taken back into itself again, a pasture, for cows or people.

The Common covers 48 acres, part of it across a slope, and the distance around the outer perimeter is three-quarters of a mile. A baseball diamond and tennis courts make the corner near Charles and Boylston streets the playing fields of the Common. Many weekday mornings, you can find mounted policemen there, schooling horses. The area lining Boylston Street further along is shady and quiet, and seems the oldest part of the Common, with its small, crooked **Central Burying Ground**. Gilbert Stuart is among those buried there.

Looking toward the center, as you walk up Tremont, you might notice the Parkman Bandstand, no longer in use. A dramatic statue nearer the street honors the contribution of black soldiers during the Revolutionary War, by depicting Crispus Attucks, an African-American who fell in the Boston Massacre. As you walk along Tremont, past the **Visitor Information Center** opposite Winter Street, you are shadowing the route of America's first subway line, which ran between the Boylston stop (at the corner of Arlington) and the Park Street stop, the first of the two and the first in this country. The entrance to it is in the Common, on Tremont Street near Park Street. Crossing Park Street at the top of the sloping Common, you will arrive at the **Shaw Memorial**, a bronze relief of Col. Robert Gould Shaw, a white Bostonian, leading a famed regiment of black troops during the Civil War. It is a moving depiction, an excellent piece of sculpture by Augustus Saint-Gaudens.

The **Frog Pond**, where cows used to drink when they roamed the Common, is spruced up for skating in the winter, with a new Pavilion. I am not against the new Pavilion, except that it is a reminder that I wish they would stop building things on the Common. The biggest statue in the whole place looms to the left, as you continue to circumnavigate the Common, a memorial to all the sailors and soldiers who fell in the Civil War. After you turn the corner and finish the lap with a last leg along Charles Street, look to the right – not to the Public Garden that is actually there, but instead, to the saltwater that used to be there in colonial days, when the west edge of the Common was a shoreline.

The Esplanade

Up until the 1930s, there was something missing between the Charles River and the townhouses of Beacon Street: what was missing was **the Esplanade**. A sidewalk with a simple lawn was all that there was, until Mrs.

Helen Storrow donated $1 million to regrade the whole strip as a parkland, with places for sailboats and for music.

The Esplanade became part of Frederick Law Olmsted's "**Emerald Necklace**" loop of green space around the city; in fact, his sons worked on the original landscaping in 1931. From the Charles River Dam to the Harvard Bridge, the Esplanade and its neighbor, **Charlesbank Park**, stretch two miles. The land is mostly flat, graded for walking, jogging, bicycling, or skating.

You can hear music on summer nights at the **Hatch Shell**, which is shaped as though it could be something called a "hatch shell," on a boat. In fact, it was named for a man named Edward Hatch. You can arrange to rent a boat at the Community Boating marina near the Hatch Shell. Or you can bring a sack of sandwiches and watch everybody else, on land and water.

THE RIVER CAME FIRST

The story of the Esplanade is linked, with some irony, to an earlier story of the Charles River. Through the end of the 19th century, the river was continually pushed and pulled by the tides of the sea. That made the shoreline messy, but the daily flushing also kept the water clean and free of mosquitos. Parenthetically – and perhaps this really doesn't mean anything – it also made the Charles a choppy river on which to row. A lot of Harvard boys spent four formative years out on the river, rowing back and forth. James Storrow did, before he graduated in the 1870s to became a lawyer and private banker in Boston. He grew to be obsessed with building a dam in the Charles, so that the riverfront could be stabilized and then beautified. Those opposing him complained that turning the Charles into a still-water would make it susceptible to disease and vermin. They also spread the rumor that the whole project was just an effort to make the river more suitable for Harvard's crew practice. Storrow drove back the dissent, however, patiently working his way through hearing after hearing, and collecting supporters on a long list of leading citizens, including John Fitzgerald, Boston's mayor and the grandfather of John F. Kennedy.

In 1909, Storrow's efforts resulted in the construction of the Charles River Dam. In the aftermath, the river did not become a scummy, germ-ridden puddle, as the pessimists had warned, but rather a contented recreational waterway. It also left the shoreline along the Back Bay empty and useless, however. In 1910, Mr. Storrow instigated the initial reclamation of the riverfront, with simple lawns and a walkway, but it was Mrs. Storrow's million dollars, donated in 1931 in memory of her late husband, that developed the Esplanade as it is today. Or almost: Storrow's beautiful riverfront gave way to a new road in the early 1950s. The whole Esplanade had to move over, onto landfill in the river, to make way for the road, the big, ugly four-lane road. James Storrow would have hated it. So they named it after him.

13. NIGHTLIFE

The first decision is when to start the night. Working backward: bars close at 2 am, and don't forget that the T stops operating with the 12:45 am trains out of Park Street.

AFTER WORK

The Littlest Bar, *47 Province Street, Tel. 523-9766,* is definitely not big enough for you and *all* your best friends, just take them there one at a time. Tucked into a nook below an old private walk, there is no room inside for pretension (there isn't even room for the liquor – the bartender has to get it from a storage shed outside). You can sit at the bar, or you can stand by the bar, or you can bump into the wall.

People leave their offices 'way behind when they cross the wand of water below the Northern Bridge and shimmy into the **Barking Crab**, *88 Sleeper Street at the Northern Ave. Bridge, Tel. 426-2722* (see also Chapter 10, *Where To Eat*): the party after work is friendly, noisy, and it is my experience that everybody talks to everybody else, perhaps because we are, after all, in a tent.

Sometimes you leave work without leaving it behind, in the person of a colleague or client. The **Rowes Wharf Bar** *at the Boston Harbor Hotel, Tel. 439-7000,* is as dapper as a Dunhill suit (and at least as English in style). It is not often crowded, but the sense of decorum prevails, in any case.

Revving up a little on the tachometer, the **23**, *161 Berkeley Street, Tel. 542-2255,* is a substantial place, a former bank near Copley Square, reclaimed as a steakhouse. According to a sign in the window, the very popular bar has been designated by a local magazine as the "best place for people-watching." Bosh – the best place for people-watching is any bus station, but 23 is unmistakably full of people who have decked themselves out and want to be looked at.

Those are places to go after work. The place to go instead of work would be the **Bukowski Tavern**, *50 Dalton Street, Tel. 437-9999*, where the bar is for leaning on, the people aren't. And where it is never required etiquette to look at the person to whom you are talking. Or punctuate your sentences, at all. The "Buke" is tailor-made for those who like bars without music and/or like the writings of Charles Bukowski.

THE LITTLEST HISTORY OF THE LITTLEST BAR

*The Littlest Bar is built under an old walking lane called the **Bosworth Street Private Way**, which connects Province Street to Tremont. To use the Way from Province Street, you'll use steps and a rail dating from 1716. Called the Province House Steps, they once led from the British Royal Governor's House to his garden. The house and garden fell out of use somewhat after 1776, along with everything else British and/or Royal, but the steps remain. By the "Way," pun intended, the Littlest Bar is across from Marliave's.*

BEFORE DINNER

The **Oak Bar** at the **Copley Plaza Hotel**, *138 Street James Avenue, Tel. 267-5300*, is a rich living room, with reliably fine piano music starting nightly at 8 pm. I used to think it was the perfect place to wait for people before going on to dinner, until somebody I know made a mistake at first and went instead to the Copley Square Hotel. So, it may not be an unimpeachable place to *meet*, but it's still a perfect place to wait.

Without spoiling supper, **Aniago** at the Lenox Hotel serves a savory menu of appetizers with drinks. The **Blue Cat**, *Mass. Ave. at Newbury, Tel. 247-9922*, is post-modern inside, tinged with the 1950s; **Pignoli**, *79 Park Plaza, Tel. 338-7690*, is also post-modern, but it has a dirigible. Both are serious restaurants, but their bars are good places to meet, even on the way to somewhere else.

THE HEART OF THE EVENING

From Memorial Day to Labor Day, the **Ritz-Carlton Roof**, *Ritz-Carlton Hotel, 15 Arlington Street,* is open for dining and dancing to the music of a swing orchestra. The Public Garden is the floor show, from 17 stories up in the summer air. **The Mercury Bar**, *116 Boylston Street, Tel. 482-7799,* took the best of a pre-war look in a nightspot: overstuffed burgundy booths, soft lighting and a long, grown-up bar. And very good food if you want it. It gets crowded, but if you (and whomever you're with) can get a booth, you'll be by yourself. The Mercury Club is a dance bar downstairs that gets going at 10 pm.

The dining tables are banked at the **Bay Tower Room**, *60 State Street, Tel. 723-1666,* looking down on Boston and the harbor from the 33rd floor; for couples, it's well-recognized as a place to get engaged, so you might want to tread lightly into an invitation to dine there. However, if all you want is a swell place to take in a stunning view, stop in for a drink at the bar, overlooking the city, the harbor, and a lot of nervous-looking couples.

MUSIC & PEOPLE

The **Grand Canal**, *57 Canal Street, Tel. 523-1112,* is a high-Victorian Irish restaurant with a Venetian name and modern American music most nights of the week. It can't be called an Irish pub, even though there is Irish music on Monday nights, but it is a beautiful place, with a polished bar and a snappy crowd.

Sometimes **Dick's**, *55 Huntington Ave., Tel. 267-8080,* books basic bands of the type that might have played down the street and around the corner in the Beatles era. Sometimes the bands are bigger and more brassy, blaring at the frat-party that is always rolling along at the bar.

The pianos – there are two – are matched at **Jake Ivory's**, *1 Landsdowne Street, Tel. 247-1222,* near Fenway Park. The musicians will play any song on request: sing along if you want. Sing a different song if you want; Ivory's is nothing if not easy-going.

JAZZ

The best thing about the jazz at **Turner Fisheries**, *off Copley Square in the Westin Hotel, Tel. 424-7425*, is that you always know it's there, every night at 8 pm. No mad dash to the newspaper listings; the pianists, quartets, and trios playing in the lounge are generally solid, and making more than background music. **Sculler's** is also at a hotel, *the Doubletree Suites in Cambridge, Tel. 562-4111*, with many national artists booked on the weekend. I never drive by without renewing my permanent disappointment at one time missing George Shearing at Sculler's; the shows were sold-out in a split second.

The **Regattabar**, *at the Charles Hotel, Cambridge, Tel. 876-7777*, is another fairly swank place to be, with a lot of jazz savvy, while the **1359 Jazz Club**, *288B Green Street, Cambridge, Tel. 547-9320*, is one of the best for rooting out the local sound. **Club Passim**, *47 Palmer Street, Cambridge, Tel. 492-7679*, schedules mostly folk musicians, with some jazz and blues, but most of its acts are leaning into the forward edge of their type of music. To hear the jazz line-up all over greater Boston, call the **Jazzline**, *Tel. 787-9700*.

IRISH PUBS

There are two types of Irish pubs running around Boston. Both are fun, but there is a difference to be noted. One type is an Irish pub because it says it is – other than that, you might think it was a bar. Having said it is an Irish pub, however, such a place must be a bit friendly and "of good character where women are concerned," to quote George Bernard Shaw. In chemical terms, it must sell Guinness, Harp, Old Bushmill's, and more Guinness. Other than that, it can have Whitney Houston wailing over the speakers, plastic chairs at formica tables, and a big screen TV where the fireplace used to be. Come to think of it, though, that is just exactly how a lot of perfectly good pubs over in Ireland actually are. Anyway, the other type of Irish Pub known around Boston works harder to be mellow in decor, and more purely Gaelic in the sense of humility, and a bit of imagination.

Many Irish pub/bars, to give the former a name, border on being sports bars; the neighborhood near North Station and the Fleet Center is crowded with them (Portland and Friend streets, in particular). A sure characteristic of the type that could be called a Gaelic/Irish pub is called a "Seisiun," a jam session of traditional Irish music. The **Druid** in Inman Square, *1357 Cambridge Street, Tel. 497-0965*, is a rustic pub with a seisiun every night on weekends, and often during the week, as well. In town, **The Green Dragon**, *11 Marshall Street, Tel. 367-0055*, near the Union Oyster House, is the oldest bar of any type in Boston, dating to well before the Revolutionary War; whatever its past, it is quite Irish these days, and you can hear a seisiun on Saturday nights there.

The Claddagh, *113 Dartmouth Street, Tel. 262-9874*, on the south edge of the Back Bay, is a comfortable, woodsy pub with hearty food. The **Grafton Street Pub & Grille**, *1280 Mass. Ave., Cambridge, Tel. 497-0400*, prides itself on a menu of true Irish cooking – not the corned beef and cabbage that everyone thinks of as the epicenter of the cuisine, but delicate fish dishes and "wheaten" breads.

O'Leary's, *1010 Beacon Street, Brookline, Tel. 734-0049*, has a contemporary look, and features traditional music one or two nights a week. If you're downtown, you can stop in at the **Black Rose**, *160 State Street, Tel. 742-2286*, a darkly lit place best for unrushed conversation.

IRISH MUSIC UPDATES

*The most complete schedule of Irish music is printed in the weekly **Irish Emigrant**, available for one dollar at many pubs, or call 296-6671 for other locations.*

COMEDY

The **Comedy Connection**, *Tel. 248-9700*, is a lodge of a club, up in the eaves of the second floor of Quincy Market. Seven nights a week, somebody is standing there trying to make everybody else laugh; about once or twice a month, nationally famous comics are up onstage. **Remington's**, *124 Boylston Street, Tel. 574-9676 or 800/401-2221,* brings in local talent, rougher, by and large, and trying a little harder than those on the Comedy Connection circuit. The Cheers pub, **The Bull & Finch**, *84 Beacon Street, Tel. 227-9605*, has a sports-and-comedy night on Thursdays.

BREWHOUSES

Boston spawned one of the first of the microbreweries, **Samuel Adams**. Now, it has become something of a big boy, but it still counts as a local. When the company opened its own pub in the Lenox Hotel on Boylston Street, it seemed a stroke of genius. Actually, the place is kind of grungy, but you can sample the whole Sam Adams line-up, even recipes that may not show up in every grocery store: Cranberry Lambric, for example.

Brew Moon, *115 Stuart Street, Tel. 523-6467; and in Cambridge at 50 Church Street*, is the sleekest of the new lot of breweries, and emphasizes international cuisine. So does **John Harvard's Brew House**, *33 Dunster Street, Cambridge, Tel. 868-3585*, which offers four-course gourmet dinners, using different beers, both in the recipes and as accompaniment. **Boston Beer Works**, *61 Brookline Ave., Tel. 536-2337*, is across from Fenway Park. You can see its brewing equipment all the way from the box office: some of it, anyway. The place is big and so is the plumbing that makes the beer.

Back Bay Brewing, *755 Boylston Street, Tel. 424-8300*, serves six ales and lagers, and is popular as a lunch spot near the Prudential Center. The **Commonwealth Brewing Co.**, *138 Portland Street, Tel. 523-8383*, has been around for over a dozen years and features live music on weekends, in addition to fresh beer.

BEER ON THE HOOF OR BEER ON THE TROLLEY

*You can take a walking tour of the **Boston Beer Co.**, which brews Samuel Adams beer. Tours start at 2 pm on Thursdays and Fridays (and Wednesdays in July and August); at noon, 1 and 2 pm on Saturdays. The brewery is located in South Boston, near the Stoney Brook T-stop; call 522-9080 for directions. The suggested donation for the tour is one dollar.*

__Old Town Trolley__, Tel. 269-7150, chauffeurs beer connoisseurs around on a three-hour excursion to three local brewhouses, for tours and samples at each. The Brew Pub Tour leaves once a week.

LATE NIGHT DANCE CLUBS

Some nightspots close at about 11 pm. Others open at that hour, for people who want the city all to themselves – at least a three-hour slice of it. The dance clubs congregate close to each other in different sections of the city. It's not always easy to tell beforehand which place you'll want to be at. A club has more moods than the average bar, and the crowd can shift with the speed and coordination of a school of fish. Rotten music can bring in rotten people. Worse yet, rotten music can bring in great people (then you're stuck).

The *Improper Bostonian's* "Boston By Night" listing will give you an idea of which spots have live music (cover of about $3-15), and which are running records (possible cover of about $3). It will also note which clubs are hosting a special night: most of the clubs change names and personalities certain nights of the week. Each will typically have a Gay Night, and a Euro, or International, Night, directed at overseas college students.

These are some of the set special-nights, for example:
- Sunday at **Avalon**: Gay Night
- Monday at **Chaps**: Open Mic
- Tuesday at **Joy**: Euronight
- Wednesday at **Mercury Bar**: Greek Night
- Thursday at **Roxy**: Latin Night.

So, you should consult the listings or call ahead to make sure that the club you set out for is the same club you arrive at. Generally, **Avalon**, *15 Landsdowne Street, Tel. 262-2424*, has a hard and loud electro-dance show on the floor, while the lounge is almost quiet enough, some nights, for a conversation. It is over twenty years-old now, a pioneer of the Landsdowne strip. For a slightly older crowd (late, rather than early twenties), **The Roxy**, *Tremont Hotel, Tel. 338-7699*, is even more devoted to dance, set up for DJ music and a dizzying laser show.

AT NIGHT WITHOUT ALL THAT JAZZ
Upper Newbury Street

Let's say you can't stand anything like a bar, but you want to be out and about until about midnight: by yourself, on a date, in a group, or with a couple of the boppers, if they can stay up late. Let's also say you don't care what's cool – but I do, and so I will observe that upper Newbury Street at night has all of the tension and excitement, and attractive people, of what is called "nightlife" without the concomitant alcohol.

To sit and jabber at the **Trident Cafe and Bookstore**, to scour **Tower Records**, to find a place on a stoop with an ice-cream from **J.P. Licks**, to sit at the juice-bar at the **Cosmic Cafe**, sipping one of their offbeat concoctions – a lot of people think that's a good night's work. None of these places is going to have a "Euro Night" in the near future, it's true. Even so, they still seem to fit into the late hours. The short list above only covers the first half-block of upper Newbury. The *piazza* atmosphere continues for at least six blocks. Take the T to Hynes or Copley; stick to Newbury Street.

HOT SPOTS

In age order (of the average patron):

Landsdowne Street. *Located next to Fenway Park, block-long Landsdowne is the Las Vegas of Boston, with bright lights all in a row, and crowds marching around on the sidewalk, deciding where to alight. Fantasy abounds, or tries to, both in the decor inside the clubs and in the growing popularity of virtual reality and other games. The street draws the youngest crowd in the city, slightly more working-class than the one flocking to Boylston Place, though there is a further variety in places and patrons to be found a half-block away on Brookline Ave.*

The Alley at Boylston Place. *It really was an alley until the early 1980s, when several developers carved into the old warehouses behind the walls to make a playground of nightspots mostly for college kids. It isn't too conspicuous from the street: go to the* **Mercury Bar,** *116 Boylston Street, sidle twenty paces to the right, and look down the rather Dickensian alleyway that is there, to the less Dickensian neon lights toward the end.*

Bulfinch Triangle. *Portland, Friend, and Canal streets have risen so quickly on the nightscene that no one knows yet what to call the lively little district: "North Station," "Fleet Center" or the original "Bulfinch Triangle." The range in nightspots is rooted in sports bars, but gentrified pubs, brew-pubs, and a couple of dance clubs have landed as well.*

Quincy Market. *You might not notice it during the day, but Quincy Market is loaded with nightlife. Places to sit and talk are the strongsuit, only a few impose any form of music louder than perhaps a Gershwin strain on the piano. There are a couple of robust pubs in the area, too, and a couple of those felicitous bars that seem to extend no special attraction whatsoever, except that they are jam-packed every night.*

14. CULTURE

Culture is Boston's response, and it has been for a long time. The idea that self-improvement is a social remedy on the large scale and a personal responsibility on the smallest scale started with the Puritans. The question from their time to this is what constitutes culture. Boston was banning racy books until the early 1970s, under the rule of the Watch & Ward Society. On a poster at the Hynes T-platform for a vaunted Museum of Fine Arts exhibition of the work of a fashion photographer in 1996, a passerby scrawled heavily, "Glamor is not art." The person who expressed that opinion might have been a Transcendentalist: in the 1840s, they also reacted against a "society they felt was lowering intellectual standards by catering to popular fads and vulgar tastes," as the historian Thomas O'Connor wrote (in his estimable *Short History of Boston.*)

Reacting to the vulgarity of popular culture, the Boston **Athenaeum** was formed in 1807 and the **Handel & Hadyn Society** in 1815, the **Museum of Natural History** (now the Museum of Science) started in 1830 and the **Public Library** in 1848. The **Museum of Fine Arts** grew out of the Athenaeum in 1870, and the **Boston Symphony** presented itself as an answer to the question of culture in 1881. All were pioneers in the nation. Culture is the answer in Boston: it's the question that has been the cause of debate, whether it is social stability, aesthetic reinforcement, or aesthetic challenge that is asked being for.

At least we know that art is not glamour. But you ask your own question, and here are a couple of the answers that Boston can give.

MUSIC

The **Boston Symphony** is a company of musicians, playing in different configurations, musical styles, and locations. Its headquarters is the elegant **Symphony Hall**, *Mass. Ave., Tel. 266-1492*, which was designed by McKim, Mead & White, along with so many other Boston landmarks of the turn-of-the-century. For the concert hall, the firm worked with a consultant in acoustics, a Harvard professor named W.C. Sabine. Their combined efforts resulted in a sober, rather clumsy red-brick building, renowned for the sound, let alone the *sounds,* within. On opening night in 1900, the first words to emanate from the stage were from a Bach chorale, "Grant us to do with zeal our portion, whatsoever."

With all kinds of zeal, the Boston Symphony expanded its portion during this century, growing in stature, as well as in activity: the **Pops**, the **Chamber Players**, and **Youth Concerts** reaching quite different audiences. The full orchestra is the main attraction, playing its series of 25 programs at Symphony Hall from October to April each year. A quarter of a million people attend the classical concerts each year, while 180,000 go to the Hall to see the **Boston Pops**, a full orchestra of a different slant, made up of most of the same musicians as the symphony orchestra. When they play at Symphony Hall, the row-seats are removed and cafe-tables dot the floor. A cafe-table is naturally a place for light refreshments, of course, and so it is at a Pops concert.

A typical program is in three parts: first, some light classic music; then a performance by a guest star, usually a singer, and finally, a selection of songs from Broadway, Hollywood, Sousa, or the like. During the first week in July, while the Boston Symphony is on its summer schedule in the Western Massachusetts music center called Tanglewood, a Boston Pops orchestra (made up of different, free-lance musicians) plays at the Hatch Shell on the Esplanade back in Boston. The concerts are free, and notoriously well-attended.

The T-stop is Symphony. Performances are normally given on Tuesday, Thursday, Friday and Saturday evenings, and Friday afternoons. Tickets for the Symphony cost $23-69. The Boston Pops perform at Symphony Hall through most of May and June, and at Christmastime. Website, www.bso.org.

Tickets cost $16-51. The concerts take place in the evening, Tuesday through Sunday.

BOSTON SYMPHONY INSIDER TIPS

• *The Symphony sets aside a certain number of "Rush" tickets to be sold the day of the performance (Friday afternoons, Tuesday, and Thursday evenings), for only $7.50, one to a customer. Get in line at the Cohen Wing entrance, at 9 am on Friday morning; Tuesdays and Thursdays at 5 pm.*

• *On some Wednesday evenings and Thursday mornings, visitors can attend an open rehearsal – the same music headed for the actual concert, with the bonus of overheard comments from the conductor; tickets $12.50.*

• *A pre-concert lecture precedes the open rehearsal and lasts about a half-hour.*

In the 1970s, Sarah Caldwell, director of the Opera Company of Boston was doing something amazing. She did not accept that the only place for opera in America was Lincoln Center in New York. Fanning a hot-blooded enthusiasm into the classic repertoire, she drew national attention even as her company drew into a position of competition with New York's Metropolitan and City operas. The Boston Opera helped to ignite the new interest in opera around the country, as companies even in small cities have found audiences far from Lincoln Center. The Opera Company has ceased to exist, but its place has been taken by the **Boston Lyric Opera**, *45 Franklin Street, Tel. 542-4912.*

More & Yet More Music

The **Handel & Hadyn Society**, *300 Mass. Ave., Tel. 266-3605*, is highly active, sponsoring concerts of works by the aforementioned, as well as other 18th century works. The Society has been performing *The Messiah* every Christmas season since 1854. The **New England Conservatory of Music**, *290 Huntington Ave., Tel. 262-1120, ext. 700 for schedule; Tel. 536-2412 for tickets,* one of the most respected schools in the country, offers at least 250 concerts per year, by students, faculty, and guests. In one week, you might have the choice of hearing the N.E.C. Percussion Ensemble, the

Jazz Orchestra, or the Youth Chorus, for example. Most of the concerts are free. The **Museum of Fine Arts**, *465 Huntington Ave., Tel. 369-3300*, sponsors a chamber-music series, with regular appearances by its own **Boston Museum Trio**, specialists in baroque music. Most of the programs take place Sunday afternoons, about twice per month; tickets cost $18.

Nearby, the **Isabella Stewart Gardner Museum**, *280 The Fenway, Tel. 734-1359*, is a memorable venue for music by soloists and small ensembles; concerts are Saturdays and Sundays at 1:30 pm. King's Chapel, *Tel. 227-2155*, and **Trinity Church**, *Copley Square, Tel. 536-0944*, both offer weekly organ concerts; in fact, Trinity Church presents a full schedule of music in voice and/or instrument each week.

Boston Musica Viva, *25 Huntington Ave., Suite 612, Tel. 353-0556*, encourages contemporary classical music; at the other end of the spectrum, the **Boston Early Music Festival and Exhibition**, *PO Box 2632, Cambridge, Tel. 661-1812*, is an on-going season of concerts using instruments rarely seen or played in the last, say, 500 years.

The **Cantata Singers and Ensemble**, *PO Box 375, Cambridge, Tel. 267-6502*, is a 44-voice chorus, while the **Boston Aria Guild**, *Tel. 267-3029*, presents light opera and programs of operatic selections. An organization called **World Music**, *720 Mass. Ave., Cambridge, Tel. 876-4275*, presents performances of distinctive musical styles not normally heard in this country.

Boston Ballet, *19 Clarendon Street, Tel. 695-6955*, is a bright, well-rounded company, with a fall-to-spring season of 133 performances at the **Wang Center**, *290 Tremont Street near Stuart Street*, a vintage stage in the heart of the Theater District. The regular season stops in late November to make way for over 50 performances of *The Nutcracker*; Boston's rendition is the most popular ballet production in the world. In the regular season, the company of about 40 dances classics, such as *Giselle*, as well as "pop" ballets, based in modern music. Tickets typically range from $16 to $48. The **Dance Umbrella**, *380 Green Street, Cambridge*, is the city's leading contemporary dance troupe, presenting a variety of styles: sometimes childlike, sometimes amazing, sometimes just this side of burlesque, but always determinedly innovative.

The **Berklee School of Music**, *136 Mass. Ave., Tel. 266-1400,* is an admirable institution that has brought the discipline and thorough training of classical music to students of jazz and rock. The school's Performance Center, *136 Massachusetts Ave. near the Hynes Convention Center,* has two free recitals per day during the school year, at 4 and 7 pm.

TICKET TRICKS

BosTix is a non-profit ticket service representing practically every theater production and concert in the Boston area, in addition to some sporting events. Half-price tickets go on sale at 11 am on the day of performance. Both full-price and half-price tickets have to be cash transactions. **BosTix**, *Tel. 423-4454, does not do business by telephone, but has three locations. Kiosk at Copley Square: Monday-Saturday, 10 am-6 pm; Sunday, 11 am-4 pm; same hours for the kiosk at Faneuil Hall, except that it is closed Mondays. BosTix also has an outlet in Harvard Square. You can also call* **TicketMaster**, *Tel. 931-2787.*

For tickets to events otherwise sold out, check with concierges at the leading hotels. They can often locate last-minute tickets, even for non-guests.

THEATER

Boston theater tends to be more rusticated than its music. If New York theater isn't what it once was in the days of Merman and the Lunts, then Boston theater has slipped even more, because the shows starring the Lunts or Ethel Merman nearly always stopped in Boston first on the way to Broadway. Sometimes a new show comes through, but more often, the Shubert, the Wilbur or the Colonial handle national touring companies on their way out of New York and on their way to Syracuse.

The Huntington Theater, *264 Huntington Ave., Tel. 266-0800,* affiliated with Boston University, is consistently the best of the Boston-based repertory companies. Located just beyond the Back Bay on Huntington Ave., it does a good job in the hardest type of theater: bringing the audience to another place entirely, and into the presence of people who are real. The more believably such theater is presented, the less I know how it is done. The Huntington season runs from September to May.

American Repertory Theater, *The Loeb Center, 64 Brattle Street, Cambridge, Tel. 547-8300,* affiliated with Harvard in Cambridge, strives for a different type of theater, emanating more from the brain than heart, and typically laden with effects, with symbolic gestures and/or brazen casting. I always know how this type of theater is done: with big, onstage ideas. ART has a national reputation for bringing new things to theater, an endeavor with which I, for one, am not automatically sympathetic.

The Lyric Stage, *140 Clarendon near Copley Square,* presents comedies and musicals in the round, usually with an uneven but altogether energetic cast. The **Nora Theater**, *1208 Mass. Ave., Cambridge, Tel. 491-2026,* is a dauntless company, one with a social conscience that produces contemporary plays: often lesser-known works by famous playwrights. Emerson College has a strong drama department; student productions run at the **Studio Theater**, *69 Brimmer Street, Tel. 824-8000.* **The Hasty Pudding Theater**, *12 Holyoke St. in Harvard Square, Cambridge, Tel. 496-8400,* stages outright comedy productions; its most notable being the annual Hasty Pudding Theatrical, an original production from the boys at Harvard. **Improv Boston** is another comedy troupe in Cambridge, writing a new script as they go along, with every production at the **Back Alley Theater**, *1253 Cambridge Street, Cambridge, Tel. 576-1523.*

The Charles Playhouse, *74 Warrenton Street, Tel. 426-5225,* has a decided hit in the interactive murder-mystery, *Shear Madness,* which opened in 1980. Other productions that have taken root in Boston are: *The Late-Nite Catechism,* a frolic having something to do with nuns at the fortress-like **Church of All Nations** in the Theater District, *333 Tremont Street, Tel. 338-8606,* and *Joe and Maria's Comedy Wedding,* fake vows that include a real dinner, at the **Tremont Playhouse**, *Tremont House Hotel, 275 Tremont Street, Tel. 800/733-5639.*

GOINGS ON, ON CAMPUS

It's hard to say that "there's nothing to do," in Boston, providing that you can find you way to any one campus in the area. During a typical week at **MIT** – the Massachusetts Institute of Technology – these are just some of the events that were on the schedule – mind you, this is one week, taken at random – the MIT African Performance Ensemble, concert of traditional East African music; Tech Jazz Singers, concert; Arty Techy Show and Tell ("Bring slides, video, poetry ..."); MIT All-Women's a capella group, comedy show; Woman's Chorale Bach and Mozart program; Schubert's Birthday, concert by a soprano who is also a library assistant; Russian photography exhibit by the Navigator Foundation; *The Importance of Being Ernest*, at the Kresge Little Theater; Folk Dance Party, no experience/partner needed.

If you can't find something on that list, then you really ought to go to the Arty Techy Show and Tell – as an exhibit. The MIT campus along the Charles River is comfortable and fairly compact, and the atmosphere around it is just a bit *grateful* – they know they don't get as many visitors as that other college further down Massachusetts Avenue. Pick up a monthly schedule of the arts at the **MIT Museum**, *265 Mass. Ave., Cambridge, Tel. 253-4444.*

That other college down Mass. Ave. in Cambridge, Harvard, is a veritable candyshop of culture. A campus guide notes that students there produce over 80 plays each year and give over 350 concerts, in addition to dance recitals, readings, and various arts festivals. The campus is host to a professional theater group (see American Repertory Theater described in "Theater," above), but the students themselves are likely to do work that is as good or better.

The **Harvard-Radcliffe Dramatic Club**, *Tel. 495-2668*, stages four major plays per year and numerous other productions. The **Harvard-Radcliffe Orchestra**, *Tel. 496-6276*, plays at least four concerts per year. The **Fogg Art Museum**, *Tel. 495-4544,* sponsors an eclectic series of musical recitals, often presenting either obscure music or rare instruments. For schedules, call the Office of the Arts, *Tel. 495-8676.*

FILM

Speaking of Harvard, the **Harvard Film Archive**, *24 Quincy Street, Cambridge, Tel. 495-4700*, shows vintage, experimental, foreign, or merely

WE HAD THEATERS, THEN

Every week, Boston is host to about a half-dozen touring theatrical companies or individual artists. Yet the theaters that put up the road companies are often the best part of the show, a collection of beautiful old theaters that puts Boston in front of every other city in the country in this respect: so many other cities – even, to some extent, Broadway in New York – demolished the irreplaceable when they tore down their show-places. Thirteen theaters were built in Boston's Theater District between 1900 and 1935: nine are still standing and five are still lit for shows. The following list is an invitation to go inside during the day and take a look; you can also use the telephone numbers to see what's going on onstage.

The Charles Playhouse (1839) - 76 Warrenton Street, Tel. 931-2787. Constructed in the Greek revival style, the Charles was originally a church, one that included storefronts, in a practical churchly measure. It became a theater in the 1950s.

The Colonial (1900) - 106 Boylston Street near Tremont Street, Tel. 426-9366. A big, very beautiful gilt-edged theater filled with ghosts of Follies past, and facing the Public Garden.

Emerson Majestic (1903) - 219 Tremont Street near Stuart Street, Tel. 482-6661. Massive from the outside, the Majestic has a rococo interior, and is being restored by the latest owner, Emerson College.

The Shubert Theater (1910) - 246 Tremont Street near Stuart Street, Tel. 426-4520. Without a grand facade to announce it, the Shubert has presented most of great dramatic actors of the past 85 years.

The Wang Center (1925) - 290 Tremont Street near Stuart Street, Tel. 482-9393. The Wang was a movie palace, renovated into a legitimate stage in the early 1980s. Lavish marble and gilt interiors evoke 18th century France, or is it 1920s Hollywood. There are 3,700 seats.

The Wilbur (1912) - 246 Tremont Street near Stuart Street, Tel. 423-7440. A Colonial-style, brick building with (fake) paned-glass windows, the Wilbur looks more like a library than a theater. Very understated on the inside. There are 1.000 seats.

The Sanders Theater (1874) – located within Harvard University's Memorial Hall, Tel. 496-2222. The Sanders is a Victorian rendition of a Gothic stage. There are 1,200 seats.

good movies nearly every night of the week. The **Boston Public Library**, *Copley Square, Tel. 536-5400,* also shows vintage or foreign movies, on most Monday nights starting at 6 pm. The **Sony Nickelodeon** at Boston University, *34 Cummington Street, Tel. 424-1500,* and the **Kendall Square Cinema**, *1 Kendall Square, Cambridge, Tel. 494-9800,* both show those arthouse movies that make "arthouse," another word for "not quite so predictable."

AUTHOR-SIGNINGS, LECTURES, & READINGS

If you like to meet writers, check with the **Barnes & Noble BU Bookstore** *in Kenmore Square, Tel. 236-7421,* and the **Lauriat's Books** *in Copley Place, Tel. 828-8300*: they have the most active roster of authors parading through.

Lectures have long been a way of life of life in Boston, but not an unchanged one, as Edward Everett Hale related, looking back on the 1830s in his book *A New England Boyhood*: "A function which brought people together, and brought them together with older people, was the arrangement for evening lectures. These were much more familiar and homelike than the lectures of to-day, to which we go hardly with any idea of social enjoyment. But, as I mentioned, the 'march of intellect' had begun ..." The march continues and several of institutions sponsor regular lectures that are indeed intellectually bracing, without quite settling into the familiar or the homelike.

Among those worth checking are: **Harvard Museum of Cultural & Natural History**, *26 Oxford Street, Cambridge, Tel. 496-6972*; **Old South Meeting House**, *Washington and Milk streets, Tel. 482-6439,* and the **Museum of Fine Arts**, *465 Huntington Street, Tel. 267-9300.*

To see the mighty **Faneuil Hall** in use, not merely on display, stop by Sundays from 7 to 8:30 pm, when you can expect a regular open-mic poetry reading. Bring your own writing or just listen to the featured poet and the rest of the roster as it unfurls. The **Phoenix Coffeehouse**, *675 Mass. Ave., Cambridge, Tel. 547-2255,* also has an "Open Mic Poetry" session every Sunday night.

The **Literary Tour**, *Tel. 74-5950*, is a four-hour trolley ride that exposes riders to that bracing air in which Boston's best writers have moved. Among the eight stops are the Longfellow National Historical Site in Cambridge and Walden Pond in Concord. Tours run Saturdays starting at 9 am and 1:15 pm and Sundays, at 1:15 pm; the meeting place is the Omni Parker House, at School and Tremont streets, and the cost is $19.

ART GALLERIES

Many of Boston's public galleries are described in Chapter 11, *Seeing the Sights*, but here are some less-trafficked art galleries worthy of your attention.

The Institute of Contemporary Art, *955 Boylston Street, across from Hynes Convention Center, Tel. 266-5152*, looks rather quaint on the outside – a narrow brick building that was once a police station. Step inside, however, and all that is gone: replaced by tall space, lined in white. The Institute stages thoughtful exhibitions that launch current ideas in art into that tall space. The **Boston Center for the Arts**, *539 Tremont Street, Tel. 426-5000,* also specializes in modern shows and installations. The **Museum of the National Center of Afro-American Artists**, *300 Walnut Ave., Tel. 442-8614,* exhibits art in a wide variety of media; the shows there usually leave a strong impression. The **Art Institute of Boston**, *700 Beacon Street, Tel. 262-1223,* is a school, with unique exhibits, often of work that is both artistic and historical.

To start the grand tour of Newbury galleries – ones that actually sell artwork, in addition to displaying it – start with a pair of venerable, non-profit organizations, located almost next door to each other. They exhibit

WHAT'S ON AT THE GALLERIES?

ArtsMEDIA is a free monthly publication with exhibit reviews and coverage of the all the local galleries. It is available at most galleries, or call 451-1887.

art for its own sake – but you can still buy it. The **Copley Society**, *158 Newbury Street, Tel.* *536-5049*, came into being in 1878, to promote American fine arts; the **Guild of Boston Artists**, *162 Newbury Street, Tel. 536-7660*, was formed in reaction, to give local artists attention and encouragement. Both stage small shows of predictably high-quality work.

The **Vose Galleries**, *238 Newbury Street, Tel. 536-6176*, has been in business since the middle of the last century, representing first-rate artists, including, to name drop ... John Singer Sargent. It is set up almost as though it were a home, and the atmosphere is not much more formal or intimidating than a nice old house. The **Mercury Gallery**, *8 Newbury Street, Tel. 859-0054*, is also worth checking, the exhibitions are wide-ranging and well-handled.

The International Poster Gallery, *205 Newbury Strret, Tel. 375-0076*, is eye-catching even from the street – that's fitting, because the advertising posters within were meant to be bold. And many were meant for the street, in cities such as Paris, Milan, or Munich in the earlier years of this century. **Skinner/Boston**, *63 Park Plaza, Tel. 350-5400*, is an auction house that produces exhibits of specialized antiques or artwork; a recent showing, for example, was of antique toys.

LIBRARIES

The Rev. Jeremy Belknap wanted to spend all his time in the late 1700s studying history, but he couldn't find the sort of original sources he wanted: not books and articles, but letters, documents, ledgers, and so on. In 1791, he founded the first historical society in the New World, the **Massachusetts Historical Society**, *1154 Boylston Street, Tel. 536-1608*. A few years later, as he wrote to a friend, he was delighted with his "depository," and was no longer "waiting at home for things to fall into the lap, but prowling around like a wolf for the prey." Bringing a new edge to the gathering of material, the Society amassed a collection including the papers of John Winthrop, the first governor of the Massachusetts Bay Colony, and of the Adamses: John, Abigail, and Samuel, among others.

It has 3,200 such separate collections, pertaining to one person or family. It has Paul Revere's own recollections of his "Midnight Ride," most of Thomas Jefferson's architectural drawings and his farm notebooks, and Francis Parkman's original Oregon Trail Notebooks. Such items are not normally on display, but visitors can request a tour of the Society by calling in advance.

The Boston Athenaeum, *10 1/2 Beacon Street, Tel. 227-0270,* is also a relatively ancient institution, in a fortress of a building on upper Beacon Street. It is a private library and gallery, to which the general public is welcomed. Most libraries built recently have sacrificed close and quiet comfort for ... for whatever is good about an airline terminal. The Athenaeum smacks more of a quiet wing of the White House. It is composed of well-proportioned rooms, rich in architectural detail and sensible furniture. And remarkable art: works by Gilbert Stuart, John Singer Sargent, Chester Harding and others, most purchased new from the artists by the Athenaeum. You can stop in, just to look around by yourself, or make a reservation (which is required) for a guided tour. The Athenaeum's gallery stages regular exhibits of painting and sculpture, often pertinent to New England.

The **Boston Public Library**, *Tel. 536-5400, ext. 216,* is the anchor of Copley Square, in more than one respect. Reasons that I have gone there in the past month: 1. to find a specific copy of a certain magazine from 1848 (first floor); 2. to take two of my little relatives to use the most convenient public restrooms off of Copley Square (downstairs); 3. to meet a friend in the garden court (sitting comfortably in the soft air, reading and not caring so much to be kept waiting 25 minutes), and finally, 4. to see the famous John Singer Sargent murals, recently restored (third floor). I'd never before bothered to glance up at the work of my all-time favorite artist. There's obviously too much to do at the BPL. Free tours start in the Dartmouth Street (McKim) lobby: Sunday, 2 pm; Monday, 2:30 pm; Tuesday & Thursday, 6 pm; Friday-Saturday, 11 am.

Boston University has strong collections of theatrical and Hollywood memorabilia, and original literary manuscript material. The revolving exhibits in the front rooms at the **Mugar Library** often pertain to great personalities, while a permanent exhibit honors a great American, and BU alumnus, Dr. Martin Luther King, Jr.

A BOSTON CHRISTMAS IN THE YEAR 3OOO

It's no science fiction. These traditions will probably be going strong a thousand years from now:

Black Nativity - since 1969. A musical play presented by the National Center of Afro-American Artists. Weekends during December; Tel. 442-9289

A Child's Christmas in Wales - since 1975. The Lyric Stage recreates the small adventures of Dylan Thomas' world. Most of December; Tel. 437-7172.

Christmas Revels - since 1970. A celebration of the winter solstice, transported from Northwestern France through the centuries. Weekends toward the end of the month; Tel. 496-2222.

Christmas on the Boston Common - since 1950. An afternoon of trees-lighting at the beginning of the month; Tel. 635-4505

Handel's Messiah - every year since 1854. The Handel & Hadyn Society (Tel. 266-3605) first performed the great 1742 work in 1814 – when it wasn't even that old. In fact, they don't even call it "The Messiah." Look for "J.S. Handel's Christmas Oratorio," and you'll have the Handel & Hadyn Society. The performance, in two parts, runs at the beginning of December. Late in the year, though, Boston will hear at least ten various renditions of the same work, in part or whole. Some days, the sidewalks reverberate from all the "Hallelujahs" banging into each other in mid-air.

The Nutcracker - The Boston Ballet production is the most popular in the country, and packs them in at the Wang Center. End of November to beginning of January; Tel. 695-6955.

Prudential Tree Lighting - The spirit of Christmas is reflected in the story of both the tree and its lighting. During World War One, two ships, one carrying ammunition, collided in the harbor at Halifax, Nova Scotia. The explosion was holocaustal, killing over one thousand people. The first rescuers, laden with supplies, arrived at the desperate city on a fast train from Boston. Ever since, Nova Scotia has shown its unforgotten gratitude by sending a great Christmas tree. Since 1971, the tree has stood at the Prudential Center, lit with ceremony in early December.

15. SPORTS & RECREATION

"As the snow melted, and the elms blossomed, and the grass came,
the Common opened itself to every sort of game."
– ***Edward Everett Hale***, *writing of his boyhood in the 1820s*

SPECTATOR SPORTS

A great sports town is a noble entity, truly. Boston, like Cincinnati –
unlike New York – shows up in droves even during a losing season.
Winning feels better than losing, of course, even for a spectator, but that
isn't the point. In a great sports town, the point is simply that seeing sports
is better than not seeing sports.

However, the other side of the coin is that you would probably have
a better shot at getting tickets in a bad sports town. Used to Boston, I
became momentarily disoriented one time in Milwaukee, on being told
that box seats were still available for a ballgame starting within minutes.
That will never happen in Boston, where some of the boxseats for the
professional teams were not only sold before you got into line at the ticket
window, they were sold before you were born.

Sports are everything to Boston. The city may have named its new
multi-million dollar sports arena, "the Fleet Center," after a bank, but take
no notice of that. The same year, it turned around and named its new
multi-billion dollar tunnel after one of Boston's all-time great athletes,
Ted Williams.

DOT-COM: SPORTS INFORMATION

The regional sports channel, NESN, updates a website concerning sports events in Boston and throughout New England: www.nesn.com.

THE BIGS

Baseball

For six months each year since the spring of 1912, baseball has been played on the same ground at **Fenway Park**. If the soil were tested, it would have baseball in it. Other cities can build "retro-classic" ballparks, but they will never capture the peculiar charm of Fenway Park. And they will probably never try, either. The whole thing is a big green monster (as they call the leftfield wall), red-brick on the outside and all green and rather crooked on the inside.

Why, it's an engineering marvel. I often ponder – and often have the time to do it – how did the builders manage to block so much of the field from so many seats, with so few columns. It's a veritable Stonehenge of alignment. If you have grandstand tickets, my insider's tip is to go with someone who doesn't know anything at all about baseball, and put them in the seat – there's bound to be one – from which you can't see the pitcher ... they won't know. Keep in mind that the boxseats are all fine, it's the "grandstand" seats that can be troublesome – but also easier to come by. Bleacher seats, also unobstructed, are often available; they are located behind center field. Bring a telescope with which to see the batter and be apprised that the people who sit out there are not necessarily students of the game, and deport themselves only about as well as a person can with a beach ball about to bounce off their head.

There is talk of building a new stadium, mostly for the sake of the enclosed, corporate "skyboxes" it could include, but I predict in print that it will not happen. For Bostonians, Fenway Park is a favorite old dog. (I don't see why they don't build skyboxes at Fenway *underground*, and the corporate types inside each one could watch the game on a giant TV screen *disguised* as a window! ... they won't know.)

Fenway Park is located at the corner of Brookline Ave. and Yawkey Way. Tel. 267-1700; TDD, 236-6644, website, www.redsox.com. T: Kenmore. The Box Office is open during baseball season: Monday-Friday, and weekend gamedays, 9 am-5 pm. Cost: $26, boxseat; $18-24, grandstand; $12-14, bleachers.

Basketball & Hockey

The basketball **Bruins** and hockey **Celtics** play in the **Fleet Center**, which replaced another beloved old monster, the Boston Garden, in 1995. The sparkling new arena is well-planned, with an enormous parking garage (entry on Nashua Street). It also adjoins a T-stop and train depot, called the North Station. The area opposite Causeway Street from the North Station/Fleet Center has always been grizzled in appearance, though it is on its way up, under its old name again, the Bulfinch Triangle. Causeway Street from Portland to Canal is lined with Irish pubs, sports bars, and subshops.

FleetCenter recorded information: Tel. 624-1000. For Bruins tickets ($29-65), Tel. 624-1900; for Celtics tickets ($10-70), Tel. 523-6050.

Football & Soccer

The **Patriots** are a football. Oh, they are a football *team*, as you know, but they are also a political football, and the truth of this chapter is that New England's favorite sport of all is politics. No wonder the Patriots are always a big story. They used to play in Boston; now they play in Foxboro, a town to the southwest, chosen because it is equally inconvenient to both Boston and Providence, and Hartford to some extent.

The stadium at Foxboro would have looked old and miserable to Walter Camp; it is an array of stands (bought surplus from a high school in Texas, perhaps) overlooking a football field, with a muddy hill for a parking lot. For a long time, the Patriots were definitely going to move, just as soon as everyone with an opinion could agree on a new site. That being the case, they are going to be in Foxboro forever, so here is the telephone number for tickets, which range from $20-78: *Tel. 800/543-1776; schedule information, Tel. 508/543-3900.* To reach the stadium by public transportation, use the special MBTA train service; *call 800/392-6100 for schedules.*

The professional soccer team, the **New England Revolution** played its first game at Foxboro Stadium in 1996. The Major League Soccer season runs from April to September, *Tel. 508/543-0350.*

Horse Racing

Suffolk Downs is a perfect place. There are probably more charming racetracks in the country, such as Saratoga or Santa Anita – but they are not 20 minutes from Faneuil Hall. You can actually sneak out to Suffolk just for a few races, it's that convenient; I've nipped out waiting for a delayed flight at the airport, two T-stops away. The track was founded in the 1930s, and it has the traditional look of a big white house about it, natty with dark green trim. Whether you bet or not, you have close access to the ceremonies of the sport: the grooms walking the horses in the paddock; the owners and trainers giving their jockeys a leg up, and a few last-minute words; the man in the red coat with the horn, calling the horses to the race; the surge of muscle at the start; the flash of speed at the finish.

Horse racing is the most intricate of sports and yet the one that is easiest to understand. And Suffolk Downs makes it easy to enjoy, as well, with all kinds of options in seating and dining, indoors and out. Suffolk Downs is open everyday for telebetting (from television simul-casts of other racetracks), with a long live-racing season January to June and other times starting in autumn. The schedule, *Tel. 567-3900*, is something of a patchwork and the best thing to do is call.

Cost: grandstand, $2; clubhouse, $4. Senior citizens, half-price. Free parking available. T: Suffolk Downs. Stop is a quarter-mile from entrance: it is a pleasant walk, or instead, shuttle buses provide frequent service.

Other Spectator Sports

Never a dull minute, in an area with 60 colleges, where men's and women's teams play every known sport. **Harvard** football is always drenched in tradition, especially the Harvard-Yale game, if you can get a ticket. The hockey team is typically excellent. **Boston College** is a fun place to see a basketball game: and it's one of the few Big East venues where you'll find more students than boosters in the bleachers! Division

III **MIT** has absolutely no reputation in sports, yet it has teams in practically every one of them; crew is probably the most conspicuous. **Boston University** has been known to have a good football team, and the stadium is easily accessible, on campus between Commonwealth Ave. and Storrow Dr. (along the Charles River).

*University sports information: **Harvard**, Tel. 495-2211; **MIT**, Tel. 258-5265 (all events are free); **Boston University**, Tel. 353-4628; **Boston College**, Tel. 552-3000.*

The Boston Marathon

You have to watch the race, if you're in Boston on Patriot's Day (the third Monday in April) - a million and a half other people do. You certainly have to watch out, anyway: much of the Back Bay is completely immobilized on race day. The 26.2-mile course starts to the west of the city in a town called Hopkinton and enters Boston from Brookline; up Commonwealth Ave., a jog over Mass. Ave. to Boylston and then down to Copley Square, the finish line. That is the hotbed for race-watching, but since the racers keep on coming over a span of about four hours (and more), you can count on having an obstructed view sooner or later. *Call 236-1652 for information on entering or watching the Marathon.*

WHERE IT'S ALWAYS SPRING ...

The New England Museum of Sports, Cambridgeside Galleria, Tel. 621-0520, is filled like a locker overflowing with memorabilia and artwork pertaining to every aspect of the sporting life in the region. The Red Sox Hall of Fame is in a separate gallery at the back.

PARTICIPANT SPORTS

You can spend a weekend in the country within the city limits of Boston, going in for some sailing or canoeing, a river walk or tennis in the shadow of downtown.

Bicycling

At **Back Bay Bike**, *33 Newbury Street, Tel. 247-3336*, most of the bicycles go out for rental before 10:30 am. The rate is $20 per day, including lock and helmet. The store also rents rollerblades. **Community Bicycle Supply**, *490 Tremont Street, Tel. 542-8623*, rents bicycles from April to September at $20 per day, including the lock, but a helmet is $5 per day.

Canoeing

If you know the basics of paddling, and safety, rent a canoe from **Charles River Canoe & Kayak**, *2401 Commonwealth Ave., Newton, Tel. 965-5110*, or sign up with the company for a trip to a nearby body of water. Cost of canoe rental: $8 or $32 per day.

Fitness

Boston Sports Club, *561 Boylston Street, Tel. 536-1247*, extends single-day privileges to members of the International Health, Raquet and Sports Association.

Jogging

The **Esplanade** is flat, devoid of cars, and catches breezes from the Charles River alongside.

INDULGENCES

• ***The Spa on Newbury***, *38 Newbury Street, Tel. 859-7600. Everything from a four-layer facial of seaweed ($102, including tip) to a Swedish full massage for $46.80.*

• ***Giuliano***, *338 Newbury Street, Tel. 262-2220. Beauty salon and spa, where a "Day of Beauty" ($379, plus tip), includes a 1 1/2-hour facial, massage, body renewer, lunch, manicure, pedicure, hairdressing and make-up.*

Sailing

A non-profit organization called **Community Boating**, *Tel. 523-1038, website, www.sailing4all.org,* has been putting people on the water since 1946. A full season membership is $195, but visitors can take out a one-month membership for $65 and have access to sailboats, kayaks, and windsurfing, including instruction if desired. The boathouse is near the Hatch Shell on the Esplanade.

Skating

Boston Common Frog Pond, *on the Common.* New facility with 16,000 square feet of ice and a pavilion offering ice skate rentals and hot chocolate. Skating is free; skate rental is $3. Hours: Sunday, 10 am-9 am; Monday 10 am-5 pm; Tuesday-Thursday, 10 am-9pm; Friday-Saturday, 10am-10pm. *Call the Boston Parks Department at 635-4505.*

Tennis

Play at the courts on the Common. If there's a more exclusive country club than one that goes back to 1634, I don't know what it would be.

EDIBLE WILD PLANT CLASSES

Ever wanted to try that interesting looking plant as you're walking or hiking around? Professional environmentalist and wild foods enthusiast **Russell Cohen** *offers a series of three hour wild plant classes at various locations throughout the greater Boston area and New England. Russ will teach you which plants are no-no's and which are safe and tasty.*

For more information and schedules, send a self-addressed stamped envelope to Russell Cohen, 90 Everett Street, Arlington, MA 02174, or you can call him at Tel. 646-7489.

16. SHOPPING

Boston stores have sorted themselves out into fairly dependable enclaves. To list them in a certain order:

For Items that You ...

	Go to ...	Such stores as ...
Really Need	**Downtown Crossing**	Filene's, Woolworth's
Sort Of Need	**Copley/Pru**	Sak's, Radio Shack
Sort of Want	**Faneuil Hall**	Disney, CelticWeavers
Really Want	**Newbury Street**	Louis, Teuscher Chocolates

To explain further, **Downtown Crossing** is the shopping district of downtown Boston, arrayed around a brick-paved pedestrian mall at the intersection of Winter, Summer and Washington streets. On noondays in the summer, the mall is usually a happenin'. Music acts or fashion shows set up in the middle somewhere and the police horses stand patiently to the side while gobs of people gather to watch whatever is put before them. In terms of shopping, Downtown Crossing is anchored by well-appointed department stores such as **Macy's** and **Filene's** (an entity separate from **Filene's Basement**). **Woolworth's** is there, and so is a large **CVS** pharmacy, a **Barnes & Noble** and an **HMV** record shop.

Small jewelry shops line West Street and fill the nearby **Boston Jeweler's Exchange**, *333 Washington Street*. And the famous Boston discount store, **Filene's Basement**, is at the intersection of Washington and Summer streets, across the street from a New York interloper, **Loehmann's**, *385 Washington Street*.

The **Prudential Center** opened in the 1960s with a slip of an indoor shopping center (nobody knew the word, "mall," then) that seemed mighty indulgent to a hardened race of Bostonians. Then **Copley Place** opened in the 1980s, a full-fledged shopping experience, and a two-level mall with boutiques, department stores and that hallmark of the good life, an atrium. In the 1990s, the Prudential renovated itself into top dog, again, a brassy, classy mall with a food court. Copley hasn't been quite as smug since then: one tip-off being that the stores have been flying around from location to location inside as though they were as easy to move as badminton birdies. You decide where the great rivalry stands, the two shopping centers are connected by a skywalk over Huntington Ave.

The Prudential Center line-up of about 45 stores includes a number of national chains, including Levi's, Warner's and the Body Shop, in addition to a post office. Copley Place's big hitters are Neiman-Marcus, Tiffany, and Louis Vuitton, though the upper floor smacks of any mall around the country.

The situation at **Quincy Market** (or "Faneuil Hall Marketplace," as it is sometimes called in the overall sense) is also more and more of an "any mall," with national chains more than happy to adapt themselves to a place that draws over 14 million people in an average year. On one hand, it's tremendous to see such an old space still in the same practical use for which it was built one-hundred-and-seventy years ago. On the other hand, it's a shame to see it become just another galleria, with its Disney, its Victoria's Secret, its Crate & Barrel and Swatch. The battle is far from lost, with Kites of Boston, Boston Cooks, and the Museum of Fine Arts stores still speaking up for one city at a time.

I have seen **Newbury Street** called the "Rodeo Drive" of Boston. It is certainly home to some pretty high-powered stuff in the first block from Arlington Street, where **Cartier**, **Bang & Olufsen**, and **Giorgio Armani** stare down the Ritz. But Newbury Street has seven blocks to go after that, before Mass. Ave. cuts off the shopping spree, and the stores are more to be heralded for their individuality than for their prices.

It is the variety that makes Newbury a street of shopkeeping, not mere retailing. The galleries are profuse, especially from Dartmouth to Gloucester streets. More and more, Newbury Street is going vertical: be sure to look up while you're window-shopping; many boutiques are locating up one flight.

BOSTON SALES TAX

*The sales tax in Boston is **five percent**, but it doesn't apply to clothing valued up to $175, or to food, except in restaurants.*

ANTIQUES

On Beacon Hill, **Charles Street** has upwards of seventy-five antique shops, including a few on the side streets. It is a charming setting, no doubt; the Charles River peeking through at one end and the Common all the way down at the other end of the shopping stretch of Charles. Sometimes I think there are too many antique stores – doesn't anyone on Beacon Hill need paint? Or hair curlers?

Near North Station, the **Boston Antique Center**, *54 Canal Street, Tel. 742-1400*, is a collection of over 100 high-powered dealers, specializing in furniture and the decorative arts. For browsers, the **Cambridge Antique Market**, *201 Mnsr. O'Brien Highway, Cambridge, Tel. 868-9655*, runs the gamut of price and category, with over 150 dealers and an active turnover of merchandise. In addition, there is a little tea-shop on the fourth floor, open on weekends. The **Minot Hall Antique Center**, *1721 Washington Street, at Massachusetts Avenue, Tel. 236-7800, minothall@aol.com*, is another bazaar and quite an elegant one, with over a hundred dealers in a restored Victorian building in the South End.

The **Skinner Auction Gallery**, *63 Park Plaza, Tel. 350-5400*, has grown in a short time to be the third-largest auction house in the country, specializing in art, antiques, and jewelry.

BOOKS

If you are looking for a certain book, and you can't find it somewhere within a whisper of Harvard Square, you ought to double-check that it has been written. There are over 30 bookstores there, and most of them make a strong effort to stock unusual or small-press books, in addition to mainstream titles.

The **Harvard Coop**, *1400 Mass Ave., Tel. 499-2000*, was the first college cooperative-bookstore in the country, founded because private booksellers were taking advantage of students in need of sweatshirts. No, sweatshirts and souvenirs came later, but the Harvard Coop is still an expansive bookstore, completely open to the public. Officially, it is the Harvard/MIT Coop, with a number of other outlets on both campuses. **WordsWorth**, *30 Brattle Street, Cambridge, Tel. 354-5201*, is an overstuffed shop, which promises to discount nearly every title. **The Harvard Book Store**, *1256 Mass. Ave., Cambridge, Tel. 661-1515*, is a dignified store that sells both new and used books.

WGBH Learningsmith, *25 Brattle Street, Cambridge, Tel. 661-6068*, sells any title that pertains directly or even glancingly to Public Television shows.

Back in Boston, the **Visitor Information Center**, *corner of State and Devonshire, Tel. 242-5642*, operated by the National Park Service, sells books on every aspect of the city of Boston and its history; many of them would be hard to fine elsewhere.

As to used book stores, I know of more of them in Boston than supermarkets. **Brattle Books**, *9 West Street, Tel. 542-0210 or 800/447-9595*, is a famous old shop, with two stories and an interesting annex next door: on clear days in winter or summer, they fill part of the empty lot there with bookscases of yet more books. **Commonwealth Books**, *134 Boylston Street, Tel. 338-6328*, affiliated with three used book stores in the South, has a comfortable shop worth visiting. The sign outside refers to "scholarly books." I found that intimidating at first, as if they might someday accuse

BOOK WORLDS

BOOKS PERTAINING TO...	BOOKSTORE
African-American life and history	*Treasured Legacy,* Copley Place, Tel. 424-8717
Computers, Math, Science, Engineering, Business	*Quantum Books,* 4 Cambridge Street, Kendall Square, Tel. 494-5042
Genealogy, New England history	*New England Historic Genealogical Society,* 101 Newbury Street, Tel. 536-5740
Government	*U.S. Government Bookstore,* 10 Causeway, Tel. 720-4180
Mysteries	*Kate's Mystery Books,* 2211 Mass. Ave., Tel. 491-2660
Swedenborg, Philosophy	*Swedenborg Bookstore* 79 Newbury Street, Tel. 262-5918
Travel	*Globe Corner Bookstores* 500 Boylston Street, Tel. 859-8008; 1 School Street (Old Corner Bookstore) on the Freedom Trail, Tel. 523-6658

me of buying books without having a doctorate. The selection inside is well-rounded, though, with literature, artbooks, travel, history and most of the usual categories. I think that "scholarly" is supposed to mean that there aren't too many romance paperbacks in the store. **Avenue Victor Hugo Books** is in the Back Bay, *339 Newbury Street, Tel. 266-7746,* selling bright greeting cards and a variety of second-hand books in the company of a big cat.

CHOCOLATE & CANDY

Teuscher, *230 Newbury Street, Tel. 536-1922*, sells chocolates from Switzerland. Not ones that people made over there a few months ago. The nougats, truffles, and bon-bons for sale at Teuscher were made on the same day, somewhere in the Alps, and shipped by jet to be eaten fresh in Boston. "Oh, come on," you say, "Shouldn't jet technology be put to better use than that?" My friends who love chocolate do not have to waste an instant thinking about their answer. A half-pound box costs about $25.

Dairy Fresh Candies, *57 Salem Street in the North End, Tel. 742-2639*, is a whole shop piled with packages of candy, nuts, and dried fruit. There are two rooms, side by side, bulging with goodies, both familiar (imported chocolates) and exotic (dried peas). The store has been in the business since 1957 and has learned at least one thing about how to sell candy: put it within reach.

CLOTHES

In women's clothes, **OKW** is a Boston company that creates a bright, but classic look. *The shop is located upstairs at 234 Clarendon Street.*

Did you come to Boston for cowboy clothes? Try **Walker's**, *122 Boylston Street, Tel. 423-9050*. For one-stop hip shopping in clothing and accessories, **Urban Outfitters**, *361 Newbury Street, Tel. 236-0088*, is a two story education in What's Coming. You get a little younger just looking in the windows every so often. Urban Outfitters also has a location in Cambridge.

Celtic Weavers, *North Market, Quincy Market*, imports contemporary and traditional clothes from Ireland. **Louis, Boston**, *234 Berkeley Street*, sells the finest clothes and shoes from makers all over the world. John F. Kennedy Jr. is a good customer, so they say. It is quite a large store, in the old Museum of Natural History building.

Those used to skiing or scuba diving might have looked upon running as a nice, simple sport, in which the only equipment necessary was a large-size inclination to go somewhere. However, **Bill Rodgers**, the marathoner, has disproved that notion flagrantly, filling a whole shop at Faneuil Hall (North Market) with all the stuff needed to be as fast as he is: from lightweight waterbottles and radios to special balm to keep your skin from chafing. There are also shorts, tops and sneakers in abundance. Of course, one can also walk 26 miles, 385 yards and most of us do, eventually. Down the row in North Market, the **Rockport Shoes "Concept"** store has shoes just for that. The concept, which includes free foot massages, is that feet need help getting through life, too, and comfortable shoes are a start.

FOOD

The Italian section doesn't have grocery stores – it has salumeria (delicatessens, more or less), and *rosticceria* (butcher shops), and other specialty stores. **Salumeria Toscana**, *272 Hanover Street*, is a spanking clean little deli, with a whole section devoted to olive oil, virgin olive-oil, extra-virgin olive oil; and someday, soon, perhaps oil from olives that haven't been born yet. Around the corner at **Pace**, the couple of aisles are stocked with imported groceries, and the deli sells especially good cold cuts. For those who want to shop the Italian North End in the company of a specialist, Michele Topor offers a three hour Market Tour on Wednesdays and Saturdays *(Cost is $35; Tel. 523-6032)*. Another classic little food store in Boston is **Savenors**, *160 Charles Street, Tel. 723-6328.*

I used to hunt all over Cape Cod for a tangy delicacy of the shore, wild beach-plum jelly. I'd find it in quaint country stores and overpriced gift shoppes, and then one day I noticed it on the shelf at **Star Market** for about half the price, or $2.89. The Star Market, *tucked under the Prudential Center, Tel. 262-4688,* is the only supermarket in the Back Bay, a big store that is open 24 hours a day, except weekend nights. The sandwiches from the deli are big for a good price; they will form the basis of a robust picnic on the Esplanade.

The Bread & Circus, *15 Westland Ave., Tel. 375-1010* (and other locations), has a pronounced respect for healthy foods and ferrets out locally grown and cottage-made products. It is also a walking seminar on

HOW TO EAT IN QUINCY MARKET - A BATTLE PLAN

Intelligence Report:

Quincy Market has a food court in the Colonnade Building, serviced by over 30 specialty stands, nearly all of them local in origin. Baked goods and beef sandwiches of one sort or another dominate an eclectic field that also includes plenty of chowder, pizza, and Asian food. However, making a choice is only half the task. Much of the time, and always on weekends, the groundfloor seating area for the food court stays full, and so does the one upstairs. Besides that, to bring food back to a (you hope) table, you have to negotiate through a dense forest of bumpy elbows.

Plan of Attack:

*• It is legal to take food off the Quincy Market premises, after all, so if you have your meal packaged for take-away at the food court, you can walk about five minutes to the east to **Christopher Columbus Park**, a large patch of grass on the Harbor. Just walk under the ugly Central Artery and you will have a beautiful place to sit, either on one of the benches or on the grass.*

*• Quincy Market has about a dozen restaurants, the kind at which you sit down and let someone else drag the food around. After you see how long the wait is at **Durgin-Park**, try **Zuma's Tex-Mex Cafe**. It has a lot of seating in the basement, which is, admittedly, devoid of the Quincy Market atmosphere – which might be taken as a good point on a very crowded day. By the way, one way to get into Durgin, even when the line for tables wends down the stairs, is to go to the bar and ask if you can have a table on the third floor. The third-floor dining room is small and rather quiet, but it is sometimes relatively empty because most people want the full Durgin charm of the second-floor dining rooms. Sometimes the bartender can make arrangements for you.*

food production, with signs and brochures on such subjects as "Produce Waxes."

GALLERIES

The Society of Arts and Crafts has been around for over a hundred years, trying to stay on the new side of old ways. The folk crafts sold are contemporary, not vintage, and they are an appealing step away from anything seen elsewhere. The Society has two shops: *101 Arch Street downtown, Tel. 345-0033, and 175 Newbury Street, Tel. 266-1810.*

Sometimes **Just Africa**, *201 Newbury Street, Tel. 536-1648*, sells sculpture and paintings, sometimes new fashions in a showcase of a specific designer. There are antique prints by the drawer-full at **Haley & Steele**, *91 Newbury Street, Tel. 536-6339.*

GIFTS

I have been in many a museum that was not half the size of the gift shop, alone, at the **Museum of Fine Arts**, *465 Huntington Ave., Tel. 369-3575.* It offers a depthful selection of art books, in addition to scarves, bags, replica pictures and sculptures, cards and jewelry. The latter – that is, everything but the books on Delacroix's middle years – is also sold at four other MFA shops, including one at Copley Place and one at Faneuil Hall. They may go even further than the original in presenting unexpected ideas for housegifts, toys for children, and offbeat souvenirs of Boston, or ancient Luxor.

The **Women's Educational and Industrial Union**, *356 Boylston Street, Tel. 536-5651,* is a charitable foundation, well over a hundred years old, that helps to support itself with an eclectic store. The finest antique grandfather clock I've seen in Boston was for sale here, next to a table of handknitted children's wear and a rack of fairly conventional greeting cards. The antiques are on the second floor, while the first floor has many handmade Yankee items, and even candy ... the best part of the WEIU being not what you take home, but that you leave a few dollars behind ($6,500 in the case of that clock) for a good cause.

FOR THE HOUSE

Lou-Lou's, *121 Newbury Street, Tel. 859-8593*, has locations elsewhere, but it seems like a one-of-a-kind place – specifically, the service pantry of the *Queen Mary*. The shop is piled with chinaware copied exactly – or bought surplus – from great ocean-liners, hotels, and other institutions. Some are long gone; in fact, most of the ships are. The appeal is half nostalgia and half terrific design. Lou-Lou's also sells authentic, original miscellany from the days of grand travel.

Sweet Pea's, *Clarenden Street*, is another flavor entirely – the flavor of chitlin's, hominey grits, and sweet peas. The store sells furnishings in a fanciful, rustic look that I'd describe as Appalachian nouveau.

JEWELRY

Shreve, Crump & Low, *330 Boylston, corner of Arlington Street, Tel. 267-9100*, has changed its name and location since it sold its first bangle in 1796, but nonetheless, for a long time it called itself the oldest continuously operating jewelry store in North America. Then someone got to thinking, and did some research, and now it is even more expansive, calling itself the oldest luxury-goods store on the continent.

The company does sell more than jewelry, though the first floor is filled with cases showing that. It sells china, silverware, and – to sum up – anything that you could possibly give to anyone as a wedding gift. It also sells antiques in a corner of the third floor, an offering of Federal-era furniture that is equal to anything in the city. Shreve, Crump & Low has been closely connected with the city's history, through the 19th century tradition of rewarding public citizens with weighty amounts of silver formed into a loving cup – or, in the case of a presentation piece given to Cy Young in 1907, a loving baseball.

MAGAZINES

The first floor of **Tower Records**, *360 Newbury Street, Tel. 247-5900*, is devoted largely to magazines, from *Woman's Day* to tiny journals in translation of obscure foreign poetry, to counter-counter-revolutionary readings to glossies about foreign sports cars. In between the extensive racks are books related to music or counter-culture.

Out of Town Newspapers, a kiosk (as is indicated by its address, *Zero Harvard Square, Tel. 354-7777*), sells out-of-country and out-of-hemisphere periodicals as well. Most people like to browse through magazine racks; personally, I don't like to look for titles where browsers are in the way. The place for grumps like me is the outdoor installation known as **Copley Square News**, *corner of Dartmouth and Boylston streets*, where service prevails and the clerks will personally hand over any title named.

MODELS

The **Lannan Ship Model Gallery**, *540 Atlantic Ave., corner of Congress Street, Tel. 541-2650*, takes up a large corner storefront. Ships fill the windows: intricate model ships of clippers, sloops, and other sailing vessels. The store has a large collection of paintings, too, and related items, but it is only open by appointment. If you are in the market for nautical antiques, you can call. If not, you can at least take a good look in the window and see if you'd like to be in the market.

MUSIC

Tower Records, *corner of Mass. Ave. and Newbury Street*, is only a block from the Berklee School of Music, and a few more to the New England Conservatory of Music. Emerson and BU are in the other direction. Braced by so many people who are serious about the performing arts, Tower has a complete inventory in practically every category of music. Where other stores pay only glancing attention to jazz or classical music, Tower has large rooms devoted to each, and I doubt there is any type of music that it ignores.

NOSTALGIA

Orpheus, *362 Commonwealth Ave., Tel. 247-7200*, sells second-hand records, compact discs, books, and autographs related to the performing arts. Its specialty is classical music and the theater. One street over, the **Nostalgia Factory**, *336 Newbury Street, Tel. 236-8754*, sells the material that advertised the movies, music, and theater in this century. Movie posters in the window will usually catch your eye as you pass the shop, located down a short flight of steps.

SOUVENIRS

Of all the souvenir shops at the attractions in Boston, the best one overall is at the **USS Constitution Museum**, *Charlestown Navy Yard, Tel. 426-1812*. While many of the goods are nautical, about half pertain to Boston in general, and the merchandise is uniformly of good quality. Among the more novel items are chunks of the actual, original *Constitution;* pieces discarded during reconstruction, they cost about $5 each. When it comes to chunks of wood, the gift shop at the **Old North Church**, *Tel. 523-4848*, has one that isn't for sale: an actual chip of the actual tree under which George Washington took command of the American army July 3, 1775. It's a good little gift shop, the back half of which is turned over to displays on colonial life.

For sports geegaws, The **Souvenir Store**, *19 Yawkey Way, Tel. 421-8686 or 800/336-9299*, is a bazaar with items ranging in price from one dollar to $300 for an autographed photo of Ted Williams. All of Boston's sports teams are represented, with the emphasis on baseball. You can buy a different style of Red Sox hat for every day in the month, without repeating once. Closer to downtown, the **Boston Bruins Pro Shop**, *North Station, Tel. 523-5242*, carries souvenirs and autographed merchandise from all of the local teams.

STATIONERY

Crane's, *Prudential Center, Tel. 247-2822*, is an old Massachusetts company that makes stationery that you can buy custom-made and printed, or in boxes off the rack. The art directors must have a sharp eye for color, because some of the combinations of ink and paper invite writing, as no plain piece of paper does. Since Crane's produces the paper on which US currency is printed, it carries a line of writing paper made out of the thoroughly shredded remains of old or rejected bills: it's that certain shade of green.

HOW QUINCY MARKET CAME TO LIFE

Faneuil Hall Marketplace consists of six buildings, one of which is Faneuil Hall itself, a historic meetingplace where retail stalls are confined to the first floor, just as they were in the mid-18th century. In those days, Faneuil Hall looked out on a trashy section of the waterfront. In the 1820s, however, Boston had a brilliant mayor, Josiah Quincy, Sr., who had the area graded as the site for an elegant new markethouse, flanked by two complementary warehouses. Long known as the Quincy Market, the North Market, and South Market, they were vital to the city for well over a hundred years.

But they fell into disrepair and were practically empty by the 1960s; Durgin-Park was a lonely hold-out against what seemed to be the inevitable demolition of the hulks. In April 1968, architect Ben Thompson was preparing a talk that would make Quincy Market symbolic of the desolation of the city – of all cities. Then Martin Luther King Jr. was assassinated. The next day, Thompson felt that he had to change his attitude, rewriting the speech overnight. As he told the Boston Globe in 1995, "I believed there was a critical need in cities – by no means in Boston alone – to reassert values of urban life and preserve urban quality and beauty on a human scale." He instigated the idea of reinterpreting Quincy Market's original use, renovating it into a collection of small shops and dining places – a modern marketplace. Enlisting the support of Mayor Kevin White and mall-developer James Rouse, Thompson oversaw the project until its opening day, August 26, 1976. Soon after, two more buildings, Marketplace Center and the Flower Market, completed the Faneuil Hall Marketplace, and dozens of imitations around the country have continued ever since to reverse that attitude so prevalent in 1968, that American cities were without hope.

But as you walk around, see if you can hear the point that Thompson made when he returned to Quincy Market in 1995: "It's run by a mall developer, applying mall principals to what was meant to be a more delicate environment."

TOYS

The giftstore at the **Museum of Science**, *Science Park, Tel. 723-2500*, is crammed with unique playthings and educational games. You need not pay admission to the museum itself to go into the store.

FAO Schwartz, *440 Boylston Street, Tel. 262-5000*, has separate boutiques within the store for each licensed character to wend its way into childhood in the past generation of more. Barbie is there in force, but many of the others are based on books, such as Madelene or Curious George, and offer related toys and costumes. The marketing zeal is overwhelming at FAO Schwartz – as is the never-ending rendition of "It's a Small World, After All."

For toys that are just toys, and not licensees, go to **No Kidding! A Toy Store**, *19 Harvard Street, Brookline, Tel. 739-2477*, where you can explore completely different kinds of toys.

THE FILENE'S BASEMENT GAME

*Edward Filene's original idea in 1909 was to operate his bargain basement as a reverse auction. If an item did not sell upstairs in the department store for $20, he would put it out down in the Basement for, say, $10. The item received a tag showing the price and the date. If it remained in the table after 14 days, it was automatically marked down by 25 percent, and cost $7.50. After 21 days, it was automatically marked down again, to half, or $5. After 28 days, it slipped by another 25 percent, and cost $2.50. And after four weeks, the item went to charity. Whether it was a pair of grey socks or a sable stole, it went to charity. The store has two floors, selling (in order of quantity, men's, women's and children's clothing and shoes; jewelry; linens; housegifts; furs; perfume; luggage; gourmet food, and travel. **Filene's Basement**, 426 Washington Street, Tel. 348-7974, is completely independent of the **Filene's Department Store** upstairs.*

The original pricing system still prevails today, though the talk of the racks, among the hardened customers, is that the store is changing Edward Filene's original rules. In the first place, many items are going out onto the racks without dates on the tags. No dates: no automatic markdown. The place is becoming a regular discount store. Second, many of us have good reason to suspect that the store goes around and puts new dates on certain items, to keep them from automatically marking-down too far. We, who go often to Filene's Basement, play this game very seriously. If you only go on one day, you may not notice these troubling trends, but keep these tips in mind:

• Once you have picked out an item, hunt around for the same exact item with an earlier date.

• If an item is four weeks past its original date, you don't get it free. You pay 25 percent of the amount on the price tag ($2.50, in the example above), but you have to pay it in cash at the "charity desk." The store will donate the money to whatever charity you chose, from a long list of them, and the item will be non-returnable.

• Ask at almost any cashier-stand and the store will loan you a big, sturdy, plastic bag to use as you go around gathering items, perchance to buy.

• The store normally opens at 9 am, but on special sale days, the time may be earlier. Check either of Boston's daily newspapers.

17. EXCURSIONS & DAY TRIPS

Just drive in any direction from Boston. If you have the spirit of exploration, you will find a reason to have gone exactly there: a vista across a rocky shore, a schoolhouse museum, a roadside pie-stand. You may not know in advance what it is that you'll find, but here is exactly how to get there: add the two digits of your birthday; go that many miles from your parking place in Boston via any road at all; turn right at big trees, left at pine trees, and straight past all the others.

That's as good a route as any for a Sunday drive in New England. Don't worry about getting lost. I'm more worried that you won't, unless you take care to pay attention to all the wrong things.

DAY TRIPS
Lexington & Concord

"Stand your ground. Don't fire unless fired upon. But if they mean to have a war, let it begin here."

A minuteman named John Parker spoke those words the night the British troops tried to pass **Lexington** on their way to confiscate ammunition stores in Concord. Today, there is a vivid statue of Parker, the quintessential Minuteman, on the **Lexington Green**. Every April, the battle is re-enacted: about 70 Americans against about 700 British.

Lexington is a charming village, still lightly gathered around the green. The 18th century houses of those Minutemen are marked with

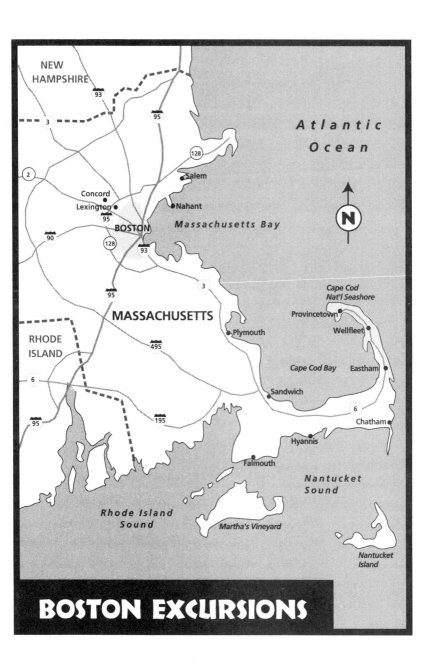

BOSTON EXCURSIONS

small signs, so you know how it was, the night the patriots rushed out to protect their green in the middle of the night. The shopping district is only a few blocks long, but it has several good places to eat. **The Museum of Our National Heritage**, *33 Marrett Rd., Tel. 861-6559*, does not stand still – any more than our national heritage does, in fact. Its revolving exhibits are well-staged and can cover any subject from Negro League baseball to the Irish Famine to cocktail shakers.

Concord is slightly bigger than Lexington, built around a slightly smaller green. It is another unspoiled New England village, with many sites of both military and literary significance. The American resistance at the Old North Bridge turned the much larger British force back in defeat. Rangers from the nearby **Minuteman National Park** give talks at the bridge through the day in the summer and on weekends in spring and fall. The National Park, *174 Liberty Street, Tel. 508/369-6993*, is open April to November. The **Concord Museum**, *200 Lexington Rd., Tel. 508/369-9609*, envelops the entire history of the region, from the Indians through the battle through the Transcendentalists who made a capital out of Concord. It has an extensive collection of antiques, many of which belonged to the famous people who lived in the area: Thoreau's bed, for example, the one that he slept on when he was living in a hut on Walden Pond.

The writers who made Concord their home in the 1840s and 1850s knew each other, and so each historic home related to their way of life usually includes references to more than one figure. Ralph Waldo Emerson grew up in **The Old Manse**, *269 Monument Street, Tel. 508/369-3909*, for example, which had belonged to his grandfather originally – but for three years, he rented it to his friend Nathaniel Hawthorne. Nathaniel was not a perfect tenant ... as you can see, he etched on the windows, as a matter of fact. Louisa May Alcott's home, **Orchard House**, *399 Lexington Rd., Tel. 508/369-4118*, is relaxed, even as it was when the imaginative Alcott family lived there.

The **COLONIAL INN**, *48 Monument Square*, has been rambling along for over a hundred and fifty years – when the Transcendentalists got hungry, they surely stopped in. It has been buffed up recently, so it no longer has its old, creaky charm: now the two-story, clapboard inn is quite swank. The bar is adorably little, the dining rooms are small and profuse, and the food is unashamedly American.

Directions: Take Storrow Drive west to Fresh Pond Parkway, following the signs for Rt. 2 west, which leads to Lexington and Concord.

Nahant

The first scheduled ferry service out of Boston went back and forth to the island of **Nahant**, about 12 miles up the coast. Actually, Nahant is not an island, but is connected to the shore by a causeway. And actually, there are two Nahants: Big and Little. Little is crowded with homes, but Big Nahant is a gentle little town, spread out over a ... a peninsula that looks like an island.

From the mainland, at the town of Lynn, Nahant offers wide and sandy beaches. Further up the hill, there are great homes dating from the early 19th century. In about 1820, developers spread rumors of a sea monster off of Nahant. No one ever saw the beast, but day-trippers keep coming to this day, though the boat from Boston is long since stopped. If you are driving, make a pit stop at **KELLY'S DRIVE-IN**, *Route 1A in Revere Beach*, for a picnic bundle of roast beef sandwiches, hot dogs, fish, or french fries.

Directions: Go through the Callahan Tunnel and follow Rt. 1A north to the Nahant traffic circle just north of the city of Lynn.

Salem

Salem is a little city – the game *Monopoly* is made in Salem by the Parker Brothers. For visitors, the **Peabody-Essex Museum** alone is worth the trip, *East India Square, Tel. 508/745-9500*; it is an excellent explanation of the sea-trade that made Boston great, focusing especially on imports from China. The collections were actually started in 1799 by the East India Marine Society, so they are, if nothing else, authentic. The **Salem Witch Museum**, *Washington Square, Tel. 508/744-1692*, is a popular attraction that tries to explain how fear ruled Salem at the end of the 17th century.

The National Park Service in Salem conducts tours of the historic waterfront, *Tel. 508/740-1660*, and **The House of Seven Gables**, *54*

Turner Street, Tel. 508/744-0991, is supposed be the one that Hawthorne used as the model for the one in his great book of the same same. The museum includes other early buildings, as well, including Hawthorne's own birthplace.

Directions: Go through the Callahan Tunnel and follow Rt. 1A north to Salem.

Plymouth

In the earliest days of New England, a plantation was not a big private farm, as it was later in the American South. It was a money-making community, somewhere between a corporation and a colony. **Plimouth Plantation**, *PO Box 1620, Plymouth, 02362, Tel. 508/746-1622 or 800/262-9356*, recreates the world of the Pilgrims in an open-air museum that shows how they lived and worked. In Plymouth, a small city, you can, of course, see the actual, exact, for-real **Rock** upon which the Pilgrims first stepped. At least, someone in about 1810 said it was the exact rock. The *Mayflower II* was built in the 1950s, and actually sailed across the Atlantic, on the route used by the Pilgrims; it is also worth a visit.

Directions: Take Rt. I-93 south from the center of Boston; it divides at Braintree, then take Rt. 3 to Plymouth.

Whale Watching

Twenty-seven miles east of Boston, the water pushes up nutrients from the ocean floor on the StellWagen Bank. That draws plankton and little fish. That draws whales. And that draws humans. Over two dozen types of whales have been spotted there, but the most common are the **humpback**, at a length of about 45 feet, and the **finback**, at about 75 feet. After spending their winters in the Caribbean, they summer off New England and Nova Scotia, and whale-watching boats go out from May to October. They leave from Boston or other seaside towns, and the tours take from 4 to 6 hours. The cost per person ranges from $20-25.

Reservations are advised: the same whales that supported a thriving industry (of killing them) hundreds of years ago are supporting yet another one today, just in getting close to them.

I have included as many companies as possible, in case reservations are hard to come by on the date you require:

From Boston
- **A.C. Cruise Lines**, *290 Northern Ave., Tel. 261-6633, 800-422-8419.* Also service to Gloucester.
- **Bay State Cruise Co.**, *Long Wharf and Commonwealth Pier, Tel. 723-7800.* Also cruises to the Boston Harbor islands and Cape Cod.
- **Boston Harbor Cruise**, *One Long Wharf, Tel. 227-4321.* Also harbor, historic and other cruises, 20 per day.
- **Boston Harbor Whale Watch**, *50 Rowes Wharf, Suite 430, Tel. 345-9866*
- **New England Aquarium Whale Watch**, *Central Wharf, Tel. 973-5277.* Also education harbor cruises.

From Cape Cod
On Cape Cod, the whale-watches are usually shorter in duration and cost around $15 per person:
- **Cape Cod Cruises**, *Fisherman's Wharf, Provincetown, Tel. 508/747-2400, 800-225-4000*
- **Dolphin Whale Watch**, *MacMillan Wharf, Provincetown, Tel. 508/349-1900*
- **Hyannis Whale Watcher**, *Millway Marina, Barnstable Harbor, Tel. 508/362-6088, 800-287-0374*
- **Portugese Princess**, *MacMillan Wharf, Provincetown, Tel. 508/487-2651, 800-442-3188*
- **Provincetown Whale Watch**, *MacMillan Wharf, Tel. 508/487-1582, 800-992-9333*

From Gloucester
- **Cape Ann Whale Watch**, *Rose's Wharf, 415 Main St., P.O. Box 345, Gloucester, Tel. 508/283-5110, 800-877-5110.* Also service to Provincetown.
- **Captain Bill's Whale Watching**, *33 Harbor Loop, Gloucester, Tel. 508/283-6995.* Also deep-sea fishing.

- **Seven Seas Whale Watching**, *Seven Seas Wharf, Rt. 127, Gloucester, Tel. 508/283-1776; 800-238-1776*
- **Yankee Whale Watch**, *Cape Ann Marina, Rt. 133, Gloucester, Tel. 508/283-0313, 800-WHALING*

From Newburyport
- **Newburyport Whale Watch**, *Hilton's Dock, 54 Merrimack St., Newburyport, Tel. 508/465-7165; 800-848-1111*

From Plymouth
- **Captain John's Boats**, *Town Wharf, Plymouth, Tel. 508/746-2643*. Also fishing boats, and service to Provincetown.

From Salem
- **East India Cruise Co.**, *197 Derby St., Pickering Wharf, Tel. 508/741-0434; 800-745-9594. Also harbor cruises.*

OVERNIGHT TRIPS
Nantucket

Other countries seem more like America with each passing year. Not Nantucket, though, which (you may have to remind yourself) *is* part of America. It doesn't seem anything like America in this century. Settled in the 1600s, Nantucket became a boomtown after a fisherman in about 1710 did something phenomenal. He went out to sea and came back with a whale. Before that, fisherman caught the occasional whale lost near the shore. Starting in the 1720s, Nantucket hauled in whales by the thousands and the money followed close behind.

By 1900, though, whale oil was out of favor and Nantucket was practically a ghost town. Finally, over the past 60 years or so, it has been appreciated as beautifully preserved sea-country. To go there, either fly (**Cape Air**, *Tel. 800/352-0714*; **USAir**, *Tel. 800/428-4322*), take the **Steamship Authority ferry** from Hynannis, *Tel. 508/477-8600*, at an hour and fifty minutes, or use the speedier **Hy-Line ferry**, at about one hour from Hyannis, *Tel. 508/778-0404*. You won't need your car on Nantucket, so don't take it unless you have to.

There are beaches close to the main village of Nantucket, and bicycles can be rented there for a further jaunt. If you want to see the whole island, you can hire a car-and-driver at about $20 for an hour, or so. Full-day whale watching is also available out of Nantucket, through **Nantucket Whale Watching**, *Straight Wharf, Nantucket, Tel. 800/942-5464.*

Rhode Island & Connecticut

Newport is still a summer outpost for New York society, as it was at the turn-of-the-century – but to live in a 200-room mansion, well, that just isn't done anymore. In Aspen, maybe, but not in Newport: so about a dozen of the great, vintage houses are now open to the public. The biggest of the big is **The Breakers** (1895), once owned by the Vanderbilts. Sometimes, in the summer, it isn't any easier to get in to it, though, than it was in the days when you had to own a railroad or two to obtain an invitation. In this day, it's first-come, first-serve, and on weekends, it can fill up quickly.

But there are plenty of houses to tour other than the Breakers; among them are **Marble House** (1892); **Rosecliff** (1902), **The Elms** (1901), and **Chateau-sur-Mer** (1852). *For information about any or all of them, call 401/ 847-1000.* The people who owned the mansions originally developed an Ocean Walk; running along the sea for about three miles, it follows a cliff that is mildly intimidating in places, but if Consuela Vanderbilt could do it, you probably can, too.

The talk in Providence is always of the avant-garde grill called **AL FORNO**, *577 South Main Street, Tel. 401/273-9760.* It started in a store-front, moved to bigger quarters, and moved again to the bottom of an old warehouse. It still isn't big enough for the crush of people from all over New England who want nothing more out of life than a perfectly cooked piece of meat and a mess of potatoes more alive than when they were in the ground. Northern Italian dishes are also on the menu. The restaurant opens at 5:30 pm, and it doesn't accept reservations. If you won't stand in line, try to arrive at around 5 pm for an early dinner; the wait later on is bound to be even longer.

Directions: Take Rt. I-93 south from the center of Boston; it divides at Braintree, then take Rt. 124 west to Rt. 24, which leads into Newport.

Block Island is a 75 minute ferryride from Rhode Island, either Port Judith or, in summer only, Providence or Newport (**Interstate Navigation**, *Tel. 401/783-4613*). Block Island has been a relatively quiet resort island for 150 years, with its fields and fresh breezes. The best way to see it is on bicycles, which can be rented.

Mystic is an old fishing village hugging the water on Connecticut's shore. The main attraction, other than meandering around the small shops at waterside, is the Mystic Seaport, an extensive re-creation that includes original buildings and houses, in addition to over 200 vintage boats, in the water or in drydock for repairs. For an extra admission, you can take a steamboat ride on the Mystic River.

Vermont

Vermont is about two hours away from Boston, a contented backwater that retains Yankee charm as though there were no choice but to be small-scale, slightly stubborn, and green. **Burlington** is the biggest city – and a nine-story apartment building there is the tallest building in the whole state. On a blue stroke in the mountains called **Lake Champlain**, Burlington is also a college town, with a world's fair of restaurants and microbreweries downtown. One of the most chic is **LEUNIG'S**, an open-air cafe that would be at home in Berlin, with its mixture of rococo fittings and industrial garage-doors (to ensure the open air).

The **Green Mountains** south and east of Burlington are unspoiled ridges of trees showing the way in every direction. **Route 89**, the interstate leading south from Burlington, is one of the most beautiful drives in New England.

Montpelier, the state capital, is the prettiest of cities – population 6,000. Brick buildings and attractive local stores share the downtown with three restaurants operated by the exuberant students of the **New England Culinary Institute**. One is a cafe-bakery, while the **MAIN STREET BAR AND GRILL**, *118 Main Street*, features the other two, a trendy bistro and a formal restaurant, both of which try to feature Vermont recipes, such as cheddar-and-tomato soup. Wandering around Montpelier is a relaxing visit to another time in America, when people were only in a hurry some of the time, not all of the time. The **Vermont Historical Society**, *109 State Street*, is next door to the capitol building, featuring bright exhibits, such as items invented through the years in Vermont: among them is the "Wonder Bra." Who would have guessed?

A great way to see Vermont would be to follow my advice at the beginning of this chapter; get in your car and drive, and don't worry about small details like getting lost! Some of the small towns that give Vermont so much of its charm – **Middlebury**, **Craftsbury**, **Woodstock** – are wonderful places to visit, but not on a summer weekend or during the peak of fall foliage. Yes, these are in some ways the most beautiful times to visit, but steel yourself against hordes of crowds in Saabs and Range Rovers who coincidentally thought, as you did, that it was a lovely day for a drive in the country. Rest assured, however, that there is plenty of fall foliage to go around in Vermont; it's quite a big little state that way.

Middlebury, Craftsbury, and Woodstock each offer another version of Vermont's special charm, and you can spend hours wandering quaint main streets admiring plucky colonial architecture and darting in and out of unique shops and stores. If you're hunting for antiques, Route 7 in the western part of the state is known as "The Antique Trail" from top to bottom.

When you get hungry, try one of the following in each village:
- **CRAFTSBURY INN** or **INN ON THE COMMON**, *Craftsbury*
- **DOG TEAM TAVERN**, *Dog Team Road, Middlebury* or **MIDDLEBURY INN**, *Court House Square, Middlebury*
- **WOODSTOCK INN**, *On the Green, Woodstock* or **BENTLEY'S**, *Elm Street, Woodstock*

NEW ENGLAND INNS -
WORTH A TRIP ALL BY THEMSELVES

Massachusetts

JARED COFFIN HOUSE, *29 Broad St., Nantucket 02554. Tel. 508/228-2400; 800/248-2405. 60 rooms. $100-200.*

A Federal-era brick inn, with a variety of different style rooms in other buildings. Perfectly situated in "downtown" Nantucket. Breakfast, lunch, and dinner.

THE RED LION INN, *Main St., Stockbridge. Tel. 413/298-5545. 111 rooms. $72-350.*

Mammoth for an inn, with over 100 rooms. The lobbies and restaurants are warm with antiques, Oriental rugs and fireplaces. Breakfast, lunch and dinner served.

YANKEE CLIPPER INN, *96 Granite St., P.O. Box 2399, Rockport MA 01966. Tel. 508/546-3407. 20 rooms. $110-239.*

Verandah after verandah overlooking the sea; most of the rooms do, too. Breakfast and dinner.

THE BRAMBLE INN, *2019 Main St., Brewster, Cape Cod 02631. Tel. 508/896-7644.*

Converted house near the North Shore of Cape Cod. Breakfast and dinner.

New Hampshire

PHILBROOK FARM INN, *881 North Rd., Shelburne NH 03581. Tel. 603/466-3831. 18 rooms. $110-140.*

A white clapboard inn of longstanding reputation; out in the country fields. Yankee dinners.

NEW ENGLAND INNS - WORTH A TRIP ALL BY THEMSELVES

Connecticut

ALTNAVEIGH INN, 957 Storrs Rd., Storrs CT 06268. Tel. 203/429-4490.

In the historic district of the university town.

BEE AND THISTLE INN, 100 Lyme St., Old Lyme CT 06371. Tel. 203/434-1667. 11 rooms. $69-125.

Near the shore, a converted 18th century house. Breakfast, lunch and dinner.

Rhode Island

THE 1661 INN, Spring St., Block Island 02807. Tel. 401/466-2421.

Overlooking the sea – as practically everything does on Block Island. 21 rooms, $75-350. Affiliated with the rustic Hotel Manisses, also on Block Island.

Vermont

THE INN AT MONTPELIER, 147 Main St., Montpelier VT 05602. Tel. 802/223-2727. 13 rooms. $99-153.

Montpelier either is a small city or a big town: whichever it is, the important thing is that it never outgrew itself, a walking town of bookstores, small museums, and country cooking. The inn is an old house right in town. Breakfast and dinner.

THE EQUINOX, Historic Route 7A, Manchester, VT 05254. Tel. 802/362-4700; 800/362-4747. 163 rooms. $140-500.

A rambling inn, doing business since 1769.

CAPE COD

Cape Cod is the arm that swings out into the ocean south of Boston, trying and valiantly succeeding to offer something for just about everyone: birds, artists and vacationers. One of the nation's protected enclaves, the Cape is changing these days, as it fills in with retirement complexes and condominium complexes and shopping complexes — and complexes of all kinds that are insinuating themselves into the basic simplicity of the place. Parts of it are actually starting to look like America. Most of it, though, still looks like Cape Cod.

And the look of Cape Cod is of small towns, little changed with time. It is the look of wooden houses in weathered grey or bright white clapboard: not crowded together, not in the look of Cape Cod. It is of open spaces, too, forever given to the bogs, the ponds, the barrens, the dunes and the sea — very much part of Cape Cod.

The pace is not slow on the Cape and there is nothing sleepy about it. But it is an ordered pace, grooved into patterns over time. That also happens to be the way that the ocean waters order the dunes and the sandbars: with slow change.

OVERVIEW

This Cape is not a cape.

A cape is supposed to be more like a bump of land than an arm. But in any case, Peninsula Cod is now technically an island, separated from the mainland by a wide canal, leading from Cape Cod Bay on the north to Buzzards Bay on the south. Two roads cross the canal: **Rt. 25**, leading generally from Providence and Southern Massachusetts, turns into **Rt. 28** at the canal and takes cars south into the part of the arm that could be the sleeve of a T-shirt, drooping down. The main city there is **Falmouth**, which is the hopping-off point for automobile ferries to Martha's Vineyard. Rt. 28 continues east as the main drag of the south shore.

The road that leads from Boston is **Rt. 3** and it turns into **Rt. 6** at the Canal. Rt. 6 was built in the 1950's as a high-speed highway, whizzing fully modern progress through the middle of the Cape. It is a divided road all the way to Orleans, at the base of the forearm, (if Cape Cod were an arm cocked up to make a fist). In reality, however, places like Cape Cod have a way of fending off modern progress and there is nothing highspeed about Rt. 6 on crowded weekends in the summer. As long as you are in no hurry, though, (and if you are in a hurry, then what are you doing on Cape Cod?), take the byway onto the Cape: **Rt. 6a.** It was old in the early 1700's, when it was already known as the Old King's Highway, and it meanders through a small wrinkle in time, the Cape's north shore.

The villages on the north shore are proud, in the well practiced New England way of being in the right about most things and disdaining action on the remainder. Neatly maintained and tightly zoned, there is nothing of the quick buck about them—even the restaurant seems to be something of a brazen new invention on the north shore, one that has only caught on sporadically. As to stores, they are hard to notice because the style in signs hasn't advanced much beyond woodcarving. The fact is that by refusing to pander to tourists, villages such as **Barnstable**, **Yarmouth Port** and **Dennis** have the most to offer to tourists, giving them a timeless sense of Cape Cod, of New England and perhaps, of America.

The south shore is different, and it has been even since before things like villages, signs and Americans arrived. Where the north shore has soil, the south shore has sand. Where the north shore sits on a protected bay, the south faces the open ocean. Because of that soil and that protection, the north shore was fully developed first, by farmers and by fishermen taking easy catches from the bay. The south shore tends to have a newer look about it. Some towns, such as **Chatham**, have 17th-century roots and retain a 19th-century look, but most of the oceanside came into its own in more recent times, with the full-scale vacation industry. The prime example is **Hyannis**, which has its charms, here and there, but much of which could actually be a small city anywhere in the country, with its strip malls and commercial priority.

Cape Cod stretches 70 miles, from the canal at the shoulder to the tip of the last knuckle at **Provincetown**. Beyond the elbow, where it turns northward, more than half of the acreage is protected as the **Cape Cod National Seashore**. The water is the whole way of life in towns such as **Eastham** and **Wellfleet**, though Provincetown is expanding fast. Half the people there seem to be looking at what happened to Hyannis with envy, and half with abject horror. For now, the former seem to be winning, as Provincetown is the fastest growing city on the Cape.

PLANNING A TRIP

Over five million visitors arrive each summer for periods ranging from a few hours to the whole season and Cape Cod has made itself ready to match each one with a custom-made holiday. That isn't to say that Cape Cod is a crass place or overtly commercial. But it has spent many a long winter sitting by the fire plotting improvements for the following summer. By this time, they have piled up and there are not many aspects of history or nature on old Cape Cod that are not duly accompanied by a color brochure. But then, what would you do if five million people were coming to see you for the summer? You'd look around and try to think of something they'd like to do.

The **Cape Cod Chamber of Commerce** offers free publications, including the annual Offic*ial Guide, Culture on the Cape, Golf Guide, Calendar of Events* and a *B&B Guide*. The chamber has visitors centers: on the way from Boston, on Rt. 3 at exit 5 near Plymouth; and on Cape Cod, on Rt. 6 at exit 6, for West Barnstable. *The chamber can be reached at P.O. Box 790, Hyannis, MA 02601; Tel. 508/862-0700; toll-free 888/332-2732; website, www.capecodchamber.org. One of the several weatherlines for Cape Cod is 508/771-5522.*

ARRIVALS & DEPARTURES

Cape Air is based at the Hyannis Airport and offers service to Boston and Providence, as well as Provincetown and the islands of Nantucket and Martha's Vineyard. *Tel. 800/352-0714; website, www.flycapeair.com.* A flight to Nantucket on its adjunct, **Nantucket Airlines**, from Hyannis, takes twelve minutes. *Tel. 800/635-8787.*

US Air Express also serves Cape Cod and the islands, as does Continental, in the summer season.

The Plymouth & Brockton Street Railway Co., *Tel. 508/771-6191, website, www.p-b.com*, offers bus service between downtown Boston, Logan Airport and two cities on Cape Cod, Barnstable & Hyannis.

If you're driving from Boston, take Rt. 3 out of the city. Rt. 3 turns into Rt. 6 at the Canal.

By Ferry To Nantucket & Martha's Vineyard

Standard ferry service from Hyannis takes about two hours to Nantucket and about one hour to Martha's Vineyard. **Hy-Line Cruises** *(Tel. 508/778-2600; 800/492-8082; website, www.hy-linecruises.com)* offer service. Round-trip fares for adult passengers are approximately $24 for either island; children under 12 half-price; children under five free. **Steamship Authority** *(Tel. 508/477-8600; 800/778-1132; website, www.islandferry.com)* also offers service to Nantucket from Hyannis. Both lines also run high-speed boats to Nantucket, which cuts the time in half (and so doubles the fare).

To save money on the trip to Martha's Vineyard, use the Steamship Authority service from Woods Hole, on the western tip of Cape Cod's South Shore. The trip is only $10 roundtrip for adults.

An alternative to Hyannis crowds on the trip to Nantucket is the ferry from Harwichport, run by **Freedom Cruise Line**, *Rt. 28, Harwichport; Tel. 508/432-8999*. It is often less hectic than the Hyannis ferries, and offers free parking.

A DAY ON THE CAPE

To someone who has studied Cape Cod horticulture solely in the aisles of a supermarket, it may seem that the only things that grow here are cranberries and wild beach plums. The **Heritage Plantation**, *Pine and Grove streets, Sandwich*, will refute that notion, with its resplendent display of thousands of plant specimens. The Heritage Plantation was developed over the past seventy years as the private hobby of the Lilley family, long associated with the manufacture of pharmeceuticals. The Heritage Plantation gardens present a gorgeous first impression of the Cape.

Hidden inside the vintage barns are displays of more modern distractions, including automobiles. One of the prizes of that collection is one car that looks a bit like a flower plucked from one of the beds outside. It is the green-and-yellow Duesenberg originally built for Gary

Cooper: a true super star — the car, I mean. The Heritage Plantation is open Mother's Day to the end of October. *Admission: $9, adults; $8, senior citizens; $5, children; under 5 free. Tel. 508/888-3300, Recorded Information, 508/888-1222; website, www.heritageplantation.org*

The village of **Sandwich** is laid out with twisting streets that give the right-of-way to waterways and old houses. One of the very oldest is the **Hoxie House**, dating from 1685, overlooking a long body of water called Shawme Pond. When Hoxie House, now a museum, was first built, it was just plain practical. But "plain practical" has a way of taking on great style on Cape Cod, and the idea of a small house with a sharply slanting roof caught on and became the colonies' first contribution to architecture: the saltbox.

Hotels in Sandwich

THE DAN'L WEBSTER INN, *149 Main St., Sandwich, Tel. 508/888-3622; 800/444-3566; website, www.danlwebsterinn.com. 47 rooms. Rates: $99-159, off-season; $119-209, summer/fall.*

This inn is a tradition in town, with its central location and private lawns with gardens. The rooms are renovated in an early Victorian motif, to a very gracious standard. If you are dining at the Dan'l Webster, request a table in the Conservatory, overlooking the gardens.

THE SPRING HILL MOTOR LODGE, 351 Rt. 6A, Sandwich, *Tel. 508/888-1456; 800/647-2514; website, www.sunsol.com/springhill/. Rates: $65-85, off-season; $85-115, summer/fall. Also cottages, i.e. two-bedroom ones: $850 per week, off season; $1,100-1,400, summer/fall. 24 rooms.*

Located just outside of town, Spring Hill is a natty white complex that includes cottages as well as tennis courts and a swimming pool.

The North Shore has its beaches and one of the finest is a long strand near **Barnstable**, on Sandy Neck. Jutting out into the bay, it forms a harbor at Barnstable from which several guided fishing boats operate. The harbor, with a tiny, lapping beach just right for tiny children, really needs no activities. It is activity enough just to take in all that the view offers, as the light from the sky and the harbor and the bay beyond blend in mysterious ways, all real.

An attentive drive through Barnstable ought to constitute one or two credits toward a degree in domestic architecture: so many styles are represented at such a peak of design, and all are meticulously maintained. I use the word "all" advisedly: the towns along Rt. 6a are chock full of homes that would be conspicuous anywhere else. Not every house is a mansion, but one after another is a treat to see, if not to study. The countryside between the villages is cushioned with cranberry bogs, in washes of burgundy and dark green. In fact, even castoff roadsides on Cape Cod fill the eye, with blooms of wildflowers always in season: daffodils in spring, for example, and hydrangia later in the summer.

The **Cape Cod Museum of Natural History**, *Rt. 6A in Brewster, Tel. 800/479-3867*, is a resource for anyone interested in the elementary beauty of the Cape, and especially its birdlife. The museum itself has exhibits reflecting both scientific and artistic appreciation of the surrounding life. However, the whole of Cape Cod is a museum, as far as the Museum of Natural History is concerned and it offers guided tours via walking, canoeing and on boat excursions. It is also a center for bird-watching, a rewarding occupation on Cape Cod. There is a shop further on in Orleans that caters exclusively to it: the **Bird Watcher's General Store**, *36 Rt. 6A, Orleans; Tel. 800/562-1512*, has everything from bird recordings to bird binoculars — which, should the name be confusing, are not made for birds, but for looking at birds.

Cape Cod has a long tradition for summer baseball, with a league that includes teams such as the Brewster Whitecaps and the Cotuit Kettleers. (Wouldn't you look good in a baseball cap for the Cotuit Kettleers?) The 44-game season runs from mid-June to Mid-August, and represents something of an all-star camp for amateur players from all over the country; hundreds of them land in the major leagues eventually. The other eight cities with teams in the Cape Cod League are Bourne, Chatham, Falmouth, Harwich, Hyannis, Orleans, Wareham, and Yarmouth Port-Dennis.

Restaurants in Brewster

ABBICCI, *43 Main Street, Brewster; Tel. 508/362-3501, Yarmouth Port.*

A modern restaurant, with a continental menu. Seafood is expertly prepared.

CHILLINGSWORTH, *2449 Main Street, Brewster; Tel. 508/896-3640; 800/430-3640.*

A favorite among locals. Lunch is low-key, but dinner is prix fixe, serving French haute cuisine. Accommodations are available.

Just outside Brewster, Rt. 124 leads directly south toward the ocean and Rt. 28. Maple trees give way to pines somewhere along the way, just as the restraint of village shoppes gives way to shopping centers and parking lots. The village of **Harwichport** offers one important element in a beachside picnic: dessert. **Lucious Louie's** has superb baked goods, including pumpkin-cream and cranberry muffins, which are local favorites. About four miles east, on the outskirts of Chatham, the **Pampered Palate**, *1291 Main Street, Tel. 508/945-3663,* sells sandwiches on homemade breads, and the fishmonger nextdoor, **Chatham Fish and Lobster**, *Tel. 508/945-1178,* has perfected lobster bisque. Ignore the styrofoam cup, the shop's bisque is flavorsome and creamy, chunked up with lobster. **Hardings Beach** is only about two miles away: a generous strip of deep, soft sand, with Stage Harbor Lighthouse and Monomoy Island in view.

Chatham is one of the most appealing towns on the South Shore, with lively shops and galleries. Between the Fourth of July and Labor Day, it revels in its Friday night concerts, a tradition of sixty years' standing in which the uniformed Chatham Band takes its place in the bandstand at Kate Gould Park and plays, while people watch and dance. Some people do neither, but add to the festivity by flying kites made of balloons. And some people don't do that either, but paint the incredible scene, and then trot their canvases down the next day to fill up all the shops and galleries in town. On the way to the band concert, stop for a lobster-roll dinner at the First United Methodist Church on Main Street.

One of the memorable ways to see the Cape is in an open-cockpit biplane. Rides are offered at the Chatham Municipal Airport, a normally quiet field restricted to private planes. You can go up the coast to Provincetown, around the Monomoy Wildlife Sanctuary, or you can specify a stunt ride, and see the Cape upside down, sideways and, perhaps, with your eyes squeezed shut. Inquire at the **Cape Cod Flying Circus**, *240 George Ryder Road, Chatham Airport; Tel. 508/945-9000.*

Hotels in Chatham

PORT FORTUNE INN, 201 Main Street, Chatham, *Tel. 508-945-0792; 800-750-0792, website, www.capecodnet/portfortune/. Rates: $85-115, off-season; $110-170, summer/fall.*

This is a quiet hotel that overlooks the ocean and is an easy walk to the beach. The rooms are furnished with antiques and reproductions.

HAWTHORNE MOTEL, *196 Shore Road; Tel. 508/945-0372, Open mid-May to mid-October. Rates: $100-120, low-season; $130-150, mid-summer.*

A well-run motel with its own beach, located in a fine residential neighborhood of Chatham. Ten of the 26 rooms have efficiency kitchens and ocean-views.

BEACH HOUSE INN, *4 Braddock Lane, Harwichport; Tel. 508/432-4444; 800/870-4405; website, www.capecodtravel.com\bhi\lowercape. Rates: $185-295, summer; $125-185, off-season, including breakfast.*

Beach House is a Victorian style hotel, with its own private beach. Most of the fourteen rooms have a view of the ocean.

From Chatham, you can continue east and north to the **Cape Cod National Seashore**, *Tel. 508/349-3785*, which covers over 45,000 acres of classic beachland, along with the wetlands adjunct to it. There is a **visitor's center** *at Eastham, Rt. 6, Eastham, Tel. 255-3421*, and a center for ten nature trails. When many other beachside parking lots are full, you have a good chance of finding a space at the Visitor's Center, from which a shuttle bus leaves for **Coast Guard Beach**. Coast Guard is a serious open-ocean beach, and the surf can be too strong for swimming. Further north, the **Marconi Beach** at South Wellfleet mark the spot at which Guglielmo Marconi sent a message by wireless telegraph (radio) to Great Britain in 1903.

However, if Cape Cod must be a daytrip, it might be better to turn west from Chatham. On the way, you can stop and buy presents (for yourself) at **Chatham Jam and Jelly**, *at the corner of Vineyard Avenue and Rt. 28, Tel. 508/945-3052.* The store, located in a private home, sells over five dozen kinds of jelly, many prepared from local berries. All of them are made right in the house. There is nothing better than wild beach plum jelly. Not even ice cream.

But Cape Cod screams for ice cream, and there are places for it at hand all along the South Shore. **Kream 'n Kone**, *527 Main St., Dennisport, Tel. 508/394-0808,* is a longtime favorite drive-in. It dates from 1933 and serves good ice cream, along with meals and the feeling that Robert Montgomery or Claudette Colbert might be in the next car.

Hyannis is not quite as it was when the Kennedys discovered it in 1926. They are still there, but just as their one house somehow sprouted into a compound, Hyannis itself has expanded into the Cape's metropolis. It is a transportation center, with airplane, bus and ferry service. It is also a busy vacation spot, with motels and fast food restaurants lining Rt. 28. Hyannis is the Cape's shopping destination, and Rt. 132 is suitably frenzied with the signs of just about every national chain.

The **Cape Cod Central Railroad**, *252 Main St., Hyannis, Tel. 508/771-3800; 800/7972-7245,* runs two-hour excursions out of Hyannis in vintage trains. Even aside from the ferries that leave from Hyannis' harbor, there are excursion boats, including the sailing ship **Catboat**, which takes passengers for one-and-a-half hour rides. The charge is $20 for adults; $15 for senior citizens, and $5 for children. *Ocean Street docks; Tel. 508/775-0222; website, www.catboat.com.*

Baxter's Restaurant has an official address of Pleasant Street in Hyannis, but it is really spread out over the docks and at least one old boat on the harbor. The dishes run mainly to crunchy-delicious fried seafood, piled high, and the plates can be taken out to picnic tables right on the water. Jack and Jacqueline Kennedy regularly purchased meals there, and the walls are hung with various receipts and orders — and accounts tallied on White House stationery. For those who want to learn slightly more about the Kennedys and their way of life on the Cape, the former Town

AT HOME ON CAPE COD

Many people actually pack up and leave Cape Cod at the height of the season. Who are they? They are the people who finance beautiful homes by renting them out by the week to the many people who arrive in Cape Cod at the height of the season. To get a feel for the market, request a copy of **CyberRentals Cape and Island Rentals Magazine,** *Tel. 800/628-0558, or see their website at http://cyberrentals.com. The "magazine" is a mostly just a classified listing of picture-ads. (The company also has a Vermont magazine).*

Typical listings are:

• Charming Harwichport 5-bedroom, across street from Nantucket Sound, $2,000 per week.

• Waterfront cottage in Truro with view of Bay, sleeps six, $1,175 per week.

• Rose-covered cottage on Nantucket, two-minute walk to beach, sleeps two, $950 per week.

Of course, everything looks good in the picture, but sometimes when one is looking at them by the hundreds, the criteria become fairly cavalier, with rejections flying around for reasons such as, "Oh my. Oh my, I couldn't possibly live with those shutters –" Try to be more practical and remember that you are not buying a manse, just renting a beachhead.

For more personalized service in locating a rental property, a small company called **Sylvan Rentals** *knows the Cape Cod market well and can answer specific needs. They're at 2469 Main Street, South Chatham, Tel. 508/432-2344; website, www.sylvanrentals.com.*

Hall is now the **John F. Kennedy Hyannis Museum**, with displays on Hyannisport's glory days as the home of the Summer White House. *The JFK Hyannis Museum is at 397 Main Street, Hyannis; Tel. 508/790-3077.*

From Hyannis, it is only about 80 miles to Boston.

Hotels in Hyannis

HI-SEAS BY THE BEACH, *395 Sea Street, Hyannis; Tel. 508/775-8675.*

Hy-Seas is a cluster of a half-dozen classic cottages, right on the beach; there is not much else to the place, which I count as its prime amenity: it is just Cape Cod and a place to live on it.

SIMMONS HOMESTEAD INN, *228 Scudder Avenue, Hyannis Port, Tel. 800/637-1649; website, www.capecodtravel.com/simmonsinn. Rates: $110-140, off-season; $140-200, summer/fall.*

Simmons' is a rambling old house, overlooking a pond. It is a friendly, even gregarious place, where each room is decorated individually in honor of a different animal. Beach and fishing equipment is available for loan, as are bikes. Pets other than cats are allowed (the inn has two cats.)

Restaurants in Hyannis

MILDRED'S, *290 Iyanough Road, Rt. 28, near the Barnstable Airport; Tel. 508/775-1045.*

A gaping chowder house, which draws people back year after year, decade after decade.

INDEX

Abigail Adams 30, 32
Abolition 33-34
Adams, Samuel 27
Adams, Samuel 27, 32
Adams, John 29, 31, 32
African-American National
Historic Site 160
Airport - see Logan Airport,
    Hyannis Airport
Anthony's Pier Four 127

Back Bay, the 18, 34, 35, 179
Back Bay Hilton Hotel 79
Bakeries 130-133
Barking Crab 120, 192
Beacon Hill 15, 183
Bed & Breakfasts 88-90
Bertucci's 98
Biba 100, 125
Big Dig (Central Artery/Tunnel
    Project) 19
Black Heritage Trail 159
Black Goose Bistro 126
Bob the Chef's 101
Boston Marriott Long Wharf
    Hotel 56, 68
Boston Architectural Center 160
Boston Symphony Orchestra 62,
    202
Boston Tea Party 28, 154
Boston Harbor 19

Boston Harbor Hotel 55, 68, 192
Boston Ballet 204
Boston Public Library 181, 212
Boston Massacre 27, 155
Bread & Circus 111, 227
Brookline 18
Bruins 216
Buckminster Hotel 85
Bulfinch, Charles 140, 152, 184
Bull & Finch Pub 126
Bunker Hill, 30, 158
Buses 46

Cambridge 18
Cape Cod 20, 248
Capital Grille 102
Celtics 216
Chandler Inn Hotel 77
Chanterelle Restaurant 117
Charles Hotel 87
Charlestown 18, 23, 157
Charley's 104
Charlie's Sandwich Shoppe 109
Cheers 126
Children's Museum 62, 160
Chinatown 16, 100, 128
Christian Science 163
Colonnade Hotel 80
Common 15, 151, 188
Computer Museum 161
Concord 21, 236

Constitution 59, 145, 232
Copley Square 181
Copley Square Hotel 81
Copley Plaza Hotel 80, 193
Copley Place 222

Dance Clubs 198
Davio's Restaurant 117
DeLuca's Market 120
Dick's Last Resort 100, 107, 194
Dixie Kitchen 111
Doubletree Guest Suites 88, 195
Durgin-Park 39, 115

East Coast Grill 99
Eliot Hotel 56, 81
Emerson, Ralph Waldo 33, 238
Esplanade 189, 191

Faneuil Hall 139
Fenway Park 215
Fifty-Seven Restaurant 124
Figs 112
Filene's Basement 235
Finagle a Bagle 97
Finale 124
Four Season Hotel 54, 78
Franklin Park Zoo 59
Freedom Trail 151-159

Galleria Italiano 106
Galleries 210
Gibson House 170
Glass Flowers 150, 173
Grillfish 121

Hamersley's Bistro 123, 126
Harborside Hyatt 87
Hard Rock Cafe 127
Hart Nautical Collections 163
Harvard University 25, 38, 58,
    174, 207

Harvard Square Hotel 88
Harvard Museum of Cultural and
Natural History 149, 176
Hayden Planetarium 39, 166
Haymarket Pizza 113
Helmand Restaurant 129
Holiday Inn Boston Airport 87
Holiday Inn-Government Center
    74
Hostelling International 91
Hotels, 52-57, 65-88
Howard Johnson Lodge 86
Howard Johnson Hotel 85
Huntington Theater 205
Hutchinson, Anne 24, 152
Hyannis Airport
Hyannis Airport 250
Hyatt Regency Hotel 70
Hynes Convention Center 110,
    180

Inn at Harvard 88
Irish Pubs 195
Isabella Stewart Gardner Museum
    148

Jacob Wirth's 39, 124
Jae's 123
Jillian's 60, 105
John Hancock Tower 182, 187

Kenmore Square 18
Kennedy, John Fitzgerald 35, 141-
    142
King's Chapel 153

La Famiglia Giorgio's 108
Le Meridien Hotel 73
Legal Seafoods 98
Lenox Hotel 54, 82, 193
Locke-Ober 100, 114, 126
Logan Airport Ramada 87

Logan Airport 45
Longfellow, Henry Wadsworth 171

Mapparium 60, 173
Marliave Restaurant 118, 193
Marriott Copley Place 83
Medical services 44
Men Tei Noodle House 130
Mercury Bar 194
Microbreweries 197
MidTown Hotel 52, 83
Milner Hotel 76
MIT 60, 164, 207
Museum of Fine Arts 142, 229

Nahant 239
New England Aquarium 59, 63, 143-145
New England Holocaust Museum 168

O'Leary's Pub 108, 196
Ocean Wealth 128
Old North Church 29, 157
Old South Church 154
Olives 122
Olmsted, Frederick Law 170
Omni Theater 166
Omni Parker House 53, 72
Other Side Cosmic Cafe 112, 199
Otis House 169

Pagliuca's 106
Parish Cafe 119
Park Plaza Hotel 77
Patriots 216
Pizzeria Regina 114
Playgrounds 59
Plymouth 20, 240
Prudential Center 188, 222
Public Garden 135

Quincy Market 222, 228, 233

Radisson Boston Hotel 76
Radius Restaurant 103
Rebecca's 97
Red Hat 116
Regal Boston Hotel 71
Restaurant Marche 104
Restaurants 92-130
Revere, Paul 29, 31, 155
Revolutionary War 26-31
Ritz-Carlton Hotel 79
Royal Sonesta Hotel 71
Rudi's 118

Sailing 220
Salem 20, 239
Science Museum 39, 58, 166, 234
Seaport Hotel 69
Sheraton Boston 84
Sol Azteca 129
Sonsie Restaurant 93
South End 16
Sports Museum of New England 168
Stephanie's on Newbury 96
Subways 48
Suffolk Downs 217
Swan Boats 138
Swissotel 74

Tennessee's 99, 100
Theo's Cozy Corner 110
Toscano Restaurant 105
Tours 51, 61, 63, 156, 174, 178
Train travel 47
Tremont Boston Hotel 75
Turner Fisheries 103, 195

University Park Hotel 88

Wai Wai Ice Cream 100
War of 1812 32-33
Warren Inn 109
Warren, Dr. Joseph 28, 32
Westin Hotel 84
Whale Watching 240
Winthrop, John 22-25

Ye Olde Union Oyster House 121
Yoshi Restaurant 130

Zoo (Franklin Park) 59

THINGS CHANGE!

Phone numbers, prices, addresses, quality of food, etc, all change. If you come across any new information, we'd appreciate hearing from you. No item is too small! Drop us an e-mail note at: Jopenroad@aol.com, or write us at:

Boston Guide
Open Road Publishing, P.O. Box 284
Cold Spring Harbor, NY 11724